Advaita

— a conceptual analysis —

Contemporary Researches in Hindu Philosophy & Religion, no. 5

Advaita

— a conceptual analysis —

A. Ramamurty

D.K. Printworld (P) Ltd
NEW DELHI-110015

Cataloging in Publication Data — DK
[Courtesy: D.K. Agencies (P) Ltd. <docinfo@dkagencies.com>]

Ramamurty, A. (Aryasomayajula). 1935-
Advaita : a conceptual analysis.
(Contemporary researches in Hindu philosophy & religion, no. 5).
xii, 256 p., 23 cm.
Includes bibliographical references (p.)
Includes index.
ISBN 8124600678

1. Advaita. 2. Philosophy, Indic. I. Title. II. Series: Contemporary researches in Hindu philosophy & religion; no. 5.

ISBN 81-246-0067-8 (Hardbound)
ISBN 81-246-0446-0 (Paperback)
First Published in India in 1996
Second impression in 1999
Third impression in 2008

Published and printed by:
D.K. Printworld (P) Ltd.
Regd. office: *'Sri Kunj,'* F-52, Bali Nagar
Ramesh Nagar Metro Station
New Delhi - 110 015
Phones : (011) 2545 3975, 2546 6019; *Fax* : (011) 2546 5926
E-mail : dkprintworld@vsnl.net
Web : www.dkprintworld.com

Dedicated to

All the Vedāntins
Past and Present

Preface

SEVERAL philosophers and thinkers have been attracted to *advaita* in modern times, and most of them have tried to understand and present it as a system of metaphysical thought or as a set of doctrines on self, world and reality (*Brahman*) and their inter-relations. Although we find in the writings of Śaṅkara an attempt to construct a system of metaphysics, or to interpret comprehensively the philosophy of the *Upaniṣads* from his perspective, he is known above all for his rigorous logical or philosophical analysis of some of the concepts fundamental to the philosophy of *Vedānta*, in which capacity, he is unmatching in the history of philosophy. And this aspect of his philosophical activity is his lasting contribution to philosophy, and is perennial in its influence. However, no significant and thorough-going work has been done on this important aspect of Śaṅkara's philosophy.

In this work a comprehensive attempt is made to present *advaita* as a philosophical analysis of some of the concepts in which man is perennially interested. The object of this work is not to present *advaita* as a system of metaphysical thought but to analyse philosophically some of the concepts fundamental to the philosophy of the *Upaniṣads*. A philosophical or logical analysis of the concepts of *ātman*, *Brahman* and World is done with a view to comprehending the meaning of the concept of *advaita*, a concept central to the philosophy of Śaṅkara. The meaning of the concept of *advaita* is sought to be understood in three distinct but significant ways which complement each other, enrich each other, and would help us in comprehending the meaning and beauty of the concept of *advaita.* In the final chapter an attempt is made, may be for the first time, to discuss and understand the meaning and function of language in relation to *advaita*, and the various problems it gives rise to.

I express my thanks to Sri Susheel K. Mittal, Director of D.K. Printworld (P) Ltd., New Delhi who has taken keen interest in publishing this book. I also thank R.C. Pradhan who has gone through the entire script.

Hyderabad
6th December, 1995 **A. Ramamurty**

Contents

Abbreviations

AitUp	—	*Aitareya Upaniṣad*
AitUpBh	—	*Aitareya Upaniṣad Bhāṣya*
BGBh	—	*Bhagavadgītā Bhāṣya*
BṛUp	—	*Bṛhadāraṇyaka Upaniṣad*
BṛUpBh	—	*Bṛhadāraṇyaka Upaniṣad Bhāṣya*
ChāUp	—	*Chāndogya Upaniṣad*
ChāUpBh	—	*Chāndogya Upaniṣad Bhāṣya*
KaṭhaUp	—	*Kaṭha Upaniṣad*
KaṭhaUpBh	—	*Kaṭha Upaniṣad Bhāṣya*
KenUp	—	*Kena Upaniṣad*
KenaUpBh	—	*Kena Upaniṣad Bhāṣya*
MāUpBh	—	*Māṇḍukya Upaniṣad Bhāṣya*
MāKāBh	—	*Māṇḍukya Kārikā Bhāṣya*
MuUP	—	*Muṇḍaka Upaniṣad*
MuUpBh	—	*Muṇḍaka Upaniṣad Bhāṣya*
PrUp	—	*Praśna Upaniṣad*
PrUpBh	—	*Praśna Upaniṣad Bhāṣya*

RVSaṁ	—	*Ṛg-veda Saṁhitā*
ŚveUp	—	*Śvetāsvatara Upaniṣad*
SūBh	—	*Sūtra Bhāṣya*
TaitUp	—	*Taittirīya Upaniṣad*
TaitUpBh	—	*Taitirīya Upaniṣad Bhāṣya*

1

Introduction

SINCE its systematic development and exposition by Śaṅkara many philosophers and thinkers have been attracted to the philosophy of *advaita*, though it seems none, including Śaṅkara, could make it completely intelligible and acceptable to the rational understanding of man, or provide an adequate explanation to all the philosophical problems it logically involves. Many have attempted in their own ways to provide more and more adequate explanation to those problems. However, most of them are aware of the fact that the philosophical explanation of the problems either seen or anticipated by them or raised by the opponents is not convincing, logically adequate and irrefutable. Yet *advaita* is not outright rejected by them. We find this ambivalent attitude to *advaita* with almost all the major thinkers of *advaita*. It may be due largely to the fact that *advaita*, at least in its original formulation in the *Upaniṣads*, is not strictly speaking speculative in character, or simply a system of metaphysical thought based on man's rational understanding, but a vision or lived experience with the seers of the *Upaniṣads*. Even in the writings of Śaṅkara, which are devoted more to a systematic and philosophical representation of the Upanisadic vision, only an attempt is made to make the Upaniṣadic vision or truth intelligible and meaningful to the rational understanding of man, but not to reduce it completely into a system of concepts. At the most his writings may help one to see the validity and meaningfulness of *advaita*, not strictly in a logical sense but in a different sense, as the primary object of his philosophical activity is not to make people understand and appreciate intellectually the truth of the *Upaniṣads* but to make them realise it directly. Just as the *Veda* becomes *a-Veda* when the truth is directly seen as the object of the *Veda* is not to describe or represent the truth in a straightforward way but to point to it, so also the writings of Śaṅkara are meant to show a discerning person the intended meaning of the *Upaniṣads*, or the truth expressed through the Upaniṣadic statements, but not to determine or demonstrate it completely logically. Concluding his *Kārikā* on the *Māṇḍūkya Upaniṣad*, Gauḍapāda says: "Having realised the state (of *advaita*) which is extremely difficult to be grasped, profound, birthless, always the same, all-light and free from multiplicity or non-dual, we adore it as best as we can."[1] Commenting upon it Śaṅkara says significantly that *advaita* which is non-empirical (*avyavahāra*) or empirically not intelligible or meaningful is viewed, represented and adored empirically to the best of our ability.[2] No one can meaningfully assert that he has completely comprehended the meaning of *advaita* as it involves a basic contradiction of making *advaita* an object of one's knowledge or attainment, and the one who has at least grasped the profundity of the concept of *advaita* will have the humility to admit that what he has comprehended is only an approximation or an empirical mode of understanding *advaita* which transcends and yet comprehends all understanding.

Expressing in a general way his attitude and approach to philosophy Śaṅkara observes: "Whenever something that is well established (*loka prasiddha*) is not admitted by philosophers (*parīkṣaka*) they may indeed establish their own views and demolish the contrary opinion by means of words, but thereby they neither convince others nor even themselves. Whatever has been ascertained to be such and such must also be represented as such and such; attempts to represent it as something else prove nothing but vain talkativeness of those who make those attempts."[3] Frequently we come across in the writings of Śaṅkara, not only while criticizing the philosophical positions of others but even while expounding his own philosophy, remarks and observations expressing his faith in what is known through various means of valid knowledge, and what is well established, as well as his opposition to all those who in their philosophical investigations try to deny validity to what is well established and acknowledged by all. He appeals constantly to what is commonly observed and experienced in refuting certain philosophical positions, like *Vijñānavāda*, which either deny validity to it, or go against it. "If you deny an observed fact saying it is impossible you would be contradicting experience, a thing which no one will allow. Nor is there any question of impossibility with regard to an observed fact because it has actually been observed."[4] Much of his thought, which is developed by way of interpreting the *Vedānta* texts from his own perspective, is positive in its outlook, and is quite intelligible to rational understanding of man. But in the final analysis he rejects validity to it. He was well aware of the arguments and philosophical positions that were current in his time, and go against the validity of his philosophy, and could also clearly foresee several possible arguments against his philosophy. Most of the problems and arguments he anticipated against the validity of his philosophy and answered are quite modern in their formulation and articulation. And he was honest to admit that all the problems which an enquiring mind could raise against the validity of *advaita* are all not easy to be explained rationally. He could see clearly where logical reasoning fails to explain certain problems involved in the concept of *advaita*, and also its incapacity to support or establish the contrary position. He tried to formulate and explain cogently the basic teaching of the *Upaniṣads* as far as human understanding with the help of reason can do, and admitted its incapacity to explain certain crucial problems. His attitude to reason is quite positive and open, but when it is seen to fail in helping human understanding at a certain point in comprehending the truth of the *Upaniṣads*, he did not dogmatically cling to it, and offer pseudo arguments.

The *Upaniṣads*, the basic source of Śaṅkara's philosophy, are also positive in their attitude to several philosophical problems. They often appeal to common human experience which is neither ridiculed nor rejected. Most of the Upaniṣadic statements are positive in their attitude towards the world, man and his problems, either empirical or spiritual. Various metaphysical views find their expression in the *Upaniṣads*, and the attitude of the *Upaniṣads* towards them is not one of clear rejection in favour of any one view. On the other hand, the validity of the various views is seen in an organic or evolutionary perspective, and each view is assigned its own place, significance and validity according to the level of growth and maturity of man's understanding in knowing the truth. The various views and doctrines expressed in the *Upaniṣads*, either about man or about the world and *Brahman*, and their inter-relations are not outright rejected in favour of one view, but are sought to be organized and integrated into a perspective. It is also true that the various views and definitions of Reality (*Brahman*) found in the *Upaniṣads* are not compatible with some of the major or basic statements of the *Upaniṣads*. But the point is that those ideas and definitions which are not consistent with the so-called fundamental statements of the *Upaniṣads* are not rejected but are sought to be seen in a perspective, and integrated into an all-inclusive world-view of the *Upaniṣads*, so that each view or doctrine finds its own place and validity within the total perspective.

These observations are made with an intention to showing how despite his positive approach and attitude to several metaphysical views and problems Śaṅkara is not able to find ultimate justification and validity for them either in terms of logical reasoning or on the basis of lived experience or realisation. Being fully aware of the strongest possible objections and arguments against the validity of his philosophy, or knowing fully well that his final position lacks real philosophical or rational justification, he was uncompromising and firm in maintaining *advaita*. And this makes one ponder why Śaṅkara was so uncompromising in his attitude to *advaita* and its validity. Normally a philosopher accepts an argument or a position as long as he is not aware of the counter argument or position, or till their logical validity is criticized and denied, but when one upholds a position knowing the possible criticisms against its validity then two things are possible. One may either consider the counter arguments and criticism as no real arguments, or they are beside the point or miss it in criticising *advaita*.

The main object of this work is to present, analyse and understand the concept of *advaita*, a concept which is central to the philosophy of Śaṅkara. The meaning of the concept of *advaita* can be approached and understood in three distinct ways, and these are not three exclusive ways of understanding the meaning of *advaita*. Each would complement the other, or each in its own way would help in shedding light on the concept of *advaita*, and help us in comprehending its meaning, profundity, richness and beauty, and also in avoiding certain major problems in grasping the meaning of *advaita* which are otherwise insurmountable.

According to one way of understanding, which is preferred mostly by those who are not for various reasons, which are not always strictly philosophical, in sympathy with *advaita* it means final negation of the reality of everything except that of *Brahman*. In absolute terms the reality of everything other than that of *Brahman* is an illusion as in reality nothing other than *Brahman* exists. And as the nature of *Brahman* is free from all types of change it is in no sense an explanation of anything other than itself. Therefore, whatever that may appear to be real to man's empirical knowledge and experience has no objective existence. As the reality of anything other than that of *Brahman* is co-extensive with empirical knowledge and experience it ceases to be the moment it is not so known and experienced. Now, the reality of anything other than *Brahman* is denied for two important and logically valid reasons. The reality of the world, and of the individual self are denied because by their very nature they do not deserve the status of Reality, and also on the ground that they are not experienced or known in that form when *Brahman* is directly realised. Furthermore, our conception of the nature of *Brahman* is such that we cannot explain in terms of it, in a logically consistent manner, the reality of anything other than itself. If, on the other hand, *Brahman* is to be the cause of the world and the individual selves the nature of *Brahman* should be so conceived as to have a capacity for change, and a will or motive to give birth to something out of itself. And in all such explanations, which are attempted by theistically minded *vedāntins*, the conception of *Brahman* falls short of absolute perfection and fullness. Without somehow compromising with the absolute character of *Brahman* we find it logically difficult to explain the existence of a reality other than *Brahman* in terms of *Brahman*. Either we have to conceive and define *Brahman* in imperfect terms or deny reality to the world, as the reality of both cannot be reconciled, at least logically. If *Brahman* is absolute and perfect it cannot be an explanation of the world, and if the reality of the world is to be accepted and derived from the reality of *Brahman*, the nature of the latter is to be conceived and defined in relative terms. If the reality of *Brahman* is to be accepted in its unalloyed purity and perfection the reality of the world, which lacks any cogent explanation, is to be denied. This position is true not only logically but also in the light of *Brahman*-realisation.

Anything that is experienced or conceived by man cannot be absolute, as strictly speaking the absolute cannot be an idea in the ordinary sense of the term. Here one important discovery of the *Upaniṣads*, which is completely accepted by Śaṅkara, is that the Self or *ātman* is absolute in the true sense of the term. *Ātman* as pure consciousness to which all that man knows, experiences and understands is given as an object is radically different from all that can be known or experienced as an object. The nature of *ātman* or Self is such that it being the principle of awareness in all human experience and knowledge it is untouched or unaffected by all that is known, experienced and conceived. All notions like finite/infinite, conditioned/unconditioned, mortal/immortal, perfect/imperfect, etc., can legitimately be attributed to or predicated of a reality that is known or experienced or conceived. In other words, all thought and knowledge can touch and be true of a reality that is given to man's knowledge or understanding as an object. Anything that is experienced or known cannot logically belong to consciousness, and since all the notions are objects to consciousness they cannot logically belong to it, and affect it. Therefore to talk of anything about *ātman* is logically impossible and inadmissible because all that we can know and speak of cannot be about *ātman* as its reality is presupposed in all that we can know and speak about. We cannot even say that the Self or *ātman* is absolute as it is not an object, either of knowledge or of thought, to which alone something can be attributed, or about which something can be said. To talk of Self as absolute, perfect, unchanging, etc., is to illegitimately transfer certain things which belong to object realm to something which is never an object. When they are applied to an objective (*viṣaya*) reality they can either be true or false or meaningful or unmeaningful, but cannot simply be applied to Self without misunderstanding the nature of Self, or without making it an object which is impossible. To admit all this we need not depend upon *śruti*. Now the distinction between the Self or subject, in a qualified sense, and the non-self or object is intelligible and clear to all, and if we admit this distinction, which is radical, we also have to admit the position of *advaita* that all that can be said and asserted truly or falsely can be about an object only but not about the Self. In this sense of not being affected or determined by any of the definitions and conceptions the Self is absolute which amounts to saying that it is outside of all the conceptions and definitions.

But we are thereby bound to admit a reality other than *Brahman* to which these notions can belong, and of which the Self or *ātman* is aware. If we admit the reality of something other than Self, as otherwise we cannot even make a distinction between the Self and non-self, and consequently deny what is true about non-self to Self, or simply talk about the Self we have to maintain a position like that of *Sāṁkhya* and reject *advaita*, the central concept of Śaṅkara's philosophy. We may accept the Self as absolute but thereby we are not free to reject duality and accept *advaita*. Now comes the greatest insight of the *Upaniṣads*, which is fully grasped and represented by Śaṅkara, that the so-called non-self is not objectively different from the Self. They are not two, or are not different. And since the *Upaniṣads* are interested primarily in instructing us the truth about the reality which we all know and experience they do it mostly by correcting our wrong or imperfect knowledge of it by pointing out that where we see duality there is in fact no duality. In intention the basic statements of the *Upaniṣads* like 'I am *Brahman*' and 'all is *Brahman*' are meant to convey the same truth by way of correcting the empirical knowledge of man whereby he sees differences. It is also a positive discovery in the sense of asserting the ontological oneness of all that is which is *Brahman* or *ātman*. The significance of *advaita* is therefore largely negative in the sense that as *Brahman* is eternally self-revealing no instruction is required to know its existence but it is required to correct the wrong or imperfect knowledge of man about its true nature. In other words, duality that is experienced by man empirically is denied so that the oneness that is objectively or ontologically real is seen or realised directly which is all the while prevented because of man's imperfect knowledge of it. And what is the nature of the state of non-difference or non-duality is something that is to be directly realised but cannot be conceptualised and expressed in language, as in the process of expressing it in language one cannot help, but following the conventions or rules of using language, introduce dualistic mode of speech to express that which is non-dual. When language which is based on differences, without which it cannot function, is used to communicate or express the truth which is non-dual, or free from all relations and differences, it loses its capacity to express it; and when it is used to communicate *advaita* it ends up in distorting it.

There is another way of understanding the meaning of *advaita*, which is equally Upaniṣadic, and is based on the realisation that *ātman* or *Brahman* which is revealed to man as his own inner self is all-pervading or all-encompassing non-dual reality. *Ātman* etymologically means all-pervading or all-encompassing, like space.[5] Since *ātman* is all-pervading its knowledge or realisation must be all-inclusive, or nothing should be excluded from such knowledge or realisation. Another basic insight of *advaita* that what all we know and experience is *Brahman* only, whether we are aware of it or not, is vital in understanding the meaning of *advaita*. Our empirical knowledge of *Brahman* and its advaitic realisation do not differ radically in the sense that both of them have the same reality as their object. What a man empirically knows is *Brahman* as *Brahman* is the only reality that is there ontologically, and the same is the object of *Brahman*-realisation. How then to distinguish empirical knowledge of *Brahman* from the true or perfect knowledge of it? Now, we can make a distinction between the two either in terms of the object known or in terms of the knower. As, according to *advaita*, there is no change of any kind in the nature of *Brahman* any knowledge of *Brahman* refers to it. We cannot also say that the empirical knowledge of *Brahman* refers to it as it is enveloped by something other than itself, or to the phenomenal aspect of it, as ontologically speaking there is nothing to cover or conceal *Brahman*. As consciousness, *Brahman* cannot be concealed or enveloped by anything as in that case the very fact of its concealment cannot be known, and in knowing it consciousness is free from it. As the ideas of concealment and the thing concealed are objects of knowledge they cannot belong to consciousness, and if, on the contrary, they belong to it then that very fact cannot be known. And as the nature of *Brahman* is homogeneous, that is, *prajñānaghana* it cannot have apparent and real natures. *Advaitins* are therefore against imposing the categories of our empirical understanding, which are based on our empirical experience, and are valid with regard to it, upon *Brahman*. Strictly speaking *advaita* cannot be presented in empirically or rationally intelligible propositions. The nature of *Brahman* does not therefore reveal itself to different persons in different ways. It is known always the same to all, and if there is any difference in its knowledge it is entirely due to knowers. "This unreal phenomenal reality created by differentiation is indeed a fact for those who do not believe in things as different from *Brahman* as well as for those who do believe."[6] "Scriptural or empirical outlooks toward Reality or *Brahman* depend entirely upon knowledge and ignorance."[7] If we try to find justification in the nature of *Brahman* for the difference between empirical knowledge of *Brahman*, and its true or objective (*vastu*) knowledge various problems arise which are logically difficult to surmount. On the other hand, if we try to find out the reason for the difference in knowledge within the knower then certain major problems, which are otherwise insurmountable, can be avoided in grasping the meaning of *advaita*. As the object of knowledge is the same in both the cases, the difference between empirical knowledge of *Brahman* and its perfect knowledge is solely due to the mode of knowing *Brahman*.

In the *Bṛhadāraṇyaka Upaniṣad* it is said that what we know empirically about the Self is true of Self, but only it is incomplete and hence imperfect, as in knowing it incompletely we do not know it in its true perfection or fullness (*kṛtsna*).[8] Commenting upon it Śaṅkara says that as long as man knows the Self as possessed of the natural functions and thinks that it sees, hears, thinks, etc., he does not know the Self in its fullness or objectively (*vasturūpeṇa*).[9] Our empirical knowledge of *Brahman* or Self is not complete and perfect as we are discriminative in our approach, and identify *Brahman* with what we know about it, and also would like it to be. To that extent we exclude something from it, and limit its definition accordingly, whereas a true knower of *Brahman* does not see anything other than *Brahman*, and hence there is nothing which can be excluded from *Brahman*, either in knowing it or in defining it. Since *ātman* by definition is all-pervading, like space, there is nothing in reality which is other than Self, and hence its knowledge or realisation must be all-inclusive, or the oneness of all that is (*sarvātmaikabhūtam advaitam*). As we ordinarily find opposition between certain ideas we cannot think them to be true with regard to the same reality, and therefore try to exclude some set of ideas in knowing the nature of *Brahman*. And as we identify and define *Brahman* in terms of certain ideas we find it difficult to explain the ideas opposed to them, and therefore try to explain them in terms of another reality, or in terms of some basic change in the nature of *Brahman*. But if we see *Brahman* as transcending the limitations imposed on it by our understanding, which is formed mostly by our empirical experience, the humanly conceived opposition between certain ideas may not be valid in relation to *Brahman*. Śaṅkara says that while day and night are not there in the sun we try to explain them in terms of the sun. The former is true objectively, and the latter is also true in a sense, but thc former is no explanation of the latter. Similarly our empirical knowledge of *Brahman* is true empirically but not in the absolute sense, and there can be no transition from the one to the other as in reality these are not caused by *Brahman*. As they are true and valid either from the standpoint of ignorance or incomplete knowledge, or true or perfect or complete knowledge the transition or movement is in the knower. In moving from ignorance to knowledge, or from incomplete to complete knowledge, we are not moving from one reality to another. The movement is from ignorance to knowledge, and the significance in the movement is for the knower, and is valid only from his point of view. Either they bind or liberate the knower without in any way affecting the nature of *Brahman*. In reality *Brahman* or *ātman* is all, and when our knowledge or realisation attains that all-inclusive character, which is however not possible at the level of conceptual knowledge, then our knowledge is complete or perfect; and that is *advaita*. "Results of knowledge and ignorance are identity with all and identity with finite things."[10] "The essential meaning of all the *Upaniṣads* is to remove all finite conceptions about *Brahman*."[11] Explaining the Upaniṣadic statement that *Brahman* wanted to create so it created, Śaṅkara says that the desires of *Brahman* are by nature truth and knowledge, and are pure by virtue of their identity with *Brahman*. "The name and form in terms of which things are differentiated are essentially *Brahman*, or are not different from *Brahman* since they cease to be when *Brahman* is not there."[12] In realising the oneness of all that is one cannot exclude one's own reality from such realisation, and therefore such knowledge cannot be of the subject-object type. It is knowledge by being. The same thing is said in a different way in a different context by Śaṅkara. It is meaningful to say that one knows all by knowing *Brahman* as *Brahman* is all, but how could *Brahman* know all? Here it is said that *Brahman* knows all not through any sort of cognitive ability but by its being all. It knows all as it is itself all. And the Self, in its true nature, being *Brahman* it is all. Furthermore, the fact that all the major statements of the *Upaniṣads* intend to convey the same truth shows that in understanding the meaning of *advaita* if we depend exclusively upon some of the statements we fail to grasp the meaning of *advaita*. The same idea is expressed in a different way by Śaṅkara when it is said that the dissolution of the world (*pralaya*) as popularly understood and believed is inferior to that which is consciously realised in realising *Brahman*.[13] The latter is supreme and radical, and happens when the ignorance is dissolved in *Brahman*-knowledge. Ordinarily by dissolution of the world we understand the dissolution of all the differences and multiplicity at the time of final dissolution of the world into its cause, and *advaita* is also a dissolution in which all the differences are dissolved due to *Brahman* realisation in which no reality other than and different from *Brahman* is experienced. Such conscious realisation of the oneness of all that is is the meaning of *advaita*.

This takes us to another central problem as to what is the relation between the various conceptions of *Brahman* and *Brahman* in itself, or between the empirical knowledge of *Brahman* and its true knowledge. We may say that *Brahman* alone is real in the absolute sense, and everything else that is empirically experienced is also real but in a relative sense. Here again we find that various thinkers, who are not in sympathy with *advaita* in its classical form, try to understand by *Brahman* or *ātman* a substance or essence, and so think that it should have certain attributes. According to this understanding, *Brahman* as substance may be eternal and remain identical, but it can undergo change or modification with regard to its attributes. But Śaṅkara nowhere uses the term substance for the Self or *Brahman*, and so we cannot bring in the analogy of substance to understand the nature of *Brahman*. If at all we are to use an analogy to understand the nature of *Brahman*, a spiritual reality like *puruṣa* is appropriate. Even otherwise,can we say that the sun is the substance and light his attribute, or fire is the substance and heat its attribute? Although in language, and also for the sake of understanding, we make a distinction between the sun and light, and fire and heat in reality they are not two. One is not related to the other as in the case of a substance and its attributes. We cannot think of any relation between the sun and light, and fire and heat as in reality the sun and fire are not different from light and heat. They are not two. Heat is the nature of fire, and so it cannot in any sense qualify or affect fire, as Śaṅkara puts it. But since we think of them as two, and hence create a difference between them *advaita* teaches that they are not two in reality. As fully developed in Kāśmīr Śaivism spiritual reality and its self-expression are in no way related as they are not two. We cannot say that the Self is different from its self-expression, or *Brahman* is different from its self-expression which is all that is. As they are not two there is no meaning in attributing some motive, and consequently some change in the nature of *Brahman*, and for the same reason the world cannot affect *Brahman* in any way. It is not possible to think of a spiritual reality without its self-expression, which is its nature. They are *abhinna*, the Śaṅkara's expression for their relation, if we call that a relation at all. Somehow, we fail to realise this and see them as different, and therefore *advaita* teaches them to be non-different in reality. When all is the self-expression of *Brahman* or *ātman* to understand and define *Brahman* in terms of some of its self-expressions is to limit it, and consequently not to know it in its fullness.

Finally *advaita* means the illusoriness of all duality, or the lack of ultimate or objective validity to all metaphysical theories. In criticising and rejecting objective validity to all metaphysical theories and doctrines, either propounded by different philosophers or are found in the scriptures, the purpose of Śaṅkara is to show that as conceptions they are merely mental (*vikalpa*), and may have at the most a pragmatic justification and validity. Only in such theories, which presuppose the duality of the world and its cause, some sort of causal explanation is offered for the existence of empirical reality in terms of *Brahman*. In other words, all the metaphysical explanations and views are dualistic, and the object of *advaita* is to show how they lack objective validity. Thus the meaning of *advaita* is to show the illusory character or lack of objective validity to all dualistic metaphysics by way of tracing them ultimately to the mind and its activity. All duality is mental or conceptual as Śaṅkara at times identifies mind with the conceptual activity of man, whereas *advaita* is objective as it is not and cannot be mental as mental activity presupposes duality. In this connection it is significant to note that *māyā* is also identified with mind by Śaṅkara. Even *nāma* and *rūpa* (name and form) can be interpreted as the creations or projections of human mind, and can therefore mean concepts and their expression in language. Mind stands for conceptual activity through which man builds various metaphysical and cosmological theories, and sees differences where they do not exist, as without differences the mind ceases to function. We find therefore in *advaita* philosophy a rich analysis and understanding of mind and its nature which is aimed at showing how its various creations, though of existential and pragmatic significance to man, do not however have objective validity. Since *māyā* is identified with mind and its conceptual activity, we can grasp the meaning of *māyā* according to Śaṅkara. The concept of *māyā* is not used in the philosophy of Śaṅkara primarily to explain the world process in terms of *Brahman*, but to explain such explanations, and also to show the mystery ultimately involved in the existence of the world. To think of *māyā* as the explanation of the world process in terms of *Brahman* is itself an instance of *māyā*. Any metaphysical or cosmological explanation, as explanation, is as good or valid as any other explanation. Only some may be more logical than others. But in the final analysis they all lack objective validity. Therefore to say that *Brahman*'s nature is dynamic, or somehow as the creative power of *Brahman māyā* is both different and non-different from *Brahman*, etc., are all metaphysical explanations, and hence will have the same status and validity as any other metaphysical explanation or view. All of them are mental or are the constructions of human mind. In comparison to these explanations experience is valid. The fact that at times we cannot understand and explain an experience does not mean that that experience is meaningless. To realise *advaita* is to overcome the temptation or urge to explain, and see or be the Reality directly which all the while is prevented because of our excessive attachment (*abhiniveśa*) to various metaphysical views. Instead of accepting the mystery as to how or why any reality other than *Brahman* is experienced at all, or how *Brahman* is seen as the world, if we try to explain it, it is due to *māyā*. *Māyā*, the irresistible urge on the part of man to explain metaphysically the nature of *Brahman*, and its relation to the world of empirical experience can be satisfied or put an end to when the mind ceases to be or ceases to function which is possible only by realising its non-difference from or oneness with *ātman*. When the mind and its conceptual activity cease the urge to create theories, and the various metaphysical theories involving duality come to an end. And unless one is weaned away from the mind and its dualistic creations or projections one cannot realise *advaita*, the negation of all duality (*dvaita upaśamanam*). As *advaita* is the nature of Reality or *Brahman*, and hence objective and eternally revealing nothing is to be done to know or realise it, but some effort is required to overcome the knowledge of differences which prevent man from realising *advaita*. So, philosophically *advaita* means negation of all metaphysical theories and views which presuppose duality, and are dualistic. This is done when the mind or *māyā* is overcome, as mind loses its identity or existence when the duality, its basis, is not there. *Advaita* means the denial or negation of all dualistic views, the creation of mind or *māyā*, and what is realised thereafter is something that cannot be conceptualised and described or determined.

References

[In this book I have followed the English translation of Śaṅkara's commentary on the *Upaniṣads* by Swāmī Gambhīrānanda and Swāmī Mādhavānanda, on the *Vedānta Sūtras* by George Thibaut and on the *Bhagavadgītā* by A. Mahādeva Śāstrī.]

1. *Gauḍapāda Kārikā*, 4.100.
2. *Śaṅkara's commentary on Gauḍapāda Kārikā*, 4.100.
3. *SūBh*, 2.2.25.
4. *BṛhUpBh*, 1.4.10.
5. *KaṭhaUpBh*, 2.1.1; *AitUpBh*, 1.1.1.
6. *BṛUpBh*,3.5.1.

7. *Ibid.*
8. *Ibid.* 1.4.7.
9. *Ibid.*
10. *Ibid.*,4.3.20.
11. *TaitUpBh*, 2.8.5.
12. *BṛUpBh*,4.3.20.
13. *Ibid.*, 2.4.11.

2

Ātman

ALTHOUGH *ātman* is not a concept basic to the *Veda*, as it is to the *Upaniṣads*, there is nevertheless a continuity in its meaning between the *Veda* and the *Upaniṣads*. In both the Vedic and Vedāntic literature *ātman* is used in three different senses, or we find in them three distinct conceptions of it. In one sense it means the self of a person, and can be true and significant of a person only. In another sense it refers to the essence of a thing or a phenomenon, and lastly to the ultimate reality in which sense it means the same as *Brahman*. The word *ātman* is used to mean all the three, and its usage is direct and primary in all the three senses. It is not the case that it means primarily the self of a person, and only secondarily or metaphorically the essence of a thing or a phenomenon other than that of a person, and ultimate reality or the reality of all that is. Only in one of its senses, that is, when it refers to the inner reality of man it means self, as the self of a person, but in so using also its usage is not incompatible with its two other senses. In other words, in using the word *ātman* to mean the self of a person its two other senses are not lost sight of either in the *Veda* or in the *Upaniṣads*. More significantly, its usage in any one sense is not inconsistent or incompatible with its usage in other senses, whereas the word **self** refers primarily to the self of a person only, as the self is not present outside of man. The self of man is not the self of anything else except in a metaphoric sense. Its usage is primary, appropriate and significant only when it refers to the self of a person, and outside the realm of human reality it has no primary application. Self is distinctive of man only while *ātman* is not distinctive of man alone. While the concept of self means primarily the self of a person, a spiritual substance or a subjective reality which knows, thinks, etc., *ātman* being an all-pervasive reality is not limited to the spiritual or inner reality of man. The words **self** and **soul** can convey only metaphorically what the word *ātman* conveys primarily. Therefore throughout this work we prefer the word *ātman* instead of rendering it into self or soul.

The translation of the word *ātman* into self or soul has given rise to certain problems in understanding the concept of *ātman* in the *Vedānta* tradition. For instance, *ātma-sākṣātkāra* or *ātmānubhava* is not the same as 'self-realisation', and *ātma-jñāna* the same as 'self-knowledge', as self-realisation and self-knowledge are subjective processes in which at no stage the subjective or personal element is transcended, as self stands for what is subjective or personal in man. The self is meaningful only in relation to a person, as it is his spiritual essence, and outside of him it has no primary and meaningful application. The self is the self of a person, and when used in relation to things other than a person it will have only a metaphorical meaning. But in the Vedic and Vedāntic traditions *ātman* is used to mean not only the inmost reality of a person but of everything, and also to mean the ultimate reality. Furthermore, if *ātman*, either in the context of the *Veda* or of the *Upaniṣads*, is to be conceived as the self or soul of a person, a distinctively human reality, we have to think of another non-spiritual reality of which *ātman* can be the self or soul. And such a dualistic world-view is not true to the spirit of the *Veda* and *Vedānta*, as ultimately all is one, or one and the same reality is the ultimate source of all.

We discuss in this chapter the meaning of *ātman* in all the major contexts of its usage, both in the Vedic and Vedāntic traditions, with a view to tracing the development of the concept from what is subjectively true of a person to its conception as absolute, before we try to understand the position of Śaṅkara. There is a significant continuity in its meaning from the Vedic *Saṁhitās* to the *Upaniṣads*, and yet it has acquired wider meaning and connotation in the *Upaniṣads* wherein it is used as a synonym of *Brahman*.

Vedic Conception

In the *Ṛg-veda Saṁhitā ātman* is used more clearly and distinctly in two different senses. It is used to mean the subjective or inner reality of a person or the animating principle in him in which sense it is similar to the concept of self or soul. Secondly, it is used more often to mean the essence of a thing or a phenomenon. And in one context it is used to mean, though indirectly, the ultimate reality. While addressing the sacrificial horse, in a horse-sacrifice, the word *ātman* is used either to mean the soul or the body of the horse. Since the hymn is addressed to the horse that is sacrificed or slain the reference is obviously to the soul of the horse, or the immortal principle in the horse that is supposed to go to the deities. "Do not burn your dear *ātman*."[1] In the same hymn the body of the horse is also referred to by the word *tanu*. In another context the seer says that he has recognised or known mentally the *ātman* of horse descending from above. Here the *ātman* of the horse is seen or known by the seer with the help of his mind, and therefore it cannot be the body of the horse. I am not interested in discussing whether, according to the Vedic seers, the animals possess souls or not, but in understanding the meaning of the concept of *ātman*. In the above context the word *ātman* should mean the soul of the horse as the seer knows that the body of the horse sacrificed will perish or be burnt, and therefore thinks and prays that the soul of the horse, which is different from its body, is not so burnt. Here the usage is clear, and means or refers to the soul of the horse. In another context, *ātman* is used metaphorically to mean the motion or animation as while referring to a ship or boat fashioned by the Aśvins the seer says that it has wings full of *ātman ātmanvantam pakṣiṇam.*[2] Here Sāyaṇa understands by the word *ātman* the strength (of the boat) and interprets *ātmanvantam* as *dhārdyavantam.* "You have a boat full of strength."[3] Or we may interpret the term *ātmanvantam* as referring to the motion of the boat or the manner in which the boat was fashioned by the Aśvins. It is well animated or can move well in waters as if the boat is animated by a soul or spirit. In a direct reference to the soul of a person it is said that the soul of a person will merge with the wind after death, as other parts of man will merge with other elements of nature, like for instance, the eyes of man, standing for light in man, with the sun.[4] When it is said that the *ātman* of man will merge with wind (*vāta*) after death, the meaning of *vāta* (wind) will have a different meaning, if we understand the meaning of the word *vāta* used in other contexts, but not simply wind, an element of nature. *Vāta* or *vāyu* (wind), or the deity which manifests itself in and through wind, a more pervasive reality, when compared to other deities like *agni* and *āpaḥ,* is identified and addressed as the *ātman* of all the deities (*ātmā devānām*) or the *ātman* of all (*ātmānām vasya abhivātam*).[5] Can we therefore say that the wind understood as *prāṇa* (vital principle), which is the form of manifestation of wind in man, is the soul of man? The Vedic concept of soul might then mean the vital principle (*prāṇa*) in man. In the later Vedic literature, including the *Upaniṣads*, *prāṇa* is discussed more widely and comprehensively, and is often conceived as the first principle of the universe. It is often identified as the essence of the world, or the reality of the world. And in this sense identification of the soul of man with *vāta* (wind) suggests that the soul of man is not uniquely a subjective principle or reality abiding in man only. *Prāṇa,* which is a form of manifestation of *vāta,* is present throughout the nature manifesting itself variously or in various forms among plants, animals and human beings, and is therefore a universal principle. It manifests itself in man in a particular form and that is the self or soul of man. Then the meaning of *ātman* as the soul or self of man will have a different significance. We cannot then say that the soul or self is distinctly a human reality or true of a person only, and is not present in any phenomenon other than man. It is a universal principle or a deity which is present everywhere, and so also in man, though manifesting itself in man in a different form. This is expressed clearly in the *Aitareya Āraṇyaka* wherein it is stated that *ātman* which is present within all is known more clearly in man as consciousness or intelligence, and one who knows *ātman* more and more clearly and fully obtains fuller being (*ātmānam āvistāram veda*). "Plants, tress and animals, in them he knows *ātman* more and more clearly. In plants and trees only sap is seen, in animals consciousness. In animals *ātman* becomes more and more clear because in them sap also is seen while thought is not seen in others. *Ātman* is more and more clear in man, for he is most endowed with intelligence. He says what he has known, he sees what he has known. He knows tomorrow, he knows the world and what is not the world. By the mortal he desires the immortal, being thus endowed. As for others, animals, hunger and thirst comprise their power of knowledge. They say not what they have known, they see not what they have known. They go so far, for their experiences are according to the measure of their intelligence."[6] *Vāta* or *vāyu* is also conceived as the *ātman* of the deities. It is the essence of all. Can we then say that *vāta* as *prāṇa* or vital principle is present only in the living beings, as *prāṇa* is known to be present within living beings only. But, according to the Vedic conception of *vāta* or *vāyu*, it is a divine principle, and is present everywhere though it does not manifest itself everywhere in the same form. We can thus explain the conception of *vāta* as the *ātman* or the essence or reality of all the deities, which is of course true with other deities also. Furthermore, *vāta* or *vāyu* is not only the essence of all the deities and man but also the source of the whole universe (*ātmā devānām bhuvanasya garbhaḥ yadhāvaśam carati devaḥ*).[7]

In these contexts *ātman* is used in the sense of that which is the essence or reality of a person, or a phenomenon or all that is. Even when it is used somewhat exclusively, but rarely, to mean the subjective or spiritual principle in man, and hence peculiar and unique to man (as soul or self of man), the sense of self or soul is much wider and comprehensive in the Vedic context than it is ordinarily understood. It is not the inner reality of man only, and therefore its usage cannot be said to be just and appropriate with regard to man only which is the case with the words self or soul. *Ātman* cannot therefore be reduced to soul or self of man in the context of the *Veda*. It means the essence or that by which a thing is what it is. *Ātman* is more frequently used in this sense in the Vedic literature.

The essence is variously identified as *agni*, *vāyu*, etc., as they form the essence of different phenomena. For instance, *agni* is the essence of all phenomena in which heat or warmth in any form is present, and water (*āpaḥ*) is the essence of all phenomena in which moisture in any form is present. The meaning of *ātman* as essence is clear in several contexts of its usage in the *Veda*. The sun is seen as the essence (*ātmā*) of all that is moving and non-moving. Here Sūrya (the sun) conceived as the ultimate reality is regarded as the essence (*ātmā*) of all that is. In the expressions such as 'the *ātman* of a disease' (*ātmā yakṣasya*), 'the *ātman* of *yajña*' (*ātmā yajñasya*), 'the *ātman* of Indra' (*ātmā indrasya*) 'the *ātman* of herbs', *ātman* is clearly used to mean the essence of things like disease, sacrifice, herbs and the deity Indra, but not to mean any animating principle that abides in them. It is their essence or that principle by which they are known as what they are. We may even say that *ātman* can mean in these contexts the nature of a thing, or the defining characteristic of a thing which is more in consistency with the whole of Vedic and Vedāntic thinking. *Ātman* cannot therefore be interpreted to mean the spirit inhabiting various phenomena of nature, as spirit being an animating principle, cannot be said to inhabit such phenomena as earth, water, fire, etc. Also the concept of spirit involves something non-spiritual or physical as its abode which is not acceptable to the Vedic or Vedāntic ontology. On the other hand, the concept of essence is wider and comprehensive in its meaning as it is that which forms the inner nature of a thing or phenomenon. It is the defining characteristic of a thing or a phenomenon, and is the reason or basis for what they are. It is present within all, though in each phenomenon it manifests itself differently. In a significant expression, while describing the deity Soma, it is said that Soma milks or sheds the essence of heaven as if it is the *ātman* of heaven (*ātman vat nabhaḥ duhyate ghṛtam payaḥ*), and Sāyaṇa interprets the word *ātman* to mean essence (*sāravat*).[8] In no other sense the usage of the word *ātman* is appropriate here. Soma milks the essence of heaven as clarified butter is of milk. In the following expressions the meaning of *ātman* is unambiguous, and is used to mean the essence or inner reality of a thing or a phenomenon. "In him (*sūrya*) is the essence of all that is moving and unmoving" (*tasmin ātmā jagataḥ tastu ca*).[9] The deity *vāyu* is addressed as the essence (*ātmā*) of all the deities, and the matrix of the universe (*ātmā devānām bhuvanasya garbhaḥ*).[10] This is meaningful as the deity *vāyu* in his different forms of manifestation abides within and sustains the deities and the universe. Each deity in its divine aspect is present within all though each deity as a manifestation of the Divine manifests itself more predominantly and clearly in a particular phenomenon, and forms the essence of that phenomenon. In all these contexts *ātman* does not mean either the vital principle (*prāṇa*) or consciousness, but simply the essence of a thing or a phenomenon. On the other hand, if we understand by *ātman* the spirit of a thing or a phenomenon we will be committing ourselves to animistic explanation of things, as spirit is that which animates a thing. But *ātman* as the essence is not present within man or other animated beings only, but in all. It is present within earth, water, fire, mind and within all as their essence.

If the Vedic seers can think in terms of essence of a thing or a phenomenon, in terms of which a thing or a phenomenon is known and identified, it is but logical to think of something being the essence of all that is, whatever may be its nature or in whatever manner its nature is conceived. The essence is that which is present commonly in a phenomenon in terms of which it is identified and distinguished from other phenomena. The idea of the essence of all that is (*ātman*) is expressed in one of the famous hymns of the *Ṛg-veda.* A seer wonders as to what is the essence (*ātmā*) of the things born, and who can tell it, or who has seen it or known it, and can tell it to us (*kaḥ dadarśa pradhamam jāyamānam bhūmyāḥ asuḥ aśruk, ātmā kvacit kah vidvāmsam upagāt draṣṭum etat*).[11] Here *ātman* as the essence of all is distinguished from the life or vital principle or blood of the universe. Who has seen the life and blood of the things born, and their *ātman*? *Ātman* is the essence of man, and it is more than his blood and life or beyond his physical and vital being. Whatever interpretation we may give to the whole hymn the meaning of the concept of *ātman* is clear. It is distinguished from the physical and vital aspects of man or his blood and life. Here Sāyaṇa understands by the word *ātman* consciousness which is aware of the physical and vital aspects of man. We may take the word *bhūmyāḥ* to mean born on earth or the earthly beings whose essence or reality is not either life or blood but something more. In the expression *ātmā eva vātaḥ svaśarirāṇi gachatam*, *ātman* is used to mean what is essential to man, as the *vāta* or vital principle is identified with the essence of man; it is his *ātman.*[12] Prajāpati is addressed as the giver of essence (*ātmā*) and strength (*bala*) to man, and as Prajāpati is conceived as the source of creation he is the giver of *ātman* as he constitutes the essence of all.[13] Expressing the same idea in a different way it is said that *ātman* is blissful (*ātmā eva śevaḥ*) 'blissful like *ātman*'.[14] *Ātman* is seen as the source of bliss to all; and this would be meaningful only if the Vedic seers had seen in *ātman* the essential and unchanging reality of man and the universe. What is not ultimately real cannot be the source of real bliss to man; he finds bliss in what is his essential nature. The Upaniṣadic idea that the ultimate good of man consists in realising *ātman* as it is the ultimate reality, and anything other than *ātman* is not the source of bliss to man is significant in this context. *Ātman*, the nature of which is not identified in these contexts, is the source of real bliss to man would be meaningful only if *ātman* is seen as the essence of man, and all that is. *Ātman* is the ultimate reality, as it constitutes the essence of all or because of which they exist, and are sustained by it. Thus in most of the contexts of its usage in the Vedic literature *ātman* is used to mean that which is the essence or inner reality of man, or a phenomenon or all that is. This is consistent with the later day usage of the word *ātman*, either in the *Upaniṣads* or in secular literature, in which it is used to mean the essence of a person, or a thing, or a phenomenon or all that is. It is not used exclusively to mean the self or soul of a person, the subjective principle in him, and because of which he has an inner dimension and acquires individuality. As a universal reality *ātman* is present within man also, as all phenomena, including man, have the same reality as their essence. This is more clearly expressed in the *Upaniṣads*.

Upaniṣadic Conception

There is a continuity in the meaning of the concept of *ātman* between the *Veda* and the *Upaniṣads*. In both of them *ātman* means the essence of a person, or a thing, or a phenomenon. But the idea of its being the essence of all that is or the world which is germinally present in the *Veda* is more clearly and fully developed and presented in the *Upaniṣads*. As the essence or reality of all *ātman* is all-pervasive, but it is known clearly and directly within man as his self.

The concept of *ātman* is central to the *Upaniṣads*, and the seers and thinkers of the *Upaniṣads* tried to understand the concept in all its dimensions, and in depth. Although the concept of *ātman* is present in the Vedic literature it is not central to it.

For the first time in the Indian tradition the concept of *ātman* received serious attention in the *Upaniṣads*. But because of the nature of the Upaniṣadic literature philosophical discussion of the problem of *ātman* as was attempted later by Śaṅkara and other commentators is not to be found in the *Upaniṣads*. However, the concept was presented in all its dimensions, and at times discussed and debated more thoroughly in a style which is peculiar to the *Upaniṣads*. The Indian philosophical understanding of *ātman* is based on the Upaniṣadic conception of *ātman*, and what the commentators, especially Śaṅkara, tried to achieve through their commentaries was to establish the concept more on philosophical grounds without at the same time losing sight of the experiential dimension of the concept. Whether Śaṅkara had gone beyond the *Upaniṣads* or deviated from them is discussed later, but if we understand the Upaniṣadic conception of *ātman* we can with sufficient justification say that Śaṅkara was more true to the *Upaniṣads*, and his understanding of the concept fully represents and reflects the Upaniṣadic view of *ātman*.

In the following I would like to maintain that the Upaniṣadic understanding or conception of *ātman* is not basically different from that of the *Veda*, or there is no radical departure from the Vedic conception in the *Upaniṣads*. The only difference is that it is not central to the Vedic thought. *Ātman* is used in the *Veda* to mean the essence of a thing, or a person, or a phenomenon or all that is, and that is the basic meaning of the term *ātman* which can be substantiated in terms of the etymological meaning given to the word *ātman* by Yāska. It is that which comprehends all, or encompasses all, or pervades all, or it is that which accompanies all notions or without which nothing is experienced (*yaśchāpnoti yadādatte yaśchātti viṣayāniḥ yaśchāsya santatobhāvaḥ tasmāt ātmeti kīrtitāḥ*). The word *āpnoti* in this context is explained to mean that which comprehends all by attaining all.[15]

In the *Upaniṣads* we find three distinct conceptions of *ātman* which are not unrelated to each other. It is often used to mean the ultimate reality, the ultimate source and ground of all that is, and in this sense it means the same as *Brahman*. Secondly, it is used to mean the essence of a thing or a phenomenon or all that is, as without it nothing can exist. Thirdly, it is used to mean the self of a person in the sense that it is the essential nature or reality of man. All the three conceptions supplement each other and enrich each other, and help us in comprehending the nature and meaning of *ātman* which in a broad sense has a unified meaning despite differences in its conception, namely, that it is the essence and inner unity of all. Towards the end of the chapter we try to understand whether all the meanings of *ātman* can be reduced meaningfully to a single comprehensive meaning, and if so what would be that meaning, and how other meanings can be seen as an extension of the original meaning. And also how the concept of *ātman* has come to be equated or identified with the concept of *Brahman* in the *Upaniṣads*.

In almost all the *Upaniṣads* *ātman* is used to refer to or mean the ultimate reality, the ultimate source and ground of all that is. In this sense its conception is purely metaphysical or ontological, and is often used as a synonym of *Brahman*, another Upaniṣadic term for the ultimate reality. However, in the later Vedāntic literature *Brahman* alone is used to mean the absolute or the ultimate reality. We do not find in the *Upaniṣads* any significant distinction between the conception of *ātman* as the ultimate source of all that is and *Brahman* as both are used interchangeably. "In the beginning *ātman* was alone there, and nothing else besides. It desired to create the worlds".[16] "*Ātman* alone was there in the beginning or before anything else came into existence. It desired to be born."[17] In another expression it is said that *ātman* was in the beginning in the manner or form of a person (*puruṣa vidaḥ*).[18] It is significant to note that *ātman* is conceived in personal terms, or *ātman* the ultimate reality is personal. Not only *ātman* is conceived in the *Upaniṣads* as the ultimate reality that was there before anything else came into existence, in several passages the origin of all that is or the universe is traced to *ātman*, or *ātman* is conceived as the ultimate explanation of all that is. "It is the great unborn (*mahān ajaḥ*). It is great, and the Lord (*mahāntam vibhuḥ*) or lord of all that was, that is and that will be. It is the lord of all beings, and their king (*sarveṣām bhūtānām adhipati, sarveṣām bhūtānām rājā*)".[19] The epithets usually employed in relation to ultimate reality, or all those terms which are appropriate to describe and signify ultimate reality or *Brahman* are equally used without any qualification to describe and signify *ātman* also. In no sense the conception of *ātman* as the ultimate reality is different from the conception of *Brahman*. "*Ātman* is immortal; it is *Brahman* and it is all."[20] It is *Brahman* the highest truth or reality (*brahman nāma satyamiti*). "Just as a spider weaves a web out of itself, as tiny sparks of fire emanate from fire, all the life, all the worlds, all the deities and all the beings originate from *ātman*."[21] While all that is or the world is real or true *ātman* is the reality or truth of the world (*satyasya satyam*).[22] It is the truth of all beings, and Being of all beings. "This world and the world beyond, all the beings and everything are the breathing out of *ātman*."[23] "*Ātman* is *Brahman*, *ātman* is Prajāpati, the source of all living beings, *ātman* is all the deities, all the beings and everything."[24] It is that by which all are endowed with existence, or they exist because they partake in *ātman* which is Existence, and all are established in *ātman* which is knowledge or consciousness. "Being the essence or reality of all *ātman* assumed different forms and names of different things." (*ekasthadā sarva bhūtāntarātmā rūpam rūpam pratirūpo babhūva*).[25] *Agni* is the head of *ātman*, the sun and moon are his eyes, the directions are his ears, all the *Vedas* are his speech or from him are born all the *Vedas*, and from him are born all the deities. "In *ātman* all that is is woven like warp and hoof. It encompasses everything and permeates everything; and without it things have no existence. By entering into all it is fully present within all, as a razor in its case. It is the world of their enjoyment and experience. It is the sweetness (or delight or joy) of all that is, and all the beings are honey to *ātman*."[26]

In all such expressions *ātman* is conceived as the ultimate source and truth of all that is. It is the ultimate reality or the reality that was before the existence of anything, and from it all came into existence. It is the one reality that is present within all, or everything is permeated by it. After the birth of the universe it entered into all as their essence or reality (*antarātmā*). In this sense *ātman* is not the essence or inner reality of man only, but of all that is. Everything is like a body to *ātman*, it being the essence and unity of all. It is the ultimate resting place of all just as a nest is the resting place of birds (*sarvam para ātmani sampratiṣṭhati*).[27] Here a distinction is made between *ātman* in itself or *ātman* that was there before anything else came into existence *para ātmā*, and *ātman* as the essence and unity of all that came into existence because of its being present within all. In the *Upaniṣads*, the concept *antarātma* is not used to mean the *ātman* that is present within man only but that which is within all. While referring to the *ātman* that is present within man the *Upaniṣads* refer to *śarīra ātmā*, the *ātman* that is within a human body.

As the *ātman* is both the material and efficient cause of the world, or as all is a manifestation or self-expression of *ātman*, all is often identified with *ātman* in the *Upaniṣads*. All the deities are *ātman*, the worlds are *ātman*, the various beings are *ātman*, all is *ātman*. (*idam kṣātram ime lokāḥ ime devāḥ ime vedāḥ imāni bhūtāni idam sarvam yadayamātmā*).[28] To know *ātman* in this sense is to know all or be all, and anyone who sees any difference in *ātman*, or between *ātman* and something other than *ātman* does not know *ātman*, as *ātman* is all, and there is no reality which is other than and different from *ātman*. It is only when the existence of something other than *ātman* is admitted it can be seen, heard and spoken about, but not when everything is *ātman*. There is not the 'other' (than *ātman*) which can be seen, heard and spoken about.[29]

Ātman as Essence

In various contexts of its usage in the *Upaniṣads* *ātman* means the essence of a thing, or a phenomenon or all. In clear and distinct terms *ātman* is used to mean the essence or inner reality of all that is. When *ātman* is used in the sense of ultimate reality it refers to what was there in the beginning or before the manifestation of *ātman* into all. It is one without a second. In this sense *ātman* is not the essence of anything, as then there is no reality other than *ātman* of which it can be the essence. The concept of essence is meaningful only when there are various things or phenomena of which something can be their essence. However, all the three conceptions of *ātman* have something in common, that is, *ātman* is the reality of all. While in the first conception of *ātman* as the ultimate reality, which is purely ontological, *ātman* means the absolute, in the second it refers to that which is within all as their essence and inner unity which it is by virtue of its being the ultimate source of origin of all. The Upaniṣadic terms for essence are *sāra*, *maya* and *antarātmā*. While the Sanskrit word *sāra* is nearer to the word essence, the other two words *maya* and *antarātmā* do not convey the sense of essence, though *ātman* in relation to the world is related in all the three ways. While essence (*sāra*) stands for what is inherent in a thing or a phenomenon or its defining characteristic, *ātman* as the essence of all or the world does not mean or convey the same sense as essence, as in the case of *ātman* in the state of manifestation as all, there is no second reality or a reality other than *ātman* which can form the outer or physical aspect of the world so that *ātman* can form the inner aspect or essence of the world. The *Upaniṣads* do not speak of a second reality to explain the origin of the world. If the *Upaniṣads* admit two independent realities to explain all that is or the world we can say that one forms the essence or inner reality of the world, while the other is the source of the physical or phenomenal side of the world. But *ātman* is all either before it gave rise to the world, or in its unmanifested (*avyakta*) state of existence or in the state of its manifestation as the world. In its unmanifested state of existence *ātman* is one only without a second, and at that level it is not intelligible to talk of *ātman* as the essence of all as there is no reality other than *ātman* of which it can be the essence. It is said in the *Bṛhadāraṇyaka Upaniṣad* that *ātman* is within earth, within water, within fire, within all the faculties of man or within all.[30] It abides within all, and all is its body. *Ātman* which is immortal permeates all from within. Or when it is said that *ātman* is that which sees, but is not seen, thinks, but is not thought of, knows, but is not known; and there is no other seer, thinker and knower, *ātman* is seen as the essence of all the faculties and senses of man in the sense that it constitutes their essence or capacity to know. It is the capacity of the eyes to see, the capacity of the ears to hear, the capacity of the mind to think, etc. Now, the idea that *ātman* controls all by being within all gives rise to the idea that the reality of *ātman* is limited to the essence of things or phenomena. In explaining the meaning of *sarvāntaraḥ* (being within all) it is said that *ātman* is within all because it breaths through *prāṇa* or lives through life (*prāṇeṇa prāṇiti*); it sees through the eyes, hears through the ears, thinks through the mind, etc., and therefore it is internal to all or within all. In this sense *ātman* is not the defining characteristic of a thing or a phenomenon, or what is intrinsic and enduring in things, but the source and basis of a thing. *Ātman* is not the essence of any one thing or phenomenon, but of all that is by being the ultimate source of all. When *ātman* is all or has become all, or when all is a manifestation of *ātman*, how could it be the essence of all as if there is some other reality which forms the external aspect or body of all. When there is no reality other than *ātman* to form the body of *ātman*, in the state of manifestation, to describe *ātman* as the essence of all is superfluous and unintelligible. But the intention of the *Upaniṣads* in describing *ātman* as the essence of all is not to make an ontological assertion but to impart knowledge of *ātman*, as the chief object of explaining *ātman* and its becoming is to instruct people about the nature of *ātman*, and to make them realise it for themselves. *Ātman* as the ultimate source of all is revealed as that which is intrinsic to all or what is essential to all but not in the forms and functions of things which differ, and are not enduring.

We find in the *Upaniṣads* a development or evolution of the concept of *ātman* and its meaning. This evolution in the conception of *ātman*, as the essence of all that is, will not be significant if we identify *ātman* as the self of a person. The evolution in the conception of *ātman* which is fully reflected in the *Taittirīya Upaniṣad* but is present in other *Upaniṣads* also shows that *ātman* is conceived primarily in ontological terms, but not in psychological or anthropological terms. In trying to understand the nature of *ātman* the object of the *Upaniṣads* is to know the nature of the essence of the world or all that is. Although *ātman* is primarily conceived in ontological terms as the ultimate reality, the Upaniṣadic insight into its nature is arrived at or based on an analysis and understanding of human reality. This we shall discuss towards the end of the chapter. In the *Taittirīya Upaniṣad* we find a development in the understanding of the nature of *Brahman* starting with the materialistic conception of it as *annam* or matter. *Brahman* is conceived as matter, as vital principle (*prāṇa*), as mind or understanding and finally as bliss. In all these attempts to understand and define the nature of *Brahman* the guiding principle is to know the nature of *Brahman* in more and more comprehensive terms so that nothing is left unexplained in terms of *Brahman*. Every preceding conception of *Brahman* is found to be inadequate as they do not satisfy the quest of the Upaniṣadic thinkers for the absolute which is the ultimate explanation of all that is. The preceding conceptions of *Brahman* are not so much rejected as are found wanting in their capacity to explain the universe. While food is the essence of body as it sustains it and helps its growth, vital principle (*prāṇa*) is seen as internal to body, and mind as internal to *prāṇa*, etc.

Prāṇa is regarded as higher to the body and mind as it can comprehend and explain the latter, but not *vice-versa*. Now in the same *Upaniṣad* the same method is followed in understanding the nature of *ātman*. It is conceived as *annam*, *prāṇa*, mind, understanding, etc., and after not being satisfied with any of them, it is conceived as consciousness and bliss. In both the contexts, that is, while trying to understand the nature of *Brahman* as well as of *ātman* the Upaniṣadic thinkers followed the same method of analysis. In most of the *Upaniṣads prāṇa* is identified with *ātman* or *Brahman*, and the discussion on *prāṇa* is more prominent and comprehensive. In the process of understanding the nature of *Brahman* or *ātman* as the ultimate reality, or as the essence and unity of all that is many conceptions were considered and transcended. We can therefore say that the concept of *ātman* in the *Upaniṣads* is not something that is revealed but is arrived at after a thorough process of critical reflection and examination which is well represented in the *Bṛhadāraṇyaka Upaniṣad* in the dialogues between Yājñavalkya and others.

In the conception of *ātman* as the essence of a thing or a phenomenon or all that is which we find in the *Upaniṣads*, essence (*sāra*) is not understood in the sense of something forming the core aspect of a thing, while some other reality forming the physical or outer aspect of a thing or a phenomenon. *Ātman* has become all this, and in so becoming it has not acquired a new nature nor has it lost any of its original nature. It also did not depend upon the help of a second or another reality in manifesting itself into many. The only difference between the two conceptions of *ātman*, that is, *ātman* in its ontological conception as the absolute or ultimate reality, and in its conception as the essence and unity of all that is, is that in the latter conception, which presupposes the process of *ātman* manifesting itself into many, without which the idea of essence as what is common to more than one thing has no meaning, *ātman* is seen as what is invariably present in all, or the notion which invariably accompanies all notions. The meaning of *ātman* as essence is well represented, and more clearly in the *Chāndogya Upaniṣad*. It is the subtle essence (*ātman*) of all, and that is truth, that is *ātman*, and that is the self of man also. Although *ātman* is the essence of all that is yet the manner of its manifestation in all or in diverse phenomena is not the same. It is common to all as it is the ultimate source of all. While as pure existence *ātman* is the existence of all as consciousness and bliss it is revealed more clearly in all living beings in different degrees, and is revealed still more clearly and distinctly in man. Thus essence in this context is not a class concept. It is the subtle and inner reality of all as it constitutes the reality of all. It is the ultimate source and ground of their existence. In all the examples given in the *Chāndogya Upaniṣad* to illustrate the nature and meaning of *ātman*, the idea of its being the subtle essence of all that is is clearly asserted. In one expression it is even said that truth is the *ātman* (essence) of *Brahman* (*satyātmā*). Here truth is seen as the *ātman* of *Brahman* in the sense that *Brahman* has truth as its own nature or essence.[31] Therefore when *ātman* is used to mean the essence of a thing or of the whole world the intention is to say that *ātman* constitutes the reality of all. It is their nature, their essence, their origin and the basis of their existence. In the other sense, which is meaningful for instructing the nature of *ātman*, *ātman* is identified with the subtle essence of all without which they are not what they are, and cannot exist. *Ātman* in relation to all that is is like the sap of a tree which permeates the whole tree subtly, and forms its life. When any part of a tree, like its branch, is cut off the tree does not die, but when its *ātman*, the living sap, leaves the tree it withers away. In this context the sap of the tree is identified with the living essence or life of the tree (*jivena ātmanā*).[32] Just as the sap of a tree permeates the whole tree, and without which the tree cannot live, so is *ātman* the subtle essence of all; and is therefore the self (*ātman*) of man. With the help of another illustration it is said that just as in a salt solution the whole water is permeated by salt, *ātman* pervades all, and is their subtle essence, and that is the *ātman* of man also. Just as the subtle essence pervades the whole seed of a *nygrodha* tree, so is *ātman* in all that exists, and that is the *ātman* of man also. In all these examples which are intended to instruct Śvetaketu about the nature of *ātman*, *ātman* is described as pervading the whole universe as its subtle essence. *Ātman* pervades the whole universe subtly as butter in milk (*sarva vyāpinamātmānam kṣīre sarpīrivārpitam*).[33] *Ātman* as the all-pervading essence of all that is is meaningful and intelligible only in the context of the universe, or in relation to the universe which is manifestation of *ātman*. Before *ātman* manifests itself or becomes many the idea of its being the essence of all will have no meaning, as then *ātman* was alone without a second. It was then not the essence of anything as there was nothing besides itself. It is the only reality which exists before the world of manifestation comes into existence. It is only after the manifestation of *ātman* into all or the world it can be seen and identified as the unifying essence of all. Thus the conception of *ātman* as the immortal subtle principle and unity of all that is involves the process of knowing the nature of *ātman* and its realisation. Its knowledge and realisation therefore mean the same as knowing and realising the absolute. When it is said that *ātman* is to be heard, reflected upon and meditated, *ātman* is not identified with the subjective principle of man. If *ātman* in this context means the subjective reality of man it is not possible to hear about it, reflect upon it and meditate on it as if it is an object of all these. It is the subject in man which sees, hears, reflects upon, etc., and therefore it itself cannot be an object of hearing, reflection, etc. "One who sees *ātman* as everything, one who sees thus, reflects thus, realises thus, for him everything springs from *ātman*."[34] Then one knows that from *ātman* springs vital force (*prāṇa*), all the faculties of man and his hopes, all the elements of the universe and all the deities, and also all the *Vedas*. In that state of realisation all that was earlier seen as something separate or different from *ātman* are now seen as springing from *ātman*, and being the same as *ātman*; one who knows thus becomes sovereign (*svarāt*). As the inner ruler and pervasive essence *ātman* is present within man also, and man can know his own inner reality directly, immediately and more clearly or distinctly than the essence of anything else.

If we ask the question whether *ātman* stands primarily for the ultimate reality or for the subjective reality or self of man, the evidence of the *Veda* and *Vedānta* is in favour of the former. If *ātman* primarily means the ultimate reality how it has come to be known as and identified with the self of man? Can we say that in the order of being or existence ontological conception of *ātman* as the absolute is prior to *ātman* conceived as the self of man, but in the order of knowledge *ātman* as the self of man is logically prior to the knowledge of *ātman* as absolute? What is the logical connection between the two conceptions? And which is logically prior to the other? Is it the case that the Upaniṣadic seers and thinkers started their metaphysical enquiry with the notion of self, the inner reality of a person, and then gradually came to know and identify that with ultimate reality (*ātman*)? Or starting with the concept of *ātman* as the ultimate reality, or as that which, as the source of all, exists before anything else comes into existence, came to recognise its presence within man also as his essence or self? In the *Upanisads* the evidence is in favour of the former, that is, *ātman* is conceived primarily as the absolute, but at the level of becoming or manifestation it is seen as the essence of all, and therefore as the inner reality or self of man. If there were to be only two conceptions of *ātman* in the *Upaniṣads*, one ontological and another anthropological, the problem of ascertaining the priority of one conception over the other would have assumed a different significance. But there are three distinct and clear conceptions of *ātman* in the *Upaniṣads*, and the conception of *ātman* as the subtle essence of all forms the logical link between the ontological conception of *ātman* and its anthropological conception.

Ātman as Self

Before we discuss this problem let us consider the conception of *ātman* as the inner reality or self of man. *Ātman* is not generally used in the *Upaniṣads* to refer to human person or human reality. The concept of *puruṣa* is used, though not exclusively, to refer to a person. *Puruṣa* refers to a human person. It cannot meaningfully be used in relation to any reality other than man, while *ātman* can be used and is used not only in relation to human beings, but all living beings (*sarveṣām bhūtānām*), and also to all that is. But *puruṣa* is used only in relation to man, or the ultimate reality conceived in personal terms, or as a person. *Ātman*, on the other hand, can be both personal and impersonal or neither. In the *Bṛhadāraṇyaka Upaniṣad* it is said that in the beginning *ātman* was alone in the manner or form of *puruṣa* (*ātma eva agre āsīt puruṣa vidhaḥ*).[35] This shows that the concept of *ātman* is different from that of *puruṣa*. But *ātman* can exist or manifest itself in a personal (*puruṣa*) form. While *ātman* can be both personal and impersonal, *puruṣa* is personal only. *Ātman* is present in all beings, but all beings are not personal; only man is personal or is a person. It is only when *ātman* is viewed in relation to man it is identified with *puruṣa*, or it acquires the character of *puruṣa* (*aṅguṣṭha mātram puruṣo antarātmā sadā janānām hṛdaye sanniviṣṭaḥ*).[36] It manifests itself in man in the form of *puruṣa*, while its manifestation in other living beings is in the form of life (*jivena ātmanā*), and in the realm of inanimate objects it manifests or reveals itself as their essence. In living beings *ātman* manifests itself as life, which is their essence, and in man it manifests itself as self. *Ātman* is to be known in the context of human reality as *puruṣa* or self (*ātmanched vijānīyāt ātmani puruṣa ayamasmiti puruṣaḥ*).[37] Further to distinguish *ātman*, that is consciousness, from *puruṣa* or the subjective reality of man it is stated that the *ātman* of the human body (*śarīra ātmā*) is enveloped and supported by *ātman* that is *prajñā* or consciousness (*prajñānena ātmanā*). "The bodily self is embraced or enveloped by *ātman* that is consciousness" (*ayam śarīra ātmā prajñānena ātmanā āruḍhaḥ*).[38] He then does not know anything either internal or external (*evamevāyam puruṣa prajñānenātmanā sampariṣavkta na bāhyam kiñcana veda nāntaram*). *Ātman* is neither internal nor external, as the spatial distinctions and relations are not meaningful in relation to *ātman*. Therefore what is unique and distinctive about man is not *ātman*, which is present within all, but *puruṣatva* which is a characteristic of man only as he alone is a person, or is known for his subjectivity or inwardness. While the various faculties of man like mind, intelligence, will, etc., constitute his person, *ātman* is free from them, and is beyond them as it is their inner principle or essence. *Ātman* is not the same as *puruṣa*. *Ātman* which assumes the form of *puruṣa* or manifests itself as *puruṣa* in man is more than *puruṣa* or transcends the concept of *puruṣa*. It is not therefore true to identify *ātman* with the self of man. The individual identity of a person or his subjectivity is due to his being a *puruṣa*.

The distinction between the concepts of *puruṣa* and *ātman* is highly significant in that *ātman* is not seen and conceived in personal terms. *Ātman* is not primarily personal, as *puruṣa* is, and therefore we cannot say that the concept of *ātman* is based primarily on the understanding of man of his own subjective reality. Its conception is not primarily anthropological or psychological though an understanding of man of himself, and his inner life may be a source of understanding the nature of *ātman*, which as the essence of all, is also the inner reality or essence of man. "*Ātman* is *Brahman* which experiences all (*ayamātmā brahma sarvānubhu*)".[39] It is within all, and is known directly and immediately (*yat sākṣāt aparokṣāt brahma*). *Ātman* is within all (*ayamātmā sarvāntarāḥ; eṣata ātmā sarvāntarāḥ*). How is *Brahman*/*ātman* within all? It is within all being the enlivening principle or the essence of all; it is that which lives through life (*prāṇena prāṇiti*). It is that by which the various faculties and senses of man are enlivened and inspired. It is that because of which the eyes see, the ears hear, mind thinks, etc. *Ātman* is that inner principle which experiences all with the aid of the various faculties of man. It is internal to all the senses by which they are able to perform their respective functions, and without it they, as instruments, will not be able to operate. Just as *prāṇa* pervades all the organs and enlivens them and makes them function, so *ātman* is that which is within the *prāṇa*, and through it it enjoys all and experiences all; and without it the various faculties and senses of man are incapable of experiencing anything. Man can live without some of his organs, like a tree without some of its branches, but cannot live without life. Life is common to all the bodily parts; it is their life. Therefore *prāṇa* is their essence or the essence of the body as without it body cannot live and sustain itself. But life (*prāṇa*) is not the ultimate essence or the innermost principle of man as above *prāṇa* or higher to it are mind and understanding, and higher to them is consciousness. Without consciousness man is not man. It is because of consciousness man knows that his body is sustained by life. It is because of consciousness all the faculties of man perform their respective functions like knowing, thinking, etc., and the functions of mind or intellect are known to *ātman* as consciousness, and are inspired by it to perform their respective functions. And without being inspired by *ātman* they cannot know, think and reflect. In this sense consciousness is the innermost principle of man, and is common to all his faculties and senses as it is present invariably within all of them, and thus comprehends them all. As it is common to all of them, and comprehends them all it is higher to them all. And in knowing the essence of himself man can know the essence of all as the same reality permeates all, and is their essence. Man knows directly and immediately his own inner reality or essence, and since the same reality is present within all, the essence of himself must be the essence of all that is. *Prajñā* which is the essence of man is therefore seen as the ultimate reality or the essence and unity of all that is. It is their *ātman*.

Ātman as Ultimate Reality

When compared to the Upaniṣadic evidence in favour of the first two conceptions of *ātman*, namely, *ātman* as absolute and as the essence of all in the state of manifestation, the evidence in favour of the conception of *ātman* as the inner reality or self of man is weak. *Ātman* primarily stands for the absolute or the reality of all that is empirically real, and therefore logically it is the essence of all that is in the state of its manifestation. If *ātman* is the inner reality or essence of all that is then it is the inner reality of man also, or his inner self. While man's knowledge of the essence of things other than himself is indirect or inferential he knows his inner reality or his self directly and immediately. The inner reality of man or his self which is internal to all his faculties, and is the source of their inspiration, is often identified in the *Upaniṣads* either as *Brahman* or *ātman*. *Brahman* is also spoken of or identified with the seeing of the eyes, hearing of ears, thinking of the mind, etc. In this respect, *ātman* cannot be distinguished from *Brahman*, and therefore cannot be identified exclusively with that reality of man which is internal to all his faculties, and the source of their inspiration. "The wise discern that as *Brahman* which thinks through mind (*manaso ye mano viduḥ te nicikyuḥ brahma*)."[40] Just as *ātman* is described in ontological terms *Brahman* is described in anthropological terms. *Ātman* is the ultimate source of all, including the various deities, and *Brahman* is the innermost reality of man, and knows and experiences all with the help of the various senses and mind. *Brahman*, which is known directly and immediately, is *ātman* which is within all (*yat sākṣāt aparokṣāt brahma yadayamātmā sarvāntaraḥ*). It is within all living beings; it lives through life. "Know that as *Brahman* which cannot be known or thought of by mind, but which knows or thinks through the mind, which cannot be seen by the eyes but which sees through the eyes, know that as *Brahman* but not anything that is variously conceived and meditated upon (*yanmanasā na manute yenāhurmano matam tadeva brahmatvam viddhi nedam yadidamupāsate*).[41]

Brahman which is the essence and unity of all is known as self in the case of man. Anyone who thinks *Brahman* as non-existence himself becomes non-existence, as *Brahman* is existence, and one who knows *Brahman* as existence is wise, and that is his embodied *ātman* (*tasya eṣa eva śarīra ātmā*) or *ātman* as present within himself. After conceiving *Brahman* as *prāṇa*, as *vijñāna* and as *yoga*, it is said that the same *Brahman* is *ātman* as embodied in the case of man. *Brahman* or *ātman* which is present within all is present within man as his inner self or essence (*antarātmā*), because of which he knows everything, experiences everything and thinks everything. As pointed out earlier, *Brahman* or *ātman*, the ultimate reality, which is present within all as their essence and guide, is known to man directly and immediately as his own self. Though *Brahman* or *ātman* is known directly and immediately to man as his inner self it is not within man only. *Brahman* which has entered into all, and is present within all, but difficult to comprehend because of its subtle nature, is known by the wise by the method of analysis and understanding of one's own reality (*adhyātma yoga*).[42] *Adhyātma yoga* in contrast to *ādhibhautika* and *ādhidaivika* methods of knowing reality means the method of knowing the nature of reality in the context of man's own reality. It is by analysing and understanding one's own reality one can know the nature of ultimate reality as present within himself. *Adhyātma yoga* is one of the methods of knowing the reality which is present within all, and the same can be known by knowing the external reality. Although *ātman* is present within all it is not seen by all; it is seen by those who can discern, and whose vision is pure and subtle. The same idea is expressed differently when it is said that *ātman*, which is one, is present within all, or being of one form or rather of no form has assumed several forms in several things. It is seen by the wise as being within themselves (*eko vasi sarva bhūtāntaratmā ekam rūpam bahudhā yat karoti tam ātmastham aṇu paśyanti dhirāḥ*).[43] It is by a process of self-analysis and self-understanding one sees *ātman* as being present within himself. *Ātman* is to be known as the reality of a person or self (*ātmānam cet vijāniyāt ayam asmiti puruṣaḥ*) or *ātman* is to be known or realised as oneself (*puruṣa*).[44] The concept of *puruṣa* is similar to the concept of person, and *ātman* abides in *puruṣa*, or *puruṣa* is the abode of *ātman*. And *ātman* is present within every *puruṣa*, and this truth is known through *adhyātma yoga*. Thus the conception of *ātman* as the ultimate reality, one without a second, and its conception as the essence and unity of all that is in the state of manifestation are logically prior to its conception as the inner reality or self of a person. Therefore in knowing oneself or one's own reality one does not simply know oneself as an individual person different from others and all, but sees the same *ātman* as being present within all, and hence comes to know all as one with one's self, and oneself as one with all. This can be meaningful and intelligible only when *ātman* is the ultimate source and essence and unity of all that is. However, in the order of knowledge, that too at *adhyātma* level, *ātman* can mean the inner reality or self of man, while in the order of being or existence *ātman* means the all-pervading and all-comprehending reality, the source and ground of all. It is the same as *Brahman*. This is the intended meaning of the various examples given in the *Chāndogya Upaniṣad* while instructing Śvetaketu about the nature of *ātman*, and his being one with it. The concluding statement in all the illustrations meant to teach the nature of *ātman* is the same. "That which is the subtle essence (*ātman*) of all that is is *ātman*, that is Truth; and you are that."[45] Just as the huge *nygrodha* tree is present within the seed in a subtle form, or as the subtle essence of the seed of *nygrodha* tree, which is homogeneous, contains within itself the whole tree, or as honey contains the essence of various trees, or as salt water is permeated by salt, *ātman* pervades all, comprehends all, and is present within all as the subtle essence of all; that is Truth; and that is your self. In all these *ātman* is conceived as the subtle essence or reality of all that is, and is therefore the inner reality or essence of man also. On the other hand, if the *Upaniṣads* assert that the self of man, his inner reality, is also the reality of all, it lacks philosophical justification as to how the reality of a person is also the reality of all, whereas it is logically meaningful to assert that *ātman* which is the reality of all, and is present within all is also the reality of man, and is present within him, as man is also a form of manifestation of *ātman*. Thus it is from the conception of *ātman* as the absolute the Upaniṣadic seers have come to see it as the inner reality of man. While *ātman* or *Brahman* is viewed as manifesting itself in the form of various deities at the *ādhidaivika* level, it is seen as manifesting itself as the various phenomena of nature at the *ādhibhautika* level, and at the *ādhyātmika* level it is seen as manifesting itself as the inner self of man through *adhyātma yoga*. Both in the *Veda* and *Vedānta* all the three methods are given equal importance in knowing the nature of ultimate reality, though in certain texts one method is given more importance. Nevertheless, they are different methods or approaches of knowing and understanding the nature of ultimate reality.

Ontologically man does not occupy any privileged position in nature, or in the realm of manifestation, but nevertheless he occupies a privileged position in knowing and revealing the nature of *ātman*. Within man, a self-conscious being, *ātman*, the inner reality of all, is seen or realised directly and immediately as it is his own being. By knowing his own inner reality, or self man can know the essence of all on the understanding that the same reality is present within all as their essence. Unless one knows or accepts that the same reality is present within all, being the source of their origin, one cannot know the unity of all by realising simply one's own inner reality or self. The unity is objective as *ātman* is that unity, and it is to be heard, reflected upon and realised; and in this process of *ātman*-knowledge and realisation man by virtue of his being a self-conscious manifestation of *ātman* occupies a privileged position. Man is the key to know or reveal the nature of *ātman* that is within all, but not to know or prove its existence. *Ātman* exists independently of man as man is only a manifestation of *ātman* which manifests itself in diverse forms at other levels of its existence. Man comes into existence only after *ātman* manifests itself. Nevertheless, man is the centre of its knowledge and realisation. In knowing or realising the nature of his own reality or self man comes to know directly the nature of *ātman* for which his understanding that *ātman* is the essence of the world of manifestation is essential. His knowledge or understanding of *ātman* as the ultimate source and ground of all that is is logically prior to his realisation of its being his inner self.

Ātman and Self

Now, the method of knowing *ātman* is not the same as the method of knowing one's self. One's self is not the starting point of knowing *ātman*, but it is the other way round. The metaphysical enquiry starts with *ātman*, the absolute, and culminates in the realisation that it is one's self. While *ātman* manifests itself in diverse forms in different realms of existence, and is known in different ways, its manifestation at the level of human existence or in man is different; it manifests itself or reveals itself in man as consciousness. Different manifestations of *ātman* reveal the nature of *ātman* in different ways, as the essence of one thing or of one phenomenon is different from that of others. Nevertheless, it is the same reality that manifests itself in and through all phenomena, though differently. Thus the nature of *ātman* in its manifestation as fire, water, earth, etc., will be known differently, as the essence of fire is not the same as that of earth or water. But as essence is understood in the *Upaniṣads* as the inner and subtle principle or reality of everything, or as that which permeates all and comprehends all as their ultimate source, the essence of man or consciousness, according to the *Upaniṣads*, is not to be seen in the same form in all other things and phenomena. However, the same reality is present within all, and that is the reason in trying to understand the nature of the universal essence or *ātman* we find in the *Upaniṣads* a gradual evolution or development in its conception starting from matter and culminating in consciousness and bliss. The guiding principle in all these attempts to know or understand the nature of *ātman* is to know that by knowing which all that is is known. In terms of their capacity to explain comprehensively or completely all that is, matter or life or mind fail as we cannot explain in terms of them all that exists, whereas consciousness is that principle or reality which can comprehend all and explain all. In this connection it is significant to note that in their quest for that principle or reality which is the ultimate explanation of all that is, the Upaniṣadic thinkers arrived at the concept of *Brahman* or *ātman* which is Existence, consciousness and bliss (*sat*, *cit* and *ānanda*). Among the three concepts of *sat*, *cit* and *ānanda*, which ultimately mean or point to the same reality, it is consciousness that is preferred by the *Upaniṣads* as forming the nature of *Brahman* or *ātman*, as without consciousness nothing is known and explained, or the whole enquiry would not be possible. Moreover, consciousness is existence and bliss. This we shall discuss soon. Consciousness is ultimate as without it existence and bliss are not intelligible and meaningful. Within man the highest principle or *ātman* is that because of which all his faculties are able to function, or that because of which the senses, mind and intellect are able to act and know their respective objects. In the *Upaniṣads prāṇa* is given importance next only to *ātman* or consciousness, because *prāṇa* is the sustaining principle of all living beings and plants, but *prāṇa* is not regarded as the highest principle in man as it cannot comprehend and explain his intellectual life though it sustains it. Mind and its various creative functions cannot be comprehended by *prāṇa*. *Ātman* is the *prāṇa* of *prāṇa*, ear of the ear, eye of the eye, as these cannot function without the presence of *ātman* or consciousness. It is the highest principle in man as it comprehends all his faculties by being what is common to them all, as well as the source of their inspiration. It is the light of man as without it he cannot know anything or experience anything. It is that because of which man knows everything, including himself. It illumines all without itself requiring any illumination. In the absence of all light *ātman* is the inner light of man because of which he knows himself and knows all. There is no principle higher than it. It is higher than the *prāṇa*, senses, mind and intellect, and without it man ceases to be man. It is in the light of *ātman* man knows what is good and what is bad. It presides over all that man does. It is because of *ātman* man conceives and creates a world of his own, and in this sense the space within man or the space of his creative life is as vast or infinite as the space without him in which are all the worlds.

In the story of Indra and Virocana, who wanted to be instructed by Prajāpati about the nature of *ātman*,[46] Indra could not be satisfied with the instruction that *prāṇa* is *ātman*, as in terms of *prāṇa* one does not known oneself, as he is such and such, or the world of creatures and deities. He is lost as it were without *ātman*. Therefore not being satisfied with the conception of *ātman* as *prāṇa* he further approached Prajāpati to know the nature of *ātman*. Though *prāṇa* is necessary for man's existence it is not the highest reality of man or *ātman*, as man does not know anything either about himself or about the world by his mere existence as a living being. It is because of his consciousness or knowledge man is what he is, and his glory consists in his knowledge of himself and of the world; and *ātman* is that because of which man knows himself and all. While all the faculties of man are inspired by *ātman* to function *ātman* does not require the help of anything else to be aware of things. All the senses and faculties of man are dead without *ātman*, while *ātman* does not depend for its existence, and for its capacity to know on anything else. It is that because of which all is known, and itself is not known through any of the sources of knowledge. It is not known through any means of knowledge as it is their source of inspiration and basis. Thus in all the *Upaniṣads*, *ātman* even in the context of man, is not conceived in subjective terms as if it is the reality peculiar and unique to man only. It is not primarily a human reality, and therefore its knowledge and description are not given in the *Upaniṣads* in purely anthropological terms. Even when it is described as that which helps man to know, or as that which is the inner sense of all his senses, like the eye of the eye, mind of the mind, etc., the intention is not to view *ātman* as a human reality or a reality that is within man only. In this respect all that is true of *ātman* in the context of man is equally true of *Brahman*. *Brahman* is also described in the *Upaniṣads* as the *prāṇa* of *prāṇa*, eye of the eye, ear of the ear, etc. In the state of its self-manifestation as the world *Brahman* or *ātman* lives within all as their subtle essence, and that essence is in man also, and is known as his inner being or self because of which he knows all. Thus *ātman* is to be seen in oneself also, and one who sees so sees all in *ātman*, and *ātman* in all. *Ātman* can thus be viewed as the self of man and identified with it not in any ontological sense, but insofar as the self, being a clear and self-conscious manifestation of *ātman*, is the centre of its knowledge and revelation. *Ātman* which is *Brahman* reveals its nature more fully and clearly in man, and in knowing *ātman* directly and immediately within himself man comes to know not only his own reality or self but *ātman* the absolute or *Brahman*, as the essence and unity of all that is. *Ātman* or *Brahman* is consciousness (*prajñā*) which the whole world has as its eye (*prajñā netra*), and everything is established in *prajñā* that is *Brahman*, and that is *ātman*. *Prajñā-netra* means that by which the world knows itself. *Ātman* is *prajñā* because of which everything is or the whole world gets its existence, and is guided or controlled. It is Indra, Prajāpati or all the deities, all the elements or all that is. *Ātman* is their eye or it is their guide and impeller. *Ātman* or *Brahman* which is identified with *prajñā* or consciousness is the inner reality of man also. Thus the self of man is *ātman* or *Brahman* but not in any unique sense, as everything is *ātman* or *Brahman*.

So far we have discussed the concept of *ātman* according to the *Veda* and *Vedānta* in both of which it is conceived as the ultimate reality or the reality of all that is. And as man belongs integrally to the universe, *ātman* is his reality also. Man is also a manifestation of *ātman*, and in man *ātman* manifests itself or reveals itself as his inner self. Thus *ātman* is seen as the self of man, and it is equally the inner reality or essence of all. As explained by Śaṅkara the term *ātman* is not confined to man only or is meaningful in relation to man only. The term *ātman* is used in relation to animate and inanimate beings as it is known by its usage in relation to all things, both animate and inanimate (*ātmā śabda cetana acetana viṣaye bhaviṣyati, bhūtātmā, indriyātmā prayoga darśanāt*).[47] It basically means the essence of a thing or a phenomenon.

Śaṅkara on Ātman

Before we discuss the concept of *ātman*, according to Śaṅkara, which is based largely on the *Upaniṣads*, we have to say something about Śaṅkara's approach to the *Upaniṣads* and the problem of *ātman*. In the writings of Śaṅkara all the three conceptions of *ātman* are present. However, the way he understands and interprets these three conceptions and their relative significance is somewhat different from that of the *Upaniṣads*. While in the *Upaniṣads* the conception of *ātman* as the ultimate reality is given more importance, in the writings of Śaṅkara much importance is attached to the conception of *ātman* as the inner reality of man or his self. In understanding the nature of *ātman* Śaṅkara follows his own analysis and understanding, though basically his understanding of *ātman* is based on or inspired by the *Upaniṣads*. He accepts the concept of *ātman* as presented in the *Upaniṣads*, analyses logically the various *Śruti* statements about *ātman*, and tries to understand philosophically the intended meaning of those statements. Occasionally, while interpreting the Upaniṣadic statements, he goes beyond the direct import of certain statements in understanding the concept of *ātman*, but that he does keeping in view the import of certain other statements of the *Upaniṣads* which in his view are more important and basic to the philosophy of the *Upaniṣads*. The object of his interpretation of the *Upaniṣads* is not just to provide an elucidatory commentary on the *Upaniṣads* but to understand and explain the central philosophy of the *Upaniṣads*, and present it in a logical form. His concern in discussing the concept of *ātman* is to make it more and more intelligible to man's rational understanding and experience. The basic reason for his approach is that *ātman* as the inner reality of man is self-evident to all. There is no need for external evidence and authority to prove the existence of *ātman*, and to discover its nature as *ātman* is present within man as his own self. *Śruti* cannot be the only source of knowledge of *ātman*; it only helps us or guides us in knowing its true nature. The authority of the *Upaniṣads* consists in their capacity to reveal the true nature of *ātman* as the ultimate reality. Man can independently of *Śruti* think of ultimate reality and conceive its nature, and understand its relation to man and world. *Śruti* is not required to induce man to metaphysical thinking, as metaphysical thinking as a rational activity is possible without *Śruti*. The *Upaniṣads* themselves contain different metaphysical theories about the nature of ultimate reality, and all those theories are not acceptable to all the *Vedāntins* as each interpreter of the *Upaniṣads* has accepted such of the Upaniṣadic statements which are more significant and basic according to his own understating, or support his own point of view. This is the case with Śaṅkara also. He not only argues against several metaphysical doctrines found in the *Upaniṣads*, but also against several conceptions of *ātman* either found in the *Upaniṣads* or upheld by different philosophers belonging to different schools of Indian philosophy. In all this he follows the method of logical analysis and understanding. His arguments either for rejecting the positions of others or for supporting his own are clear, cogent and precise. Most of his arguments against his opponents are clear and formidable, and those in favour of his own position are subtle and cogent. Most of his arguments or explanations on the nature of *ātman*, seen as man's inner reality or self, are meant mainly to deny validity to the arguments forwarded by various thinkers in support of their own views and theories rather than to establish his own view of *ātman*, as *ātman* seen as the self of man does not require any proof, and its nature is revealed to all though not in the same way and form. It is self-revealing and self-evident to all. Arguments are required to demolish different conceptions of self and to uphold the Upaniṣadic conception of *ātman* as pure consciousness. Śaṅkara resorts to *Śruti* only while upholding the Upaniṣadic conception of *ātman* but not in criticizing and rejecting the rival views which he does solely on the basis of logical reasoning or *tarka*.

In accepting the authority of the *Upaniṣads* as a means of knowing the nature of *ātman* he gives basic importance to those statements whose meaning is clear and definite, and are intelligible to man's rational understanding, and can be supported by experience. He starts with an analysis of man's experience, especially of himself, and tries to understand its meaning through a process of reasoning which is not speculative but is based on or guided or supported by experience, which includes the experiences of the Upaniṣadic seers. Śaṅkara's approach to the problem of *ātman*, as it is in most of the *Upaniṣads*, is aimed at discovering the immutable principle that is revealed in and through human experience, and makes it possible. Experience is analysed and interpreted not so much to know the object of experience, but to know the nature of experience itself, and its possibility. What is it to experience, and how is it made possible? Although some object is involved or is present invariably in all our experience it is not sufficient to know and explain the nature and possibility of experience. The guiding principle behind Śaṅkara's concern for an analysis of experience is to discover the reality which commonly or invariably accompanies all our experience, and is essential for any experience to take place. Is there any reality which underlies all our experience, and does not, like the objects of experience, go on changing? The presupposition of this search or enquiry is the notion of essence which, according to both Śaṅkara and the *Upaniṣads*, is that principle or reality which does not change its nature along with the changes in its manifestation, and is at the same time the ground of change. Is there any reality which persists without any change in its nature amidst all that is changing in our experience? The objects of our experience are not free from change or mutation which, according to Indian tradition, means coming into existence, persisting for a while and then disappearing. Whatever may be the nature of change, the objects of experience undergo change, and what is changing cannot be regarded as the essence of a thing. Since there is no doctrine of creation of something completely new, either in the *Veda* or in the *Upaniṣads*, anything that comes into existence is only a form of manifestation of something which does not change in its identity or essence. All change is a change in form of manifestation of the reality that manifests itself in diverse ways and forms. And to know the nature of ultimate reality is not only to know the source and ground of all that is manifested but to discern within the changing forms of manifestation that which abides without any change. The unchanging reality which is at the same time the source of all change, whatever may be the theory of change, is *ātman*, and the same is known as self (*ātman*) in the context of man. Thus to know the existence and nature of what is unchanging in man an analysis of man's experience is sufficient. The insights of the *Upaniṣads*, which often followed the same process, will be of significant contribution in our analysis and understanding of our experience, and Śaṅkara accepts the insights of the *Upaniṣads* into the nature of self, as they help us in understanding the reality of man which however can be known independently of *Śruti*.

Out of the three conceptions of *ātman* available in the *Upaniṣads* Śaṅkara favours the conception of *ātman* as the self of man. In man the revelation of *ātman* is clear, and is self-evident to all as consciousness is known directly and immediately to all (*pratyak cetanah svasamvedyaḥ*). In the order of knowledge, *ātman* is directly known to man as his own self, though in order of reality it is the reality of all. And in knowing his own reality or self man need not depend upon any external authority or source of knowledge as it is his own inner reality which by its very nature cannot be an object of knowledge. The self or consciousness is not at all an object of knowledge (*aviṣaya*). It is beyond all empirical relations and knowledge though it is very much within the empirical realm (*avyavahāryam sarvaloka vyavahārātītam*), just as rope is present in all the notions superimposed on it.[48] It is only for the purpose of a philosophical enquiry and understanding into the nature of *ātman* it is viewed and identified as the self of man as the enquiry has to have a starting point. It also serves the practical purpose of instruction about *ātman*, for which some distinctions like the knower, the object of knowledge and the method of knowing are to be made as without such distinctions no instruction about *ātman* would be possible. Otherwise the reality of *ātman* is really beyond the scope of the term and concept of self. Neither the *Upaniṣads* nor Śaṅkara says that in knowing *ātman* one knows one's own self only. If one could know *ātman* by knowing one's self the scriptures would have asked one to know oneself, as if *ātman* is his own self only, instead of knowing it as *Brahman*, the reality of all that is. The conception of *ātman* as the ultimate reality or the reality of all that is is logically prior to its conception as the self of man. As the essence of all *ātman* is the inner reality of man also, though in man its revelation is direct and clear. It also reveals itself in man in its essential nature of consciousness. This is not lost sight of in the philosophy of Śaṅkara. However, he starts his philosophical enquiry into the nature of *ātman* with the conception of it as self of man for methodological purpose of basing the enquiry on what is self-evident and universal. No one can deny his own existence or self as in denying it its existence is proved or asserted. Denial of one's own self involves contradiction. Whatever one may think about the nature of self one cannot, without committing contradiction, deny one's own existence or self. Śaṅkara accepts the Upaniṣadic conception of *ātman* as the ultimate reality, one without a second. *Ātman* which is one without a second and all-pervasive like space cannot be identified with the self of man, if we understand by self the reality of a person or what is unique and peculiar to a person. No one can think of all-pervasive *ātman* to be contained by a human body just as a pot can contain a fruit. Even the *Śruti* cannot teach us so for it goes against its own basic teaching that *ātman* is all that is, and it is one without a second. "Not even a fool can wish to conceive mentally that *puruṣa*, (which is most often used as a synonym of *ātman* both in the *Upaniṣads* and by Śaṅkara) who is the cause of space can be encompassed by the body like a pot enclosing a small fruit, much less can a Vedic text does so which is a valid means of knowledge."[49] Śaṅkara admits that any talk of *ātman*, like it is self-luminous, it is the self of man, it is bound or liberated is possible only within the state of ignorance. But still as *ātman* in the state of its manifestation is within all as their essence its nature is revealed clearly and directly within man as his inner self or consciousness. Man thus occupies a significant place in revealing the nature of *ātman*, or his knowledge of himself is significant in knowing the nature of *ātman*. In the case of man his inner self or essence is clearly and directly known to him when compared to the essence of anything other than himself. In man *ātman* reveals itself as clearly as an object in a mirror. Knowledge of self is common to all, and is self-evident to all though people do not agree about the true nature of *ātman* that is revealed in and through man. "Here alone in the body (of man) it is possible for the vision of *ātman* to be as clear as that of a face in a mirror." "It is not realised outside the body and senses for it is inmost self or essence of all."[50]

Ātman and Man

What is *ātman* as revealed in man? Is it the body and the senses, or vital principle or mind or intelligence or the soul or self in the ordinary sense? When we look to man to know the nature of *ātman* as revealed in and through him we are to look for that in man which constitutes his essence or his essential being, as *ātman* is the essence of man as of everything. Essence of man is that which not only is present invariably in all that he knows, thinks and experiences, but also forms the ground of his existence, or that without which his existence as man is meaningless. It is his self or the subject to which everything is an object. Self or subject is that to which everything is given as an object, but itself is never an object. *Ātman* in man is identified with consciousness or the knower as consciousness or knower invariably accompanies all knowledge, or is invariably present in all that man knows or experiences, and without which no knowledge or experience is possible. It pervades the whole being of man, and is known through all that man knows and experiences. "*Brahman* is reflected (in man) in the form of a clear reflection of the light of knowledge as though it is of that form."[51] "Like salt dissolved in water cannot be perceived directly but in relation to water, so is the case with consciousness or existence."[52] Is self or consciousness a quality or an attribute of human body? "Whenever something exists if some other thing exists, and does not exist if the other thing does not exist we determine the former to be a mere quality of the latter."[53] According to this definition of quality it may be argued that as movement, consciousness, thinking, etc., the characteristics of self are observed only within bodies, and not outside bodies, self cannot be regarded as something different from the body, but only as an aspect or quality of body. To this it may be said that if the self is a quality of a body it should be found in a dead body also. It should be present when the body is present, but it is not the case as in the case of a dead body.

Human knowledge involves two factors basically, the subject or the knower and the object of knowledge. The objects of knowledge may be external to man, like the world of objects, or internal to him, like his own internal states. Both the subject and the object or the knower and the known are interdependent as in the absence of one the other is not known. Man knows himself as the subject of knowledge while knowing the objects, which may be external or internal. Just as man knows the external objects he knows his internal states also as objectively as he knows the external objects. Therefore what we ordinarily mean by the self of man is also an object of knowledge as it has a content which can be communicated. As one is aware of one's body and senses one is aware of his mind and its various functions, and by self we normally mean the unity of body and mind. The objects are known to a subject, and as the subject knows itself in the process of knowing the objects, which may be external or internal, we think that the subject knows itself directly; and this is regarded as the highest principle in man. While in object-consciousness some object is present to consciousness, in self-consciousness some idea or notion about itself or of oneself or the very process of knowing is the object of consciousness. Thus 'I know myself' means I know myself as a thinking or knowing being, or as one who is thinking or knowing, or as immortal or finite, etc., as without some object element self-consciousness is not possible, and is also not intelligible. In being aware of himself one is aware of his mental or intellectual processes, or of an idea of himself which he has formed of himself either independently or as inherited from his tradition. In both the cases the principle of awareness or consciousness and some object in the form of an idea or notion, or the very process of knowing or reflecting are present. And what is experienced as an object of experience is not the same as experiencing, or what is being aware of is not the same as being aware of, as otherwise there would not be knowledge or experience, and the self which is an idea or notion which one forms about himself is also an object of experience. The idea of self is formed by man about himself and is known internally, and what is so known can be communicated to others. We talk about ourselves to others and hear from others about themselves as we can talk about any other object. While the world of objects is external to man his self is internal to him, but both are given to consciousness as objects.

Without some object-content, which can be communicated, there can be no notion of self whether one means by self his body and senses, or his feelings and emotions, or his mind and its creations, or some idea he has formed about himself, or a unity of all these. The self has a content of which one is aware, and it can be communicated to others. There is some kind of knowledge or awareness about the self which can be communicated, as what cannot be known cannot also be communicated. Thus the idea of self involves some objective content, and is given to consciousness as any other object is given. Only the mode of knowing the self, and the means of knowing it are different from the mode and means of knowing an external object. Furthermore, one's understanding or idea of oneself goes on changing from time to time depending upon the situation of one's life. No one idea of self remains unchanging in the life of a person. But the consciousness to which the notion of self is given as an object remains unaffected despite changes in the notion of self. "Since the aggregate of the body, etc., is substantially indistinguishable from sound, etc., it too is equally a knowable. It cannot be the knower."[54]

The following analysis of Śaṅkara may help us in knowing the nature of *ātman* in the context of man. In the *Upaniṣads* *ātman* is identified as the seer, hearer, thinker, etc. Naturally all these functions are possible in the presence of some object, the object of seeing, hearing, thinking, etc., and the *ātman* as seer, hearer, thinker, etc., is known only in relation to the objects it knows (*pratibodha viditam*). In the absence of objects to be known, or when man is not knowing he cannot be called a knower. When there is no thinking man cannot be known as thinker, as when there is no seeing or hearing he cannot be called a seer or hearer. In all these the vision of *ātman* is temporary and intermittent. Seeing or hearing or thinking are not always present in man. At times he sees, at times he hears, at times he thinks, etc., and if *ātman* is to be identified with these functions and defined as seer, hearer, thinker, etc., *ātman* cannot be identified with consciousness as consciousness revealed in and through these functions of seeing, hearing, thinking, etc., is intermittent and fleeting, and cannot therefore be the nature of *ātman*, if by *ātman* we mean something unchanging and enduring. If these functions were to constitute the nature of *ātman* either *ātman* should not be found without them, or they should always be present in *ātman* which is not the case as in the state of dream less sleep. Even during the waking state these are not present always. If consciousness is to be identified with these functions we have to think of its being a quality of a substance called *ātman*. Then consciousness forming a quality or attribute of *ātman* need not be unchanging and eternal, for as a quality of *ātman* it can manifest itself at times. But on this assumption we cannot know what *ātman* in itself would be. Such an *ātman* will be an unknowable reality posited only to explain consciousness and its passing states. If, on the other hand, consciousness and *ātman* are one and the same consciousness should never be absent as it is the very nature of *ātman*.

Ātman and Experience

In this context Śaṅkara's analysis of experience is highly instructive and significant. He makes a distinction between two kinds of vision or awareness (*dṛṣṭi*) in man, one temporary and intermittent, and the other eternal or ever present. The temporary vision whereby one sees, hears, thinks, etc., is fleeting, and lasts as long as the functions of various sense-organs and mind through which it is known last. For instance, the vision of a jar lasts as long as the eyes are in contact with the jar, and the consciousness that is revealed in thinking lasts as long as thinking lasts or persists. When there are no objects of vision the vision also (of objects) will not be there. Seeing of a jar lasts as long as jar is seen. This vision which depends for its manifestation or revelation upon the sense-organs and mind has a beginning and an end. It begins with the perception of an object, and ends when the object is not there or is removed from the field of perception.

The other vision (*dṛṣṭi*) which Śaṅkara identifies with *ātman* or is seen as the nature of *ātman* (*svarūpa*) is eternal, and does not depend for its revelation on the instruments of knowledge, like the sense-organs and mind. The temporary vision of man depends for its manifestation or revelation on the senses and mind as it is known through the operations of different sense-organs and the diverse functions of the mind. It is known through seeing, hearing, thinking, etc., and is not revealed in the absence of those functions. Depending upon those functions it is regarded as having a beginning and an end, as it is known along with the functions of the senses and mind. The knowledge of a pot requires the operation of sense-organs and the presence of pot. When either of them is absent the resultant knowledge and the vision or consciousness that is revealed through such knowledge are absent. It is an act, and hence has a beginning and an end. It depends on the presence of mind, the operation of the senses and the availability of an object. In the absence of any of these the vision also is absent. It comes into existence when these factors are available and comes to an end when any one or all of them are absent. This vision is temporary and changes along with the objects of knowledge.

Ordinarily the soul or self is identified with the totality of the functions of mind and senses, and is seen as manifesting itself through those functions, or is conceived as a substance manifesting itself in and through those functions. This conception of self involves consciousness but is not identified with consciousness, as consciousness is only its manifestation. *Ātman* is not the self understood in this sense, but is the knower or witness of the self, or to which the self is an object of knowledge. *Ātman* witnesses the self which experiences various objects during waking and dream states. *Ātman* is that vision or consciousness to which the self in the ordinary sense is an object of knowledge. The self knows or experiences the various sense-objects through the senses, and the objects of mind through mind. It sees, hears, thinks, etc., and comes to know the various objects. Now *ātman* witnesses the seeing, hearing, thinking, etc., and while these functions are intermittent and temporary, *ātman* or eternal vision which witnesses these functions is not so. It does not depend for its revelation upon any instruments of knowledge. It witnesses the functions of mind and the operations of the senses, and as mind and senses are active throughout the waking and dream states, *ātman* or the eternal vision is ever revealed along with the functions of the mind and the senses. Seeing a pot is temporary, for as an act it begins when the pot is present and ceases along with it, but *ātman* as the witness of seeing is ever present, and is eternal. And in being aware of seeing, hearing, thinking, etc., *ātman* does not require any instruments. Furthermore, the objects of knowledge change or are affected by time as they are related to past, present and future, but the eternal vision is not affected by time since its nature is eternal presence (*sarvadhā vartamāna svabhāvāt*).[55] Eyes are required to see colour, ears to hear sound and mind to think and remember, but eternal vision does not depend on any means to be aware of these functions. It is not therefore an act, and hence has no beginning or end.

One may point out here that seeing, hearing, thinking, etc., as functions of the senses and the mind are also temporary as seeing is not possible in the absence of an object of seeing and thinking in the absence of an object of thought. Cannot we therefore say that the other vision or *ātman* which is aware of seeing, hearing, thinking, etc., is also intermittent and changing along with the functions of the senses and the mind? Is not the eternal vision or *ātman* affected by the changing functions of mind and the senses, just as seeing is affected by the objects seen? As sense-objects influence or affect sense perception, do not the functions of the senses and the mind, which are witnessed by *ātman*, influence or affect *ātman*? Can we say that consciousness which is aware of seeing, hearing, etc., is not affected by them? Here we have to make a distinction between perceiving, thinking, etc., and witnessing or simply being aware of. In perceiving and thinking the senses and the mind are involved, and are active, and are therefore affected by the objects of perception and thinking, whereas in witnessing these functions or in simply being aware of them *ātman* is not involved, and is not active, as witnessing is not an act. *Ātman* witnesses them by its mere presence. As one or the other functions of the senses or of mind is active during the waking and dream states, and as these are witnessed by *ātman* which is the same as eternal vision (*dṛṣṭireva svarūpamasya*) *ātman* is not at all involved in witnessing them. "Through the unfailing eternal vision which is identical with (*ātman*) and is called the self-effulgent light *ātman* always sees the other transitory vision in the waking and dream states."[56] The eternal vision is the nature of *ātman* like heat of fire. Just as light by its mere presence illumines objects or reveals them without itself being active or being the agent of illumination, *ātman* or consciousness is aware of the functions of the mind and the senses without involving itself or without intending to do so, but by its mere presence. It is not an agent of awareness nor does it intend to be aware of them.

The eternal vision of man which is consciousness or *ātman* witnesses the other vision which is transient, and by which man knows the world. The transient vision, which is ordinarily identified with the self of a person, is also an object of knowledge to *ātman* (*ahaṅkārasyāpi upalabhyamānatvāt*).[57] The transient vision also involves consciousness as without it no knowledge is possible, but it is affected by the objects of knowledge and by the instruments of knowledge. According to the terminology of *advaita*, when *ātman* is identified with the functions of the mind and the senses it is known as self, while in reality *ātman* witnesses the self, and is therefore not the same as self. In the absence of objects to be known or when there is no knowing it is not meaningful to identify oneself with knower. Therefore to talk of *ātman* as the knower is to use the language which is meaningful in relation to self. Therefore Śaṅkara says that when *ātman* is termed as knower it is used to mean that which is pure knowledge.

Ātman as Consciousness

We find in the writings of Śaṅkara another approach to the problem of *ātman* which is presented and analysed more effectively. *Ātman* is identified with consciousness as that is the innermost principle of man. Consciousness is innermost in the sense that it is never an object to which alone the terms outer or inner, or external or internal can be applied. Consciousness to which everything, either physical or mental, is given as an object (*viṣaya*) is present invariably in all that a man knows and experiences. "*Ātman* follows (*anugata*) all ideas such as 'I am this or that', for it is invariably present in all of them as rope is present in all its illusory appearances or in all the ideas superimposed on it."[58] "The *ātman* in the case of all creatures is well-known to be the inmost consciousness known directly, and is self-revealed (*pratyek cetanah svasamvedyaḥ*)."[59] All knowledge involves awareness and the objects known. The objects may be physical or mental but no knowledge is possible in the absence of an object. The subject and the object are essential for any kind of knowledge, and each is revealed or known in relation to the other. Things may exist independently of a subject but are known as objects only when they are presented to some subject. And in relation to the act of knowing an object consciousness is known or identified as the knower or the subject. In the absence of objects to be known there can be no notion of knower also. Knower-known or subject-object distinction is present in all knowledge, and in the absence of either no knowledge is possible. The objects of our knowledge are of different kinds, and in relation to them the knower is known differently as seer, hearer, thinker, etc. Thus seer, hearer, thinker, etc., are functional names of the knower, and what is commonly revealed in all the functions of knower is the capacity to know or the principle of awareness. Consciousness is invariably present in all the functions of a knower, or in all the modes of acquiring knowledge. Both the subject and object are equally real at the level of knowledge as without one the other is not known. Both are revealed or known together in the act of knowing. Seeing involves the object seen, whether real or illusory, and the act of seeing. Is there anything present invariably in all knowledge and experience so that it can be identified as what is essential to all knowledge, and can be the basis of all knowledge? It cannot be the object of knowledge as objects of knowledge change constantly. While physical objects are objects of our waking experience, mental objects or mental impressions of physical objects experienced during waking experience form the objects of our dream experience. And what persists unchanging, and is present invariably in all knowledge and experience is the principle of awareness or consciousness. It is the reality underlying all knowledge, and without it no knowledge is possible. All our knowledge and experience presuppose consciousness, and are based on it, the reality commonly revealed in all our knowledge and experience. Everything is based on it, and is comprehended by it, but itself is not based on anything and comprehended by anything. It is presupposed by all but it does not presuppose any other reality. It reveals all but itself is self-revealed, or does not depend upon anything else for its revelation. We cannot think of anything as being the basis of consciousness without consciousness being the precondition for thinking or saying so. If *ātman* as the essence of all, including man, is identified with consciousness certain things follow logically. Consciousness which is present invariably, and is revealed in and through all that man knows and experiences is by its very nature distinct from and opposed to all that is known and experienced. "In both waking and dream states we observe that the gross and subtle worlds consisting of actions, their factors and results are but objects for the seer. Therefore the seer, the *ātman*, is different from its objects, the world perceived in these states."[60] Because of this distinction and opposition in nature between consciousness and the objects of consciousness all that is known as an object cannot belong to consciousness, and affect it. On the other hand, if things known or experienced belong to consciousness then they cannot be known, as to be known a thing must be given as an object to consciousness. Anything that is an object of consciousness is other than consciousness, and therefore cannot belong to it. By presupposing or being the basis of all our knowledge and experience consciousness is not affected by what is known or experienced. If the things known or experienced were to belong to consciousness then there would not be any knowledge or experience of them. We cannot even say that consciousness exists or does not exist as in saying so the ideas of existence and non-existence are given as objects to consciousness. In asserting or denying anything about consciousness, consciousness is presupposed, or it is the precondition for saying so, and therefore it is not in any way affected by whatever we say about it. All that we say about consciousness cannot belong to consciousness, and if anything were to belong to consciousness it could not be known and asserted of it. *Ātman* or consciousness is always the knowing principle, and cannot therefore become an object of knowledge, and an object is always an object, and cannot become the knower. "Cogniser is ever the cogniser and cognised is always the cognised (*jñeyam jñeyameva tadhā jñātāpi jñātaiva*)."[61] *Ātman* is never an object of knowledge (*aviṣaya*), or there can be no knowledge of *ātman* in the ordinary sense of knowledge. It is only to objects of knowledge we can predicate or attribute something, but not to a reality which is not an object of knowledge. All that can be asserted or denied can be asserted or denied in relation to an object of knowledge but not to *ātman* or consciousness which is never an object of knowledge. Even knowledge and ignorance of which one is aware and can be communicated to others do not belong to *ātman*. They are also known by *ātman* as desires or any other mental states. The so-called knowledge of *ātman*, which the *Śruti* and other enlightened people talk about and communicate, is not really the knowledge of *ātman*, as in being communicated by one and in being grasped by others, it is known by both as any other object of knowledge (*vidyā avidyā nāmarūpā ca na ātmadharma*).[62] "All the opposing ideas like it (*ātman*) is or is not, is one or many, is with attributes or without attributes, it knows or does not know, it is happiness or misery, is inside or outside may indeed wish to roll up the sky like leather or to ascend there or trace the footprints of fish and birds in water and sky."[63] It is logically impossible or rather self-contradictory to talk of knowledge of *ātman* or consciousness. Even if we admit some sort of *ātman*-knowledge then we have to ask as to whom that knowledge is given and by whom. This would be possible only if *ātman* is an object of knowledge. One cannot have knowledge of *ātman* as the one who wants to have knowledge of *ātman* is *ātman*. Secondly, as there are no qualities or characteristics of *ātman*, as qualities can belong to something that is an object of knowledge, there can be no knowledge of *ātman*, as knowledge involves attribution of something to some other thing. There can be no inferential knowledge of *ātman* as it is that which wants to prove its existence and nature inferentially. And we cannot think of two consciousnesses, one trying to prove the existence and nature of consciousness, and the other to which it is proved. Thus it is said by Śaṅkara that "all such talk about *ātman* starting with self-luminosity and ending with emancipation is within the range of ignorance."[64] Therefore nothing can be said about *ātman* though all that can be said about anything is said because of it. It is not an object of knowledge but no knowledge is possible without it. It is not an object of sight but because of it all is seen. It is not an object of thought but because of which thought is possible.

From the above discussion it is clear that neither in the *Upaniṣads*, nor in the philosophy of Śaṅkara *ātman* is conceived as a spiritual substance or reality peculiar and unique to man only. As consciousness, *ātman* is indistinguishable from person to person, and also from those living beings in whom consciousness is present. What distinguishes one person from the rest and also from other living beings is the mind and the ways and forms in which it manifests itself in different persons. Since consciousness is the same in all living beings, and as without it no knowledge and experience are possible it pervades and comprehends all that is known. The word *ātman*, as pointed out earlier, is traditionally derived from the root *āpnoti* (attaining) which it does by pervading all and comprehending all. It enjoys all and knows all, and because of which the world has continuity and unity. Therefore all that is knowable, or about which anything can be said is not *ātman*. All that is known as an object, and of which something can be said presupposes *ātman*, and is an object to it. In this sense the self of man as constituting his various aspirations and achievements, his feelings and emotions, his knowledge and experience is an object to *ātman* though given internally and known in a different manner. "Since the aggregate of the body, senses, etc., is substantially indistinguishable from sound, etc., it too is equally a knowable, and therefore cannot be the knower."[65] *Ātman* cannot therefore be defined in terms of or identified with the self of man though we may conventionally or for practical purpose identify *ātman* with the self. There can be no definition of *ātman* (*nirdhāraṇa*) as *ātman* is not basically an object of knowledge. Therefore to talk of *ātman* as witness, hearer, thinker, etc., is inconsistent with the true nature of *ātman* which is consciousness. "They only represent conventional ways in which people express. They do not seek to define or determine the truth of *ātman*."[66]

Although there can be no knowledge of *ātman* as pure consciousness, and therefore nothing can be said about it, yet for the purpose of instruction the *Śruti* creates some kind of distinction within the nature of *ātman*, like the knower and the known, or imposes certain characteristics upon it so that instruction about *ātman* is made possible for those who are ignorant, and are in need of instruction. The creation of some distinctions in the nature of *ātman* for imparting knowledge about *ātman* is admitted as a concession to the ignorant. Or we can talk of *ātman* as if it is the ultimate object or goal of attainment only from the state of ignorance in which all distinctions are meaningful. But in the state of enlightenment or *ātman*-realisation there is no duality of any sort (*jñāte dvaitābhāvaḥ*). It is like creating signs like '1', '2' or 'A', 'B', etc., to teach numbers and sounds.

Thus *ātman* is conceived both in the *Upaniṣads* and in the philosophy of Śaṅkara as the absolute or ultimate reality, and at the level of manifestation as the essence and unity of all that is, and therefore as the inner reality or self of man. And the inner reality or self of man is identified as consciousness. As the inner reality or self of man *ātman* accompanies (*anugata*) all his knowledge and experience, and comprehends all that is known or experienced. It is the basis of all knowledge and experience as without it no knowledge or experience is possible. Its non-existence cannot be conceived as in the process of proving its non-existence its existence is presupposed and proved. *Ātman* as the self of a person, as ordinarily understood, involves consciousness as without consciousness the idea of self is untenable and meaningless. Self as the ideal image of a person or as the spiritual reality of man involves consciousness though mixed up with other things like mind, body and senses, which as objects of consciousness, are different from and other than consciousness. Thus though consciousness is involved in the concept of self it is not the same as self. There can be knowledge of self which can be communicated, whereas *ātman* or consciousness by its very nature cannot be an object of knowledge. Moreover, *ātman* which is all-pervasive and all-comprehending cannot be identified with what is unique and peculiar to a person or man. *Ātman* the essence of all that is is not the reality of man only. It is the reality of all, whereas the notion of self is limited to and intelligible in terms of man only. Nevertheless *ātman* is revealed clearly and directly in man. Therefore understanding of man's reality or self is a direct means of knowing the nature of *ātman*.

If, on the other hand, the intention of *Śruti* is to identify *ātman* with the self of man, and if *ātman* can be comprehended by the term and concept 'self', *Śruti* should have insisted upon meditating on the self of man and knowing it. Then the statements of *Śruti* like *tat tvam asi* (you are That), *aham brahmāsmi* (I am *Brahman*), 'all is *Brahman*' and *ātman* is all would be meaningless. They will then have no import and validity. And the ultimate purpose of *Śruti* would have been served by simply instructing us to know *ātman* as the self instead of instructing us to realise its identity with *Brahman* or all that is. *Śruti* would then have negated the truth and validity of itself if its intention were to identify *ātman* with the self of man. "The truth of *ātman* is really beyond the scope of the term and concept 'self'. Otherwise *Śruti* would only say one should meditate upon the self. But this would imply that the term and concept of *ātman* were permissible with the self only. That however is repugnant to *Śruti*."[67] Therefore when *Śruti* teaches the identity of *ātman* with the self of man its purpose is to teach or instruct man about the nature of *ātman* but not to identify *ātman* with the self of man. It is the starting point of enquiry or instruction but not the culmination of it. One has to know oneself to know *ātman*, as *ātman* is clearly revealed within oneself, and is known directly and immediately, but in knowing *ātman* fully or perfectly one sees *ātman* as transcending self. Then one realises *ātman* as the ontological reality or the reality of all. Just as we identify some signs with numbers to teach numbers, *ātman* is identified with the self of man for the purpose of instruction, otherwise instruction about *ātman* is not possible. "After *Brahman* realisation as the only reality there is neither instruction nor the instructor nor the self receiving instruction, we admit. But before that if we accept it it will contradict the assumption of all believers."[68]

References

1. *ṚVSaṁ*, 1.162.20 ***see also*** 1.163.6.
2. *Ibid.*, 1.182.5.
3. *Ibid.*, 1.182.5 ***see also*** Sāyaṇa's commentary.

4. *Ibid.*, 1.115.1 **see also** 10.16.3.
5. *Ibid.*, 10.92.13.
6. *Aitareya Āraṇyaka*, II.iii.2.5.
7. *ṚVSaṁ*, 10.168.4.
8. *Ibid.*, 9.74.4.
9. *Ibid.*, 1.115.1 and 7.101.6.
10. *Ibid.*, 10.168.4.
11. *Ibid.*, 1.164.4.
12. *Ibid.*, 1.34.7.
13. *Ibid.*, 10.121.2.
14. *Ibid.*, 1.73.2.
15. *KaṭhaUpBh*, 2.1.1; *AitUpBh*, 1.1.1.
16. *AitUpBh*, 1.1.1.
17. *BṛUp*, 1.4.17; **see also** 1.4.1.
18. *Ibid.*, 1.4.1.
19. *KaṭhaUp*, 2.22; *BṛUp*, 4.4.22 and 25; 2.5.14 and 15.
20. *BṛUp*, 2.5.1; **see also** *ChāUp*, 8.14.1.
21. *MuUp*, 1.1.7.
22. *BṛUp*, 2.1.20; *ChāUp*, 6.8.7.
23. *BṛUp*, 4.5.11; 2.4.10.
24. *AitUp*, 3.13; *BṛUp*, 2.1.20.
25. *KaṭhaUp*, 2.2.9-10.
26. *BṛUp*, 1.4.7; 2.5.1; *ChāUp*, 7.26.1.
27. *PrUp*, 4.7; 4.9.
28. *BrUp*, 2.4.6; 4.5.7.
29. *Ibid.*, 2.4.14; 4.3.24-30.
30. *Ibid.*, 3.7.3-23.
31. *TaitUp*, 1.6.2.
32. *ChāUp*, 6.11.1.
33. *ŚveUp*, 1.16.
34. *ChāUp*, 7.25.2.

35. *BṛUp*, 1.4.1.
36. *KaṭhaUp*, 2.3.17.
37. *BṛUp*, 4.4.12.
38. *Ibid.*, 4.3.3.
39. *Ibid.*, 2.5.19.
40. *Ibid.*, 4.4.18.
41. *KenaUp*, 1.6.
42. *KaṭhaUp.*, 1.2.12.
43. *Ibid.*, 2.2.11.
44. *BṛUp*, 4.4.12.
45. *ChāUp*, 6.9.4.
46. *Ibid.*, 8.7; 8.8; 8.9; 8.10.
47. *SūBh*, 1.1.6.
48. *MāUpBh*, 1.9; *MāKāBh*, 2.37.
49. *PrUpBh*,6.2.
50. *KaṭhaUpBh*,2.3.4 and 6.
51. *ChāUpBh*, 8.1.2.
52. *Ibid.*, 6.13.1-2.
53. *SūBh*, 3.3.53.
54. *KaṭhaUpBh*, 2.1.3. If the body constituted by various elements like colour, sound, etc., can perceive colour, sound, etc., then the elements outside the body of man may know each other as well as themselves. But this is not the case.
55. *SūBh*, 2.3.7; ***see also*** *BṛUpBh*, 1.4.10.
56. *BrUpBh*, 1.4.10.
57. *SūBh*, 2.3.40.
58. *MāKāBh*, 2.32.
59. *ChāUpBh*, 8.14.1.
60. *BṛUpBh*, 2.1.18.
61. *BGBh*, 13.2.
62. *TaitUpBh*, 2.8.5.
63. *AitUpBh*, 2.1.1 introduction.

64. *PrUpBh*, 4.5.
65. *KaṭhUpBh*, 2.1.3.
66. *BṛUpBh*, 3.4.2.
67. *Ibid.*, 1.4.7.
68. *Ibid.*,2.1.20.

3

Brahman

As presented and discussed in the previous chapter there is a discernible continuity and even unity in the conception of *ātman* among the Vedic *Saṁhitās*, the *Upaniṣads* and the philosophy of Śaṅkara. There is no radical departure in the conception of *ātman* from the *Veda* to the *Upaniṣads* though the *Upaniṣads* and Śaṅkara paid more attention to the concept of *ātman*, and developed it more fully and comprehensively. The basic meaning of *ātman* as the essence of a person, or a phenomenon, or all that is is common to both the Vedic and Vedāntic conception of *ātman*. As the essence and unity of all that is it is also the inner reality or self of man. However, the idea that the nature of *ātman* is known clearly and directly within man, a self-conscious being, is well developed and presented in the Vedāntic tradition. But we do not find in the *Veda* a clear conception of *ātman* as the ultimate reality.

Now, when we try to understand the concept of *Brahman* it may appear that there is no logical or conceptual link or continuity between the Vedic concept of Brahma and the Upaniṣadic concept of *Brahman*. Even if there is a discernible continuity, and even a sort of unity it is not clear and explicit. Before we try to understand whether there is any continuity and unity in meaning, or at least a conceptual connection between the Vedic concept of Brahma and the Vedāntic concept of *Brahman* we have to understand the meaning of the concepts of Brahma and *Brahman* as presented in both the traditions. While the concept of Brahma in the *Veda* is not metaphysical meant to explain the reality of anything or the world, in the *Upaniṣads* *Brahman* is mostly conceived as the ultimate reality, the ultimate explanation of the world. It is conceived both in the *Upaniṣads* and in the philosophy of Śaṅkara as a metaphysical reality capable of explaining the reality of the world. But in the *Veda* Brahma is not a metaphysical concept but a descriptive term. However, the concept of *Brahman* in the sense of ultimate reality or the ultimate explanation of all that is is not completely absent in the *Veda*. A few of the Vedic hymns contain metaphysical speculation, and in all those hymns Brahma is not used either directly or indirectly to mean the ultimate reality, the source of all that is.

Vedic Conception

In all the speculative hymns of the *Veda* the terms such as *ekam* (One), *tat* (That), support or ground (*skamba*) are used to mean that which is the ultimate source and ground of all that is. At times, the concept of *puruṣa* is also employed to mean the ultimate reality. But the primary concern of the *Veda* is not metaphysical speculation about the existence and nature of ultimate reality as it is in the case of *Upaniṣads*. Moreover, the Vedic seers are not, in general, interested in understanding the existence and nature of ultimate reality as in most of the speculative hymns the Vedic seers are sceptical about man's ability to know the existence and nature of ultimate reality. "Who hath beheld him as he sprang to being, seen how the boneless (formless) one support the bony (formed). Who may approach the man who knows to ask about it (*kaḥ dadarśa pradhamam jāyamānam astanavantam yat anasthā bhibharti, kaḥ vidwānsam upagāt pṛṣṭam etat*).[1] "What was that one who in the unborn's image hath established and fixed these world's six regions?"[2] The seers often wonder whether anybody could answer these questions or whether these questions could be answered by anyone, including the deities, with certainty. Even the deities are incapable of knowing the One or Unborn as they belong to the realm of becoming or manifestation. Nevertheless, the idea of ultimate reality, the explanation of all that is is present in the *Veda*, but that is not indicated by the term *Brahman*. Can we then say that the Upaniṣadic concept of *Brahman* has nothing to do with the Vedic concept of Brahma, as Vedic Brahma is not a metaphysical reality meant to explain the world and its origin? Is *Brahman* a purely Upaniṣadic concept having no history in the *Veda*? Is it the case that the Vedic concept of Brahma and the Vedāntic concept of *Brahman* are completely different and unrelated? Is the Vedic scepticism about the existence and nature of ultimate reality overcome in the *Upaniṣads*? Or can we say that the Upaniṣadic *Brahman* is the answer to the Vedic quest? Is the Upaniṣaidc *Brahman* a purely metaphysical concept having no foundation in human experience? And how are we to understand and explain the synonymous use, in almost all the *Upaniṣads*, of the terms *Brahman* and *ātman*, and their common import? Is it then the case that *ātman* is also purely a metaphysical reality having no basis in human experience? If *Brahman* and *ātman* are only metaphysical concepts having no basis in experience it would be futilc and superfluous to search for any unity in meaning between the Vedic concept of Brahma and the Vedāntic concept of *Brahman*. Is the similarity between the Vedic Brahma and the Vedāntic *Brahman* only linguistic but not conceptual?

In the *Upaniṣads Brahman* is not purely a metaphysical concept, and its identity with *ātman* is not based on any mystical experience. The oneness or unity of *Brahman* and *ātman* is inherent within the meaning of these concepts as they do not mean two different realities. They refer to the same reality in its two different states. As both these concepts are based on experience we cannot say that one (*ātman*) is based on or derived from experience while the other (*Brahman*) is based on man's rational understanding. If the concepts are identical in their import and refer to the same reality what is the philosophical justification for developing two different concepts to refer to the same reality? Do they then at least point to two different contexts out of which they are born and developed, or are the methods of arriving at these concepts different, that is to say, the concept of *ātman* is born and developed out of a context in which the starting point of man's search for reality is his own reality, and the concept of *Brahman* is born and developed out of man's search for the reality of the world? Can we say that the concept of *ātman* is born and developed when man's starting point of enquiry is himself or his own reality, and therefore it represents primarily the reality of man which is somehow extended to mean the reality of all that is? In other words, can we say that *ātman* means primarily the inner reality or self of man, and is based on man's understanding of his own reality, and *Brahman* primarily means the reality of the objective world and is born of man's enquiry into the reality of the world? Is *Brahman* primarily the reality of the world and *ātman* the reality of man, and somehow they are seen to be identical, or a sort of unity is established between them?

Ātman-Brahman Equation

As shown in the previous chapter, *ātman* does not mean either etymologically or in its actual usage in various contexts, either in the *Veda* or in the *Upaniṣads*, the inner reality of man or his self only. It is all-pervasive, like space, comprehending all by being their essence (*sarvāntara*). It is also the inner reality or essence of man, or is present within man also as his self. We cannot therefore say that the concept of *ātman* is born and developed out of man's self-understanding, though man's understanding of his own reality helps him in knowing the nature of *ātman* directly and immediately. It is one thing to say that as the inner reality or essence of all, *ātman* is also the essence of man, and quite another to say that *ātman* is primarily man's inner reality and is therefore also the inner reality of all. If we accept the latter it would be difficult for us to understand and explain intelligibly the connecting link between the reality of man and the reality of the world, or to universalise the nature of a reality that is known primarily as the reality of man. But *ātman* which in its conception is not different from that of *Brahman* as it pervades all, comprehends all and holds together all is not the reality of a person only, though its nature is revealed clearly and directly in man. And whenever *ātman* is used in the *Upaniṣads* to mean the absolute its usage is synonymous with *Brahman*, but as being present within all (*sarvāntara*) and experiencing all (*sarvānubhu*). In most of the contexts of its usage all the attributes that are appropriate to *Brahman* as the ultimate reality are equally attributed to *ātman*, and the qualities and functions peculiar to the self of a person are not exclusively attributed to *ātman*. If *ātman* primarily means the self of a person, or is discerned in the context of man's self-understanding, characteristics proper and appropriate to the reality of a person should invariably be attributed to *ātman*. This is not however the case with the *Upaniṣads*. Likewise, if *Brahman* refers primarily to the reality of the world or its ultimate explanation, and is born in the context of man's enquiry into the nature of the world, the characteristics peculiar to the reality of a person should not have been attributed to *Brahman* as it is often done in the *Upaniṣads*. *Brahman* is known in the context of man's self-understanding as *ātman* is known in the context of man's understanding of the reality of the world. "Before the creation or manifestation of name and form they were one with *ātman* and are known by the term *ātman*, and the reality of *ātman* is known after the manifestation by means of name and form as well as by the term *ātman*."[3] If the contexts of their origin and development are really different we cannot explain the fact that in most of the *Upaniṣads* where the employment of the concept of *Brahman* would have been logically more proper and appropriate the concept of *ātman* is used, and *vice-versa*. In several Upaniṣadic statements *ātman* is not only identified with the reality that was in the beginning but is described in ontological terms such as great (*mahān*), unborn (*aja*), the maker of all (*viśvakṛt*) or (*viśvakartā*), the ruler and king of all (*sarveṣām bhūtānām adhipati; sarveṣām bhūtānām rājā*). All the beings, all the deities and all the worlds are in *ātman* as they are in *Brahman* (*sarvāṇi bhūtāni, sarve devāḥ sarve lokāḥ sarve prāṇāḥ sarva eta ātmani samarpitāḥ*).[4] We can quote any number of Upaniṣadic passages in which *ātman* is described in cosmic and ontological terms, and is conceived as the ultimate source and ground of all that is. All this would be highly inappropriate and unintelligible if the primary meaning of *ātman*, and the context of its origin is the self of man.

In the context of Indian tradition in general, and in the context of *Vedānta* in particular, there is nothing unique about an individual person (*puruṣa*) who is known by the term *vyakti*, and significantly the word *vyakti* means that which is an expression or manifestation. Accordingly we may say that an individual person is an expression or manifestation of the reality whose manifestation is the whole world. There is nothing unique about man so that what is revealed in him is revealed in him only though certain characteristics of reality are manifest in him more fully and clearly. Therefore anyone who knows and thinks anything as different from *ātman* is not a knower of *Brahman* or *ātman*, for all are *ātman*.[5] *Brahman* is identified in the *Upaniṣads* with the internal ruler or the invisible principle of unity, or the thread (*sūtra*) that binds all and unites all, and *ātman* is conceived as being within earth, within water, within fire, within air and within all as their indwelling reality or essence. Thus it dwells not only within man but within all. Just as a spider weaves a web and withdraws it into itself, as the sparks emanate from fire, so from *ātman* all life, all the worlds, all the deities and all the beings come into existence. In all such expressions *ātman* is conceived as the inner reality and unity of all that is, and therefore it cannot be regarded as the inner reality or self of man only. Similarly the attributes and functions which will be appropriate to *ātman* conceived as the subjective reality of man like thinking, reflection, etc., are equally attributed to *Brahman* (*yanmanasā na manute yenāhu mano matam tadeva brahmatvam viddhi*). It is that which cannot be thought of or understood by the mind but that because of which mind can think and understand. Know that as *Brahman* which cannot be perceived by the senses but by which the senses perceive (*yaḥ cakṣusā na paśyati yena cakṣumsi paśyati tadeva brahmatvam viddhi*). Those who know it as the life of life, eye of the eyes, ear of the ears, mind of the mind can discern the nature of *Brahman* which is ancient and primordial.

Though in certain contexts of its usage *Brahman* refers to the ultimate reality, the ultimate explanation of the world, in most of the cases in which it is used more significantly *Brahman* refers to the reality that is known directly and immediately (*sākṣāt aparokṣāt brahma ayamātmā sarvāntaraḥ*). Thus not only the concepts of *ātman* and *Brahman* are used synonymously or interchangeably in all the *Upaniṣads*, but the same qualities are attributed to both without any discrimination, and this would not be meaningful if each has its own primary meaning and context of origin which are different from that of the other. On the other hand, if *Brahman* refers primarily to the reality of what is empirically real or the world, and is developed in the context of man's search for the reality of the world, and *ātman* refers primarily to the self of a person, and is born and developed in the context of man's understanding of himself each concept should have certain basic characteristics which cannot be attributed meaningfully to the other. If the source of the concept of *ātman* is man, and that of *Brahman* the world then what is significant and true of *ātman* like thinking, knowing, etc., may not be significant in relation to *Brahman*, and those characteristics of *Brahman* like its being the ultimate source of all and the ruler and unity of all cannot be true of *ātman*, the reality of a person. *Ātman* then should be conceived in personal terms, as the characteristics of a person are not intelligible outside man. Then *ātman* cannot be said to be the reality of anything other than man.

Furthermore, though it may look trivial but nevertheless significant that in the *Upaniṣads* it is the reality of man (*ātman*) that is identified with *Brahman* but not *Brahman* with the self of man. In all the illustrations given in the *Chāndogya Upaniṣad* to elucidate the meaning of the statement *tattvamasi* like the homogeneous substance of a seed which is the source of the tree, or salt solution, etc., the idea sought to be conveyed is that the same reality which permeates all, as the source and essence of all, is also the reality of man. It is not the other way round.

But how to understand as to why two distinct concepts are developed to mean the same reality if there is no basic difference either in their conception or in the context of their origin and development? Can we then say that *ātman* simply means the essence of all, which sustains all and unites all, and *Brahman* is that essence, or the nature of that essence is defined in terms of *Brahman*? It is significant to note in this connection that all the definitions of ultimate reality that are attempted in the *Upaniṣads* like *satyam jñānam anantam, sat cit ānanda*, etc., are the definitions of *Brahman* but not of *ātman* though *Brahman* and *ātman* in a sense mean the same. *Brahman* is formally defined in the *Upaniṣads*, but there is no such definition of *ātman* in the *Upaniṣads*. It is therefore meaningful to assert that *Ātman* means the all-pervading essence, and *Brahman* is the nature of that essence. *Ātman* means the essence of a thing, or a person, or a phenomenon, or all that is, and the nature of that essence is sought to be defined or understood in terms of *Brahman*. And in knowing the nature of that essence man's reality occupies a central place as in the case of man his essence is known directly and clearly. As Śaṅkara says that though *Brahman* is present everywhere or in all, and is ever revealed its revelation is direct and clear in the case of man as a face in a mirror.[6] We can thus understand the concern of the *Upaniṣads* for knowing and identifying the nature of that reality which permeates all and comprehends all by being their essence. It is variously identified as *agni*, water, *prāṇa*, mind, knowledge, etc. For instance, in the *Tattirīya Upaniṣad* the nature of *Brahman* is defined variously as matter (*annam*), life (*prāṇa*), mind, understanding and bliss. In this process the nature of *Brahman*, the essence and unity of all that is, is sought to be defined and identified more and more comprehensively. Though in the *Upaniṣadś ātman* is more often used to mean the ultimate reality it is not formally defined in them as *Brahman* is defined. Thus we can say that *Brahman* and *ātman* are not distinguished in the *Upaniṣads*, either in their conception or description, and both refer to something that is experienced, or both the concepts are based on direct experience. What is that experience which is the basis of these concepts? If we are clear about it we will be in a position to understand and appreciate that *Brahman* of the *Upaniṣads* is not unrelated to Brahmā of the *Veda* as both the concepts refer, in a broad sense, to the same experience. Therefore what Śaṅkara tried to achieve in asserting that *ātman* is *Brahman* is to bring to a clear focus or to express in a logically cogent and intelligible manner the idea that is central to the philosophy of the *Upaniṣads*.

We now discuss briefly the Vedic concept of Brahmā with a view to showing the continuity and inter-relatedness between it and the concept of *Brahman* of the *Upaniṣads*. We are not therefore discussing the Vedic concept of Brahmā in all its details and dimensions. At the same time the object of the discussion is not to force any interpretation on the concept of Brahmā so as to show the continuity between it and the Upaniṣadic *Brahman* but to understand whether the two can be shown to be conceptually related, and if so what would be the nature of that relation.

Vedic Brahma and Vedāntic Brahman

The term *Brahman* occurs thrice in the *Ṛg-veda*, and in all the contexts of its usage the deities Indra and Agni are addressed by that term. In its Vedic usage it does not show any conceptual similarity with the Vedāntic concept of *Brahman*. When Indra and Agni are addressed as *Brahman* the intention is not to identify them with *Brahman*, the ultimate source of all, but to indicate their greatness or glory which is ever-increasing or expanding, as all the deities grow or expand in terms of their glory. This meaning of *Brahman* as ever-increasing or expanding is not stressed so much in the *Vedānta* but instead it is taken to mean what is great or the ultimate reality. The term which is frequently used in the Vedic literature is Brahma which is, as said earlier, conceptually akin to the Vedāntic *Brahman*. In the Vedic literature the word Brahma does not always mean one and the same, but nevertheless it has a primary meaning which can be discerned in all the contexts of its usage. It primarily means divinely inspired devotion, and by extension the prayer or praise, and the hymns of the *Veda* which express the prayer or praise and devotion. The devotion experienced inwardly is expressed in the form of a prayer or praise which the hymns of the *Veda* express. Every hymn of the *Veda*, which in its intent is either a prayer or praise or both, expresses the divinely inspired devotion of the seers. Brahma can also mean the state of devotion experienced inwardly though it is not known to others unless it is expressed in the form of a prayer or hymn. Although a hymn is an expression in language of the inwardly experienced devotion, they are distinct as at times a hymn may not be able to express adequately the devotion experienced. While a hymn as an expression of devotion depends on devotion, devotion need not express itself in language or find its expression in language. And to the extent the state of devotion is ineffable, or the language of hymns is inadequate to express devotion, to that extent they are different though without its expression in the form of prayer or praise the nature and meaning of devotion cannot be communicated to others, and known by them, unless they experience it themselves. This distinction is to be made, and is to be kept in mind so that we can understand the primary meaning of the term Brahma, for it means in the *Veda* devotion as well as a hymn or prayer. In more contexts of its usage it means a hymn of the *Veda*. Though the word has been used more frequently to mean a hymn it is not its primary meaning. In the sense of a hymn Brahma is that which is made or created by a seer, and addressed to a deity as a prayer or praise. In this sense a seer makes or creates Brahma (hymn) and all the Vedic hymns are the creation of several Vedic seers, created according to their mental abilities. And a person is known as a *ṛṣi* or a *kavi* or becomes one when he is inspired to create or make a hymn (Brahma). In this sense the term Brahma refers to something that is made or fashioned by a seer according to his creative ability. It cannot therefore have any conceptual affinity to Vedāntic *Brahman*, the uncreated. But a hymn is indicated by the word Brahma only by extension as a hymn is the chief mode or form of expression of Brahma or devotion which is the primary meaning of the word Brahma.

Brahma as inwardly experienced devotion is divine, and is due to divine inspiration. Devotion is a divine gift (*devattam brahma*) to man, and man experiences it when he is divinely inspired. It is not due to his own effort a person experiences devotion. The seers clearly admit that it is not by their own efforts they have come to know the Divine, and its glory. They comc to know the Divine or the Divine is revealed to them in the state of devotion (Brahma) or as devotion which is due to divine inspiration. Each deity is a source of inspiration of devotion, and the deities are prayed and praised by the same devotion which is their gift to man (*imā brahma brahma vāhaḥ kriyante*).[7] This prayer is given birth to by those who are attainable by devotion. The devotion is generated in the seers by the deities (*ajanayan brahma devāḥ*) or (*brahma naḥ deva kṛtasya*). Each deity is a source of divine inspiration to the seers, and the seers create a hymn and address a deity or pray to it with the same devotion that is received from the deities as a gift, or that is inspired by the deities. Each deity is prayed with the prayer or devotion that is generated by the deity, and the chief object of most of the Vedic prayers is to receive divine inspiration or to be divinely inspired because of which one becomes a *kavi* or a *ṛṣi*.

The deities are revealed, or a seer comes to know a deity when he is divinely inspired or is in the state of devotion. It is not the case that the deities are there and they are prayed by the seers for the gift of devotion, but the existence of deities or seeing in a phenomenon of nature the presence of a deity or the Divine because of which a phenomenon of nature is seen to be the abode of a deity or a manifestation of the Divine, is basically due to divinely inspired devotion. It is the divinely inspired devotion, which is experienced inwardly, that impels one to pray. One comes to know the meaning of divine in the state of divinely inspired devotion though logically or ontologically the Divine as the source of devotion in man is prior to it. However, from the point of view of man or a seer it is the devotion that is divine as without it one cannot know the presence of the Divine and its nature. The existence of the Divine is known to man only when devotion is born in him. Man sees the Divine, and knows its meaning in the light of devotion which is directly experienced by him. Without experiencing devotion (Brahma) man does not know the existence of the Divine, and its nature. It is one thing to speculate rationally about the existence and nature of ultimate reality, and quite another to know directly in one's own inward experience the presence of the Divine, and its meaning. The experience of the Divine in the state of devotion may lead one to pose and understand certain problems related to the Divine, like its ontological status, its relation to the phenomenal reality, etc. But phenomenologically devotion is the meaning of divine, and the Divine is not known to the Vedic seers independently of devotion, or the Divine is revealed to the seers in the state of devotion or as devotion itself. Devotion which results in man's spontaneous bowing down (*namaḥ*) to the deities or the Divine is described by the seers in ontological terms. It is extolled and identified with the Divine. It holds together the earth and heaven, comprehends within itself all the deities, and rules over them. It saves man from sin.[8] Thus man's awareness of the Divine is the same as to experience Brahma (devotion), and with the growth and maturity of devotion man's awareness of the Divine becomes more and more comprehensive, and transforms his entire being and vision divinely so that whatever he does will have divine significance. Then the distinction between the secular and sacred is obliterated, and the whole creation is seen as an abode of the Divine or its varied manifestation, and hence holy. It fulfils man's life supremely, or, according to the *Veda*, the ultimate meaning of human existence is to experience Brahma and become a *kavi* or a *ṛṣi*. The same thing is said in a different way when it is said that all the deities make hymns their abode.

The deities are known because of Brahma, and they grow in terms of it. It is with the birth of devotion the nature is seen in its hidden divine aspect, or is seen as being filled with and controlled and guided by the same divine principle. Then each aspect or phenomenon of nature is seen as the dwelling place of the Divine or a deity, the poetic way of saying that the entire nature is a manifestation of the Divine. To a divinely inspired person the nature is not only the source of divine inspiration but is itself divine or a manifestation of the Divine. Each deity dwells within a phenomenon of nature, manifests itself within it, and reveals itself in and through that phenomenon of nature which it represents. Each deity as a manifestation of the Divine is divine, and the Divine is known to man or is revealed to him in and through a phenomenon or a deity which is the immediate source of divine revelation to the seers. In the *Veda* all the deities are a source of divine inspiration, and the deities, either individually or collectively, are prayed with the prayer inspired by them. The capacity to inspire devotion in man is common to all the deities, or all the phenomena of nature, and the nature is seen as divine because of its capacity to inspire man divinely. As the capacity to inspire man divinely is intrinsic to all the phenomena of nature they all share something in common, besides their phenomenal qualities, which are peculiar to each phenomenon or a deity that represents it. Each phenomenon of nature or a deity that dwells within it is different from other phenomena and deities insofar as their phenomenal attributes are concerned. The capacity to inspire man divinely is what is common to all the deities, and that power or capacity constitutes their divine nature and unity.

Since devotion is divine the Divine is the common source of all the deities, and is therefore their essence and unity. The inner divine unity of nature is revealed to man in the state of inspired devotion, or devotion is the reason or basis for seeing the inner divine unity of all that is. In the *Veda*, as pointed out earlier, we find metaphysical speculation about the existence and nature of ultimate reality, but in most cases such speculation ends in scepticism, whereas the divine power which inspires Brahma (devotion) in man is seen not only as what is common to all the deities, but also as that which comprehends all the deities, and as forming their essence and unity. Devotion is more significantly the meeting point between man and the Divine. Thus the divine unity of all that is is a matter of direct experience, and is experienced by the Vedic seers in the state of devotion or Brahma. Brahma is an end in itself, as it is not sought by the Vedic seers for attaining something by means of it. It is a divine gift, and is returned to the Divine by way of prayer and praise, and in the process the existence of man is supremely fulfilled. The object of expressing the inwardly experienced devotion in prayer is primarily to praise the Divine or glorify it, and to return the gift of devotion to the Divine as a sort of debt. The nature of devotion is really ineffable (*acittam brahma*). It is extolled by Brahma, and is perfected by Brahma.

The all-comprehensive nature of Brahma is clearly indicated by saying that its extension is the same as the extension of *vāk* (*yāvat brahma viṣṭitam tāvati vāk; brahma ayam vācaḥ parame vyomaḥ*).[9] Here Brahma can mean either devotion or the divine reality because in certain contexts of its usage, when a deity is addressed as Brahma or *Brahman* the intention is not to address a deity as *Brahman* or identify it with the ultimate reality, for in the *Veda* the deities are regarded as only manifestations of the Divine. They are born of the Divine. All the deities are divine but the Divine is not identified with any one deity. Similar is the case with *ṛtam* and *satyam* the other forms of manifestation of the Divine. If we agree with Sāyana we have to understand the meaning of the term Brahma as that which expands or grows, as every deity grows or expands by means of manifesting itself in newer and newer forms. Even the term *maha*, used as a synonym of *Brahman*, means that which grows (*mahīyante*). In this sense devotion increases, and helps the increase or growth of a deity; all the deities increase or grow by means of prayer. *Vāk* in this context may mean wisdom (*kāvya*), besides language or speech, and the extension of it is the extension of Brahma. *Vāk* as divine wisdom encompasses all, and Brahma is the birth place of *vāk*, and the limits of one are the limits of the other, or both are limitless. Thus the Vedic concept of Brahma though refers primarily to divinely inspired devotion, and by extension to prayer and hymn, it has its ontological significance. The source of its inspiration is the Divine, and the nature of the Divine reveals itself in devotion or as devotion. Devotion not only purifies man, fulfils his existence and makes him divine, but reveals at the same time its ontological character. The capacity or power to inspire devotion in man is intrinsic to all the deities; it constitutes their divinity. As each deity is the unity of a phenomenon of nature, and as all the deities are manifestations of the Divine, the Divine is not only the essence and unity of all the deities but of the whole world. The deities have their origin in the Divine, and are divine in terms of their capacity to inspire devotion in man, which is divine. Man may not be able to comprehend fully the nature of the Divine in itself but what is divine is known to him in the state of devotion. Therefore devotion is described in ontological terms in the *Veda*. Though we cannot identify devotion with the Divine the latter is not known to man without devotion. So from the point of view of man devotion is the meaning of divine, or the Divine is what is revealed in the state of devotion or as devotion. Thus Brahma as divinely inspired devotion, though refers primarily to what is experienced inwardly and directly by a seer, is at the same time ontological. It is the Divine as directly revealed to man in the state of devotion. It is both ontological, and what is directly experienced.

Upaniṣadic Conception

This is our point of departure in understanding the Vedāntic concept of *Brahman* in relation to the Vedic concept of Brahma. They are not unrelated, or there is no radical discontinuity between them. They point to the same reality though viewed from two different perspectives, and are formed on the basis of two kinds of experience. We cannot nevertheless say that as concepts they mean the same though we can assert that they are intended to mean the same reality. In the *Upaniṣads*, as in the later Vedāntic tradition, *Brahman* stands for the ultimate reality, the ultimate explanation of all that is. However, we find in the *Upaniṣads* two distinct ways of knowing *Brahman*, one metaphysical or speculative, and the other experiential. As a metaphysical concept *Brahman* is the ultimate explanation of all that is, and it is also known directly and immediately (*sākṣāt aparokṣāt brahma*). Thus we find in the *Upaniṣads* a metaphysical conception of *Brahman*, and *Brahman* which is revealed or known directly and immediately. In the *Veda* also we find speculation about the existence and nature of that which is the ultimate source and ground of all that is, but the Upaniṣadic speculation is more sustained and thorough. But the *Brahman* that is known directly and immediately is distinct from *Brahman*, the metaphysical concept, meant to explain the world. However, the object of both the approaches is to know that which is the origin of all as well as the inner unity of all. What is *Brahman* (*kim brahma*) is answered variously by different thinkers in the

Upaniṣads as matter, mind, vital force, knowledge, etc., in all of which attempts are made to understand the nature of *Brahman* which is the ultimate source of all that is. Whether matter or *prāṇa* or mind is *Brahman* is sought to be determined in terms of their capacity to explain all that is. *Brahman* is the truth or the reality of the reality that is empirically known and experienced, or the ultimate explanation of all that we know and experience. It is that by knowing which all that is is known. In the *Upaniṣads*, as in the *Veda*, all that is is classified into three realms of *ādhidaivata*, *ādhibhautika* and *ādhyātma*, and attempts were made to see and identify *Brahman* as being manifested within all the realms. Though *Brahman* is conceived to be present within all the realms it is known differently in different realms as it manifests itself differently in different realms. Or according to another Upaniṣadic classification of all that is into *nāma* (concept), *rūpam* (form) and *karma* (action or function) *Brahman* is regarded as that which holds within itself all the three, or which is pointed to by all the names, forms and actions (*trayam va idam nāmarūpam karma brahma tadvit sarvāṇi nāmāni bhibharti*).[10] *Brahman* is the inner thread or principle that holds together all, unites all and governs all. It holds all, unites all and governs all by being within all as their essence. It is that which is the origin of all, and into which all are ultimately dissolved (*tajjalāniti*). *Brahman*, the origin of all, is present within all, and being within all holds together all, controls all and rules over them all. It is the *ātman* or the essence or inner reality of all. In the expression which is often repeated in the *Upaniṣads*, "this is *ātman*, it is immortal, it is *Brahman* and it is all (*ayamātmā idam amṛtam idam brahma idam sarvam*)"[11] the underlying unity of all or the essence of all, which is unchanging or immortal, is identified with *Brahman*. After defining the nature of *Brahman* it is identified with all in the sense of its being the *ātman* (essence) of all. *Ātman* is the inner reality or essence of all, and that essence is *Brahman*, or the nature of the essence is defined in terms of *Brahman*. In all the statements made about *Brahman* in the

Upaniṣads we can use either the term *Brahman* or *ātman* without disturbing or changing the meaning of the expression. The meaning of both the terms, as far as their Upaniṣadic usage is concerned, is almost the same. *Ātman* means the all-pervading reality which is within all as their essence, and *Brahman* is that essence. Although in the *Upaniṣads* the concepts of *Brahman* and *ātman* are interchangeable or are used almost synonymously, however, when they try to define the nature of ultimate reality the term *Brahman* is invariably preferred. In all the statements in which the reality is sought to be defined or described as *sat, cit, ānanda*, etc., the term *Brahman* is used, and there is no attempt to define *ātman* in the *Upaniṣads* though *ātman* is used to mean the ultimate reality. This can support our view that *ātman* means basically the essence or inner reality of anything or all, and *Brahman* is the nature of that essence or the nature of the essence is defined as *Brahman*. Attempts are made in the *Upaniṣads* to understand and define the nature of *Brahman* which is the essence (*ātman*) of all. "That (*Brahman*) which controls all by being within all is *ātman*, which is within all, and immortal (*yaḥ sarvāṇi bhūtāni antare yamayata eṣa ta ātmā antaryāmī amṛtaḥ*)."[12] *Ātman* which is the inner reality or essence of all is equally the inner reality and ruler of man. It is present within all the three realms, and is the essence and ruler of earth, water, air, heaven, the sun, the quarters, etc., or it is the essence and unity of all that is. And *Brahman* as that essence and ruler (*ātman*) is present within all the realms. In this context the observation of Śaṅkara is significant. "The words *ātman* and *Brahman* are the adjectives and substantives of each other. The word *Brahman* rules out that the *ātman* (self) is limited by body, and the word *ātman* rules out the meditation on the sun etc., which are different from the self, as *Brahman*."[13] In other words, *ātman* does not simply mean the reality of a person, and *Brahman* the reality of all-except man, as both the concepts refer to the reality, which is all-comprehensive and all-pervasive. *Brahman* defined as *sat, cit*, and *ānanda*, etc., is the *ātman* of all, and therefore in reality *ātman* and *Brahman* mean the same reality. Nevertheless, *Brahman* is the definition of the essence (*ātman*) or it is the nature of the all-pervading essence (*ātman*). *Brahman* is *ātman* which is within all, and experiences all.

Brahman and Ātman

Brahman as *ātman* (essence) of all is known by man directly and immediately as his own self. In this sense *Brahman* is not a metaphysical concept but the reality that is directly and immediately known to everyone as his own *ātman* or self. Thus to realise the reality of one's own self is to realise the inner reality and unity of all that is, or *Brahman*, as *Brahman* is the *ātman* of one's own self. The *Upaniṣads* say that *Brahman* which is direct and immediate is the *ātman* which is within all (*yat sākṣāt aparokṣāt brahma ya ātmā sarvāntaraḥ*).[14] The philosophical significance of *ātman* as the self of a person is that a person knows directly and immediately his own reality or self. It is self-evident and self-revealed. *Brahman*, the ultimate reality, is revealed to man directly and immediately as his own self or his inner reality or essence. Therefore much importance is given in the *Upaniṣads* to man's self-analysis and understanding as it leads to direct and immediate knowledge of *Brahman*. The knowledge of *Brahman* as revealed within one's own reality is clear and direct, whereas one's knowledge of *Brahman* as present within the reality of the world is indirect or inferential. Man does not depend upon any means of knowledge to know his own reality or self.

However, the identity of *ātman* with *Brahman* is meaningful only at the level of manifestation, as when there is no manifestation there is no sense in saying that *Brahman* is the essence or inner reality of all. We can talk of *Brahman* only when there is the world of manifestation in which *Brahman* is revealed as the essence and unity of all that is manifested. Accordingly, the *Upaniṣads* speak of *Brahman* in almost all the contexts of its usage as that which is present within all as their essence and unity, and is therefore known directly and immediately by man as his self. Even to talk of *Brahman* as having two forms, one personal and another impersonal, one mortal and another immortal, one limited and another unlimited or defined and undefined is possible only when *Brahman* is viewed in relation to its manifested and unmanifested states. When the *Upaniṣads* speak of *Brahman* as the internal ruler of all that is manifested, it implies the possibility of its unmanifested state. But what could be the nature of *Brahman* in its unmanifested state can be known or understood only in relation to its manifested state. Without *Brahman*'s manifestation there can be no world, and no enquiry into the nature of *Brahman*, and there will be no one to enquire into and know the nature of *Brahman*. The state of *Brahman*'s manifestation is a presupposition for any enquiry into the nature of *Brahman*. However, an attempt to know *Brahman* in itself, or the nature of *Brahman* prior to its manifestation, is possible and significant. Here again we have to face the problem whether *Brahman* as pure being or consciousness can be without any form or completely unmanifested. It is only a reality which is completely static or dead, or without any inner dynamism can be devoid of any self-expression or manifestation. The primary meaning of the word *brahman* or *mahā*, which are synonyms, is that which is ever expanding or increasing (*mahīyante*). The term *Brahman* is also defined as great (*bṛhat*), but there is no contradiction in both the meanings as greatness or vastness does not negate the capacity or power to expand itself or express itself, as self-expression of a spiritual being is not something extraneous to its nature. Expansion or growth by way of self-expression or self-manifestation is the very nature of *Brahman*. It is not prompted by any reason or motive. It is only when we view *Brahman* as something static we can think of its growth or self-expression as something contingent and accidental due to some reason, but not when we understand *Brahman* as that which by its very nature ever expands or increases by way of self-expression. If we deny self-expression to *Brahman* we cannot intelligibly think of its state prior to its manifestation into all.

However, these are the problems with which the *Upaniṣads* are not seriously concerned. We do not find in the *Upaniṣads* any significant discussion of these problems. Nevertheless, the *Upaniṣads* have tried to understand the problem in terms of certain expamples which are highly significant. Most of the examples or analogies adduced in the *Upaniṣads* to illustrate the relation between the world of manifestation and *Brahman*, like the spider weaving the web and sparks emanating from fire, should not be taken literally as these examples are taken from the realm of physical reality, and cannot therefore help us in understanding the nature of the relationship between a spiritual being and its self-expression or manifestation. However, in one example or analogy, that is, the breathing in and breathing out in man, which are spontaneous and natural, and without which man cannot be a living being, the *Upaniṣads* have tried to understand the nature of relation between *Brahman* and its manifestation as something natural and spontaneous. If manifestation is natural and spontaneous there can be no beginning to it logically. These problems are discussed fully in the next chapter.

Before we discuss Śaṅkara's understanding of the concept of *Brahman*, which is not completely different from that of the *Upaniṣads*, as it is based on or inspired by the *Upaniṣads*, we have to say a few words about Śaṅkara's approach to and understanding of the *Upaniṣads* in relation to the concept of *Brahman*. When most of the Upaniṣadic statements about *Brahman* talk of *Brahman* in its relation to the world, and are meaningful and intelligible only in relation to the world, how can Śaṅkara talk about *Brahman* in itself or in its transcendental aspect? Here we have to consider whether the majority of the Upaniṣadic statements in which *Brahman* is viewed in relation to the world, and is conceived as the inner ruler and unity of the world, are to be given secondary importance only, or are to be regarded as not basic to the philosophy of the *Upaniṣads* in relation to certain other statements in which all this is denied, or both the kinds of statements are to be given equal importance and validity. How to reconcile both the kinds of statements or how to decide the validity and authority of each kind of statements?

Śaṅkara's Conception

In interpreting the Upaniṣadic statements about *Brahman* Śaṅkara is guided mostly by reason or logical understanding as otherwise it would not be possible to reconcile and harmonise the various statements which do not say the same thing about *Brahman*, and at times appear to contradict each other. It is reason or logical understanding which can guide us in comprehending the true import or the intended meaning of the scriptural statements. The attempt to reconcile or harmonise the various mutually conflicting statements of *Śruti* about *Brahman* is meaningful as different conceptions of *Brahman* or ultimate reality are possible. But how to judge which conception of *Brahman* is true to the *Upaniṣads*. While most of the statements speak of *Brahman* as the source of all that is, and as being present within the world as the underlying unity and inner controller of all, some of the statements deny validity to those statements in which something is said or asserted about *Brahman*. The basic position of Śaṅkara with regard to *Brahman* is that it being an objective reality (*vastu*) one need not necessarily depend upon *Śruti* for its knowledge. Just as any objectively existing reality can be known by appropriate means of valid knowledge, *Brahman* can also be known by appropriate means of valid knowledge, and therefore need not depend entirely on *Śruti* whose main object is to reveal that which cannot be known by any other means of valid knowledge, like the nature of *Dharma*. Although *Brahman* is objectively real it being pure consciousness cannot be an object of any means of knowledge, including *Śruti. Brahman* as consciousness is the presupposition or the very basis of all the means of knowledge, and therefore all the means of knowledge, including *Śruti*, can reveal it indirectly without making it an object of knowledge. It makes all knowledge possible without itself becoming an object of knowledge. The various means of knowledge can reveal a thing when it is given to them as an object (*viṣaya*) but not their very basis, or that because of which they can know. The sense-organs can perceive a thing which is given to them as an object but not their very capacity to perceive. Man can think of something but not the very capacity to think. Nevertheless, all the means of knowledge reveal *Brahman* all the time without ever making it their object as that which is revealed invariably along with the objects of knowledge. This is the case with *Śruti* also as a means of knowledge. *Brahman* is known to all, whether one is learned in scriptures or not, for it is their *ātman*, and is revealed equally in the state of enlightenment or *turīya* as well as in the state of ignorance. There may be a doubt about the existence of a thing which is other than one's own self, and appropriate means of knowledge are of use in clearing the doubt. But this is not relevant and meaningful in the case of *Brahman* as it is the very basis and possibility of all knowledge. In saying that 'I am not' one is asserting one's existence, and therefore no one can deny the existence of *Brahman* without self-contradiction.

Since by its very nature *Brahman* is self-evident and eternally revealed to all one need not depend on any means of knowledge, including *Śruti*, to know it. *Brahman* is not an object of knowledge but it is nevertheless known to all. It is both known and unknown, according to the *Upaniṣads*, and this can be intelligible and significant only in the case of one's self. *Ātman* is known to all, for it is their self, and at the same time it is not known in the ordinary sense, as it is not an object of any means of knowledge. It is by its very nature a non-object (*aviṣaya*). Now the self of man is only a source of *Brahman*'s knowledge, but not *Brahman* itself. Here I am using the word 'self' in the ordinary sense of that which is the inner reality or subject of a person. In this context the observation of Śaṅkara that *Brahman* is within a human body, but not only in a human body is significant, whereas an individual self or ego is within a body only (*satyam śarīre bhavati na tu śarīra eva bhavati, jīvantu śarīra eva bhavati*).[15] The self of man or consciousness is the direct and immediate source of *Brahman*'s knowledge as *Brahman* is revealed clearly within the self of man like a fruit in one's palm. It is revealed in and through all the functions of all the faculties and senses of man or revealed in all knowledge, and makes the objects known by illumining them. If by *ātman* we mean the self of a person only then it is not the same as *Brahman* as *Brahman* is the essence or inner reality of all that is. Śaṅkara understands by *ātman* the inner reality or essence of a thing or a phenomenon or all, and *Brahman* is that essence which is present within all. Thus 'self-knowledge' is not the same as '*Brahman*-knowledge' though through knowledge of self one knows the nature of *Brahman*. In one sense self-knowledge is the same as *Brahman*-knowledge, and in another sense it is not. If by self we mean the self of this or that person which gives him his individuality, and is unique to a person its knowledge is not the same as *Brahman*-knowledge, whereas if by self we mean *ātman* which is all-pervasive, and is within all then knowledge of self (*ātman*) is the same as *Brahman*-knowledge. Since we normally understand by the term self the self of a person, which is not intelligible in relation to a non-person, the knowledge of self, which may differ from person to person, and even in the case of the same person from time to time, the self-knowledge in terms of which a person knows himself, is not the same as *Brahman*-knowledge. On the other hand, in knowing *ātman* one does not know simply one's own self but knows all or the essence and unity of all. In this sense *ātman* realisation is the same as *Brahman* realisation. There is no difference between *Brahmadarśana* and *ātmadarśana*.

Brahman as Sat

As pointed out earlier, *Brahman* is not unknown to anyone whether one is learned in the scriptures or not. It is the same reality conceived and known differently by different people and philosophers (*sarve prāṇibhiḥ tārkikaica sarva prakāreṇa jñāyate vikalpyate*).[16] Though *Brahman* is known to all and conceived by all scriptural instruction is required to know *Brahman* truly or objectively (*vasturūpeṇa*). When there are several conceptions of *Brahman*, according to different systems of philosophy, and are present even within the *Upaniṣads* the enquiry into the true nature of *Brahman* is meaningful and legitimate, as all the conceptions of *Brahman*, which in certain cases contradict each other, cannot be true of it, as *Brahman* is an objectively existing reality but not a matter of human imagination. "If the ignorant man fails to reach or know *Brahman* though it is the common source of all then the attainment of *Brahman* by an enlightened man may as well be doubtful."[17] Is it possible to have knowledge of Brahmā which is completely objective or universally valid? If the knowledge of an objectively existing reality does not depend upon human ingenuity, as it is in the case of *dharma*, the different conceptions of *Brahman* cannot be true of it, especially when they contradict each other. The differences in the conception of *Brahman* may either be due to subjective or psychological factors (*kalpanā*) or that *Brahman* has no definable or identifiable nature. Even if we deny objective validity to the various conceptions of *Brahman*, as no conception is valid universally, for different conceptions of *Brahman* are held by some and rejected by others, we have to admit Existence as the universally valid conception of *Brahman*. In denying objective validity to every conception of *Brahman* the intellect of man ends up in admitting existence as something irrefutable, for its denial involves contradiction. All negation or denial ends up in the idea of existence which is the ultimate limit of all negation. It is the root of the universe for the negation of the world presupposes existence as its basis and limit. In other words, "the world when traced back to its ultimate root in an ascending order (*tāratamya pāramparyeṇa*) of subtleness makes one apprehend the idea of existence (*sat buddhi niṣṭha*) as its ultimate resort or ground."[18] Or when the intellect is attenuated through the process of negation of all objects and thought it gets itself dissolved but as pregnant with the idea of existence (*sat pratyaya garbhe vilīyate*).[19] Even utter scepticism about *Brahman* has to end up with the idea of existence as without the existence of the sceptic no scepticism is possible. It is possible to doubt and deny the reality of the world but such a denial presupposes the existence of one who denies, as well as existence as the ultimate ground of the universe, which may be illusory, for without existence as its ultimate limit and ground the denial of the world would not be meaningful and intelligible. One should have the idea of existence before he denies the reality of the world, or the validity of any conception of *Brahman* as otherwise there would be no valid reason or justification to deny validity to various conceptions of *Brahman*. Different conceptions may be superimposed on existence, and therefore can be explained away as mental constructions, but all this process would not be intelligible without the idea of existence on which the various ideas of reality are superimposed. Unless one knows what is real one cannot judge something to be unreal. Unless one has the idea of existence one cannot say that certain things do not exist. Now is it intelligible to think of existence as such or pure existence? The idea of existence as such or pure existence is unintelligible. We can think of existence of things, or understand the idea of existence in relation to things which exist, but can we think of existence as such (*sattāmātra*)? Now *Brahman* is defined as pure existence or *Brahman* is pure existence (*sanmātram he brahma*). How intelligible is the idea of pure existence? As we have just pointed out the existence of anything other than one's own existence can be denied but not the existence of the one who denies the existence of all. "If anyone knows or thinks *Brahman* as non-existing he himself becomes non-existence."[20] "By speaking of *Brahman* its existence is asserted."[21] And in the case of man existence and consciousness are one and the same. One can doubt and deny the existence of external reality as well as the world of internal experience, but such denial does not affect the pure 'I' which is the limit as well as the possibility of all doubt and denial. The pure 'I' is pure existence as well as pure consciousness. We cannot say that consciousness exists as pure consciousness is not a thing to be asserted or denied. Assertion and denial are possible with regard to a thing which can be an object of knowledge, and pure consciousness is not an object of knowledge. Thus Śaṅkara asks, "how can we admit or think of consciousness (*bodha*) apart from existence?"[22] They do not exclude each other. Existence is consciousness, and consciousness is existence. As the denial of pure consciousness is not intelligible and meaningful its assertion is equally meaningless and superfluous. Assertion and denial presuppose pure consciousness which is pure existence. *Brahman* which is pure existence and pure consciousness cannot be denied by anyone without contradicting himself. It is the absolute as it is not conditioned by any other reality, or limited or determined by any other reality. "The word *sat* means mere existence, a reality that is subtle without any distinction and all-pervasive, one taintless and partless consciousness which is known from all the *Upaniṣads*. It is not existence in the ordinary or *Vaiśeṣika* sense of the term in which it is understood in relation to something, like pot exists or earth, etc., exist. Existence is absolute."[23] We cannot think of existence being derived from other reality, or having an origin. We cannot also think that there was nothing or non-existence in the beginning, and from that the universe came into existence, for nothing or non-existence can have no essence, and therefore cannot be the cause of anything. In being the cause of something it should have some nature or essence which can give birth to an effect, or in terms of which an effect and cause can be casually connected or related. Furthermore, if non-existence (*asat*) were to be the cause of the world there could not be several different conceptions of it, for it would not be meaningful to conceive non-existence severally. It is utterly unintelligible to call non-existence by several names or to have different conceptions of it. And if there is no relation between an effect and its cause it would not be possible to think of a cause by seeing an effect. If it is not possible and meaningful to identify non-existence as the cause of the world, as it has no nature or essence, then the world should not be seen as an effect. On the other hand, if the universe is originated from non-existence then there can be no knowledge of it as it will have no essence or reality. Only an existing reality can give rise to another reality. If an entity can spring up from a non-entity then the assumption that this or that is the cause of something would be pointless since non-entity in all cases and for all is one and the same. Moreover, one cannot deny reality to what is normally experienced by all if one does not have the notion of reality. To deny reality to something is meaningful and valid only with reference to the idea of what is real. Mirage water is unreal only in relation to pond water which is real, or dream objects are unreal only in relation to objects of waking experience. Otherwise the term unreal will have no meaning. "Whenever we deny something as unreal we do so with reference to something real."[24]

In trying to know the truth and nature of reality one should not propound something which is not intelligible to man's understanding, or which is absurd or which goes against or contradicts what is experienced by all. Its knowledge should be definite (*niścita*) as man's liberation from ignorance depends on a definite and clear knowledge of reality. Therefore when the validity of a concept of reality can be doubted and criticised in terms of man's rational understanding it cannot be definite and valid. In the process of ascertaining the true or objective nature of *Brahman* reason can help us, as otherwise man cannot determine the true conception of *Brahman* when he finds several conceptions of it. Even within *Śruti* there are several conceptions of *Brahman*. Although reason cannot give us knowledge of *Brahman* it can help us in understanding the validity of a conception in the face of several contending conceptions. If reality is a matter of assumption, but not objectively real, there is no valid reason why we should not accept several such assumptions depending upon the level of understanding of the person who makes such assumptions. Then we will have no reason to deny validity to any assumption. If, on the other hand, what is there objectively is a matter to be decided upon on the basis of valid means of knowledge, the possibility or impossibility of what is objectively there does not arise. Whatever is apprehended by some means of knowledge is possible, and what is not so apprehended is not possible. As all the speculative conceptions of reality, or the various metaphysical doctrines about it are not based on any source of knowledge, but on reason, which can vary from thinker to thinker, and in the case of the same thinker from time to time, there can be several conceptions of reality, and no such conception of reality can give us definite knowledge of reality. Reason thus lacks finality when it is employed to know what is not within the realm of empirical experience. Its operations are valid within the realm of empirical experience but not when it is applied to non-empirical realm; it then becomes blunt as when a knife is used to cut a hard stone.[25] Reason which operates with the help of categories which are formed on the basis of man's empirical experience cannot simply operate in the non-empirical realm as then there would be nothing for it to think, or there would be no ground for it to think. Thus the limits of perceptual knowledge are also the limits of reason. Whatever is known through the senses can also be thought of, and what cannot be known through senses cannot be thought of. As pointed out earlier, reasoning or intellect of man can, at the most, assert existence as *Brahman* or *Brahman* as existence, and beyond that it cannot say anything about *Brahman*. Though *Śruti* is also not a source of knowledge of *Brahman*, as *Brahman* is self-evident to all, it nevertheless can help us in knowing the true or objective nature of *Brahman*. Not only *Śruti* but the direct knowledge or experience of those who had realised *Brahman* can also be the source of *Brahman* knowledge. *Śruti* statements about *Brahman* or *ātman* are authoritative as they in the final analysis emanate from the seers who had realised *Brahman*.[26] But then how to reconcile several conflicting statements about *Brahman* found in the *Śruti*, or made by those who had realised *Brahman*.

Brahman as Objective Reality

If *Brahman* is not a matter of speculation or mental construction (*kalpanā*) but an objectively existing reality then its knowledge should be the same to all; there cannot be several mutually conflicting conceptions of it. "Perfect knowledge of *Brahman* should be of one form because it is objective (*samyak jñānam eka rūpam vastu tantratvāt*)."[27] Anything that is known in one form is the ultimate meaning of a thing, and it is ultimately valid, and such knowledge is regarded as perfect knowledge in the world (*eka rūpeṇa vyavastito yo arthaḥ sa paramārthaḥ loke tadviṣayam samyak jñānam iti ucyate yadhā agni uṣna iti*).[28]

Alternately, as *Brahman* is not an object in the ordinary sense of the term having a fixed and determinable nature but infinite and spiritual in nature what the various conceptions of *Brahman* can reveal about it represent different aspects of *Brahman*, but not *Brahman* in its perfection or wholeness. The existence of several conceptions of *Brahman* not only in the Indian philosophical tradition but even within the *Śruti* tradition cannot allow anyone to be dogmatic about the nature of *Brahman*. Even if one wants to hold on to any one view of *Brahman* one has to argue his case and reject other views on rational grounds. Here we want to confine our discussion to those conceptions of *Brahman* which are found within the *Śruti*. How can anyone say that one definition or conception of *Brahman* is more valid and true than the others? Is there any *Śruti* justification for that? The approach of Śaṅkara in this regard is not to apply reason to understand and decide the validity of each conception, but following the word and spirit of *Śruti* to take those definitions of *Brahman* seriously in which *Śruti* itself negates its own definitions of *Brahman* on the ground that those (negated) definitions or conceptions are not all-comprehensive. If *Brahman* is the reality of all that is it should comprehend within itself all that is, and nothing should be left unexplained in terms of *Brahman*. An example of Śaṅkara can help us in understanding this principle of scriptural interpretation. A ruler of the whole world can be called the ruler of a particular country, as it is included within the concept of the world, but he cannot therefore be identified and called the ruler of this or that country, as in that case his sovereignty gets limited, though as a matter of fact one who is the ruler of the whole world is also the ruler of a particular country.[29] Thus to define *Brahman* as matter, *prāṇa*, *vijñāna*, etc., is to limit *Brahman* though *Brahman* does not exclude in reality anything from itself. The various definitions of *Brahman* exclude something from *Brahman*, and leave something unexplained in terms of *Brahman*. Can we then have a definition or conception of *Brahman* in which nothing is excluded from *Brahman*? A definition (*lakṣaṇa*) is different from predication or attribution (*viśeṣaṇa*). In attribution an individual belonging to a species is distinguished from others of the same species in terms of a quality or attribute, whereas the object of definition is to distinguish the thing defined from everything else in terms of the definition. Unless there is something from which a thing defined can be distinguished definition is not possible and meaningful. Accordingly, no definition of *Brahman* is possible as there is nothing different from *Brahman* from which *Brahman* can be distinguished in terms of a definition. Even the most comprehensive definitions of *Brahman* found in the *Upaniṣads*, such as *sat cit ānanda*; insofar as they presuppose the reality of *Śruti* as the definer of *Brahman*, and those for whom the definition is meant are distinguished from *Brahman*, and the nature of *Brahman* can be limited by them. No definition of *Brahman* can be all-inclusive and absolute as all the definitions presuppose the one who defines and the others for whom the definition is meant. On the other hand, if we admit that the one who defines *Brahman* is not different from *Brahman* then there is no meaning in defining *Brahman*. Even if the definition of *Brahman* is attempted by one who knows himself to be Brahman it cannot be for himself. It should be for someone as otherwise there is no purpose of definition. If we then say that the one who defines and the other for whom the definition is meant are real, and *Brahman* is the object of definition then to that extent *Brahman*'s reality gets limited. Can we then say that *Brahman* is that which comprehends all within itself and excludes none is itself a definition of *Brahman*? If we accept the above as the definition of *Brahman* we cannot say that *Brahman* is undefinable, but according to the meaning of definition given above it cannot be a definition of *Brahman* as it does not distinguish *Brahman* from anything.

Brahman as pure existence is the reason for the existence of anything, and existence is one only. But what about the existence of different things, like pot? Do they point to difference in existence? Existence is not qualified or differentiated in terms of different existent things, but existence is revealed in and through all existing things. Existence is known or revealed but not differentiated in relation to various things existing. Existence is one though it is revealed in and through different things. For instance, the existence of a pot is not different from the existence of clay, and therefore when the pot is destroyed the existence is not destroyed, as clay exists. All the modifications of clay show the existence of clay; only they acquire certain forms and characteristics which are different from those of clay, and help to differentiate them from clay. As different forms of clay they come into existence and cease to be. However, clay is distinguished from existence as we say clay exists. But *Brahman* as pure existence is common to all, and is revealed by all. Is pure existence then a notion as we do not see existence as such but understand it in relation to various things? Independently of things or apart from them existence is not intelligible. This is not however the case with *Brahman* which is direct and immediate. This we can understand by knowing the nature of consciousness which is *Brahman*. In saying that *Brahman* is consciousness it may appear that something substantial is said about *Brahman*. But in saying that *Brahman* is consciousness we are not saying anything about *Brahman*. In asserting that *Brahman* is existence as well as consciousness the intention is to show that existence is not an empty notion or an abstract idea. Pure consciousness, which is direct and immediate, is pure existence as well.

Brahman as Consciousness

According to Śaṅkara, everything is given to consciousness as an object of experience or knowledge. A thing is an object only when it is given to consciousness. Because everything is given to consciousness as an object all that is known or experienced as an object is different from consciousness, and cannot therefore belong to consciousness. Not only physical objects but even mental states and ideas are objects to consciousness, and therefore they cannot belong to consciousness, and affect it. Therefore all that we can say about consciousness do not belong to consciousness. On the other hand, if certain qualities and characteristics belong to consciousness then they cannot be known. If anything really belongs to consciousness there can be no knowledge of it, that is to say, anything that is known or can be known in the ordinary sense of knowledge, cannot belong to consciousness. Mind and its various functions are objects to consciousness, as physical things are. While physical things are outside of man the mind and its functions are internal to man, but they are equally given to consciousness as objects. If pain and pleasure or any other feeling or thought were to belong to consciousness then there could be no knowledge of them. For instance, if pain belongs to consciousness it cannot experience pleasure, and pain should have been present in all states of consciousness. In that case we should say painful consciousness instead of consciousness of pain. Consciousness is present in all our knowledge and experience but is not the same as any knowledge or experience. If we identify any experience with consciousness then it would not be possible to have different experiences. For instance, if a particular colour perceived by the eyes belongs to the eyes then they cannot perceive other colours. Similarly if what is experienced or known belongs to consciousness it cannot be experienced or known in the first place, and secondly, there can be no consciousness of different things. Even to say that such consciousness is a void is invalid as the notion of void is an object to consciousness, and so cannot belong to it. Similarly any idea we have about consciousness cannot belong to it, and affect it because all of them are given to consciousness as objects, and are therefore different from it, or are other than it.To be an object of consciousness it must be different from consciousness. Thus nothing can be said about consciousness, and therefore there can be no knowledge of consciousness. It is as good as nothing or *śūnya* but in saying so consciousness is revealed. Its denial reveals its presence. The only thing that can be significantly said about it is that it is existence. We cannot say that consciousness exists as it is not an object of knowledge. It is only when we can say something about consciousness it would be meaningful to assert its existence, as when we say such and such a cow exists. Therefore consciousness is existence, or pure existence is pure consciousness. Pure existence, insofar as it is not possible to say anything about it, is as good as non-existence (*asat*), and so is the case with pure consciousness. Thus pure existence as pure consciousness is not an abstract idea or an empty notion but something that is direct and immediate, and is revealed in all our knowledge and experience. *Ānanda* can be taken to mean absolute perfection as it is not any kind of bliss that is experienced. *Ānanda* can mean absolute perfection which is neither the experience of pleasure nor the absence of pain. *Cit* is *ānanda* as it is not affected by anything that is experienced or known. While the terms *sukha* and *duḥkha* can be understood in relation to each other, the term *ānanda* has no contrasting term in terms of which its meaning can be grasped. There is no opposite of *ānanda*. It is not a state of experience, but is the very nature of *Brahman*, and therefore can mean absolute perfection (*pūrṇatva*) which is *Brahman*. A state of non-perfection is the source of pain, while the state of perfection, which cannot be anything acquired or achieved, must be *Brahman*'s own nature, and that is the state of perfect bliss, or simply the state of perfection.

The other concepts like *satyam*, *jñānam* and *anantam* in terms of which *Brahman* is sought to the defined do not mean in relation to *Brahman* what they mean ordinarily, or in the context of man's empirical experience. These do not try to define or describe *Brahman* but only point to *Brahman*'s nature. For example, *jñānam* which means knowledge is meaningful only as involving a knowable and a knower. In the absence of any of these knowledge will not be possible. Ordinarily knowledge originates and comes to an end depending upon the availability or non-availability of a knowable. Since knowledge is dependent upon the knowable and knower, and is circumscribed by them it cannot be the nature of *Brahman* which is absolute or unconditioned. Śaṅkara while explaining the concept of *anantam* (infinite) makes a distinction between what is infinite from the point of view of space and what is infinite from the points of view of time and substance. A reality may be infinite from the point of view of space when it is not limited by space, but nevertheless can be limited by time. Similarly that which is infinite in time can be limited by space. Even when a reality is infinite with regard to time and space it may still be finite in respect of substance as when there are several substances each limiting the other. Therefore *Brahman* to be really infinite must be identical with all the three, space, time and substance. It is only when *Brahman* is conceived as different from any of them they can limit *Brahman*. If *Brahman* is spatially infinite it need not be so in respect of time, and even if it is infinite with regard to space and time, which is meaningful only when they are not different from

Brahman, still it can be limited by other substances. In other words, anything that is empirically known or experienced cannot be truly infinite as it is limited by all the three or by any one of them. When we think of something we distinguish it from other things, and to that extent it is limited by those from which it is distinguished. And if *Brahman* is a reality which likewise is thought of or known as something it cannot be infinite. Therefore, infinite in relation to Brahman means that it is all as in that case it cannot be limited by itself, or there is nothing other than *Brahman* which can limit it, and make it finite. In this sense *Brahman* is *bhūma* (great). *Bhūma* is that different from which nothing exists. *Bhūma* is that where one sees nothing, knows nothing, thinks nothing, etc. Anything that is not *bhūma* or *Brahman* is limited and finite, limited by space time and other substances.[30] If by *Brahman*-knowledge we mean that kind of knowledge, which involves knower and known, we cannot talk of *Brahman* as infinite, and if Brahmā is truly infinite there can be no knowledge or definition of *Brahman*.

Definition of Brahman

However, in all the attempts to define *Brahman* in which care is taken to eliminate all the factors which limit *Brahman* one basic limiting factor is present, and that is the definer who conceives *Brahman*, and tries to understand its nature progressively in more and more comprehensive terms. The reality of the definer as something other than *Brahman* is presupposed in all the definitions of *Brahman*. The reality of one who attempts to define *Brahman* is a precondition for any definition of *Brahman*, and acts as the limiting factor of *Brahman*. In terms of man's capacity to understand subtle and philosophical problems the reality grasped and conceptualised by the human mind will share the limitations of the mind. Man views and understands the nature of reality in terms of what is meaningful and intelligible to him. Thus all the definitions of *Brahman* are for man, and the meaningfulness and validity of the various definitions depend upon man's interests, and his level of understanding. A definition of *Brahman* may be meaningful and valid to someone but it may not be true of *Brahman* in itself as in all the definitions of *Brahman* the definer and his limitations are involved. The true nature of *Brahman* in itself may elude all definitions as in all the definitions, even in those definitions which are purported to be of *Brahman* in itself or in its true nature (*svarūpa lakṣaṇa*) like *sat, cit* and *ānanda*, the definer is involved. However, all the definitions of *Brahman* are about *Brahman* as ontologically speaking it is the only reality that is there. Therefore all the definitions of *Brahman* reflect something about *Brahman*, and ultimately refer to or point to *Brahman*. But no term or concept can have *Brahman* as its object, or describe *Brahman* directly as if it is an object of man's understanding or knowledge. Nevertheless, they all point to *Brahman* as in reality *Brahman* is the basis as well as the object of all description. All the definitions and descriptions of *Brahman* indirectly refer to *Brahman* or point to it as their basis or ground as well as their ultimate object of reference. This helps us in understanding and appreciating the significance of the method of *via-negativa* (*neti, neti*) in knowing the nature of *Brahman*. This also is the method followed by Śaṅkara.

The significance of the method of *adhyāropa* and *apavāda*, superimposition and negation, in comprehending the nature of *Brahman* lies precisely in its attempts to eliminate all the subjective factors in knowing the true nature of *Brahman*. All that can be negated is to be negated about *Brahman* so that what cannot be negated meaningfully remains, and that is the true or objective nature of *Brahman*. It is pure existence or pure consciousness. In this process mind or intellect of man becomes free from all ideas and concepts, and that state of mind in which it is free from all imagination and construction (*vikalpa*) is the same as *Ātman* which is *Brahman*. Then we can no longer call mind as mind as it is then devoid of all the functions of mind. "*Brahman* is known as the root of the universe for the denial of effects presupposes existence as the ultimate limit."[31] Thus as any conception or definition of *Brahman* involves a process of selection in terms of what is meaningful and intelligible to man, and also man's capacity to comprehend subtle things it is bound to be limited, and without such involvement there can be no definition of *Brahman*. In any definition something is excluded and something is attributed to the thing defined, and the thing so defined is limited by what it excludes and gets determined by what is positively attributed to it. Thus if all is negated about *Brahman* it may appear to be non-existence or void, but the consciousness to which the notion of void is given is real, and therefore cannot be negated. And consciousness is *Brahman*. It is not a defining characteristic of *Brahman* but *Brahman* itself.

Matter and Consciousness

How can we know and say that *Brahman* is pure consciousness? To our empirical consciousness so many things which are unconscious are given as objects of knowledge, and without these objects consciousness is also not intelligible. Why not we accept matter as the ultimate reality as matter is more pervasive compared to consciousness which is present only within living beings or more specifically in man only? Why not consciousness be derived from matter or explained in terms of matter? Apart from the Upaniṣadic assertion in which it is said that *Brahman* thought of becoming many, and that means *Brahman* is a spiritual reality, Śaṅkara has put forth some significant arguments against matter being the ultimate reality. We present here some of the important arguments of Śaṅkara against the validity of materialism. There is opposition between matter and consciousness. Matter is an object (*viṣaya*) to consciousness, and consciousness by its very nature is that which knows matter as an object. It is never an object. This opposition in nature between consciousness and matter is a matter of fact. And if matter were to be the primordial reality the problem of understanding the origin of consciousness from matter, keeping in view the opposition between them, would be formidable. If we suppose that matter at one stage evolved itself into consciousness we have to admit that at that stage the matter ceased to be matter in evolving itself into consciousness. Matter as matter cannot be both subject and object, and in becoming consciousness matter should become its own opposite or negate itself which is logically impossible. Matter cannot know itself, and if it knows itself it ceases to be matter. And when matter ceases to be matter in evolving itself into consciousness we cannot say that matter is the origin of consciousness. In other words, if matter has an identifiable essence of its own in terms of which it is defined and identified, and when that ceases to be in giving rise to consciousness it can no longer be called matter. One may here adduce the example of light, which is matter, but can illumine matter. But there is no opposition between light and the objects it illumines. Both are matter. Matter in becoming light does not cease to be matter. If we take the example of Cārvākas that certain ingredients when combined produce intoxication, which is not there in the individual ingredients, is not valid. There is no opposition between intoxication and the ingredients which produce it. Both are matter. Matter can manifest itself into various things, but all that it becomes is still matter only. There is no opposition between clay and clay objects. But how to explain consciousness, the opposite of matter, in terms of matter? If in becoming consciousness matter ceases to be matter then matter cannot be the explanation of consciousness. How can a thing become its own opposite without losing its own nature or essence? Even if we suppose that matter has become consciousness then we cannot prove that fact as the essence of effect (consciousness) is different from that of cause (matter); and unless there is something common in both cause and effect we cannot relate them causally. On the other hand, if we suppose that consciousness is somehow inherent within matter then how to explain the inherence within a thing of two natures which are opposed to each other. If there is no opposition between matter and consciousness the problem of explaining consciousness in terms of matter or *vice-versa* would be no problem. But after recognising the opposition between the two, as matter is not consciousness and consciousness is not matter, we cannot derive one from the other, or explain the one in terms of the other. This of course, would be a problem for those who admit the ultimacy of consciousness also. But according to Śaṅkara there is no matter, as the so-called matter in its true nature is nothing but consciousness, though it is not known to empirical consciousness of man. If Brahman, which is consciousness, is the material cause of the world, the world should have the nature of *Brahman* as things of an altogether different kind and character cannot stand to each other in the relation of material cause and effect. For instance, golden ornaments cannot have earth as their material cause. If the material world is different in nature from *Brahman* they cannot stand in the relation of material cause and effect, but as master and servant or creator and created. Then the world is to be regarded as serving the purpose of *Brahman*, the intelligent principle. Now can we say that the world in its material aspect, as a manifestation of *Brahman*, is also intelligent or spiritual. If the world is really spiritual or consciousness why not we experience it as such instead of experiencing it as something physical or non-spiritual. No means of knowledge can support the claim that the world is consciousness. To this it may be replied that the apparent absence of intelligence or consciousness in the world is to be ascribed to the particular mode of manifestation of *Brahman*. This is the case even with intelligent beings like man. Though man is a conscious being in certain states, such as deep sleep and swoon, consciousness does not manifest itself in the way in which it manifests itself during the waking state. Similarly consciousness though present within all does not manifest itself in the same manner in all. And even when for the sake of argument we assume matter to be the material cause of the world all the objects or phenomena of the world do not manifest matter in the same form or manner. Some of the material objects stand in the relation of subserviency to other material objects, as for instance, the human body and food stand in the relation of eater and eaten though they are basically modifications of earth or matter. On the same analogy, it may be pointed out that *Brahman* and world in certain cases stand in the relation of matter and spirit or subject and object though they are basically of the same substance, that is, matter. But, as pointed out earlier, it cannot be valid as there is opposition between subject and object. Can we then say that the seeming absence of consciousness in certain things is not due to non-existence of consciousness in them but due to its different mode of manifestation. For instance, if we try to define life in terms of its capacity to experience pain and pleasure we have to exclude nails and hair from the sphere of life. Moreover, consciousness manifests or reveals itself in man in and through the functions of the senses and mind, and without which consciousness cannot manifest itself in the way it manifests itself in man. That means, the manner of manifestation of consciousness in man through the functions of knowing, thinking, etc., is due to the involvement of instruments of knowledge like the senses and mind. As the instruments of knowledge are absent in other beings consciousness in them does not manifest itself in the same form or manner as in man. Though nails and hair are biological they do not share some of the characteristics which are common to all biological things like experiencing pain and pleasure. Similarly, consciousness as it reveals or manifests itself during the waking and dream states is not different from consciousness that is present in deep sleep. And if we define consciousness in terms of knowing or thinking or seeing and identify consciousness with those functions we may be forced to admit that consciousness as it is known through its manifestation during waking and dream states is not there in deep sleep. On the other hand, if we admit that what is revealed during waking and dream states is only a form of manifestation or revelation of consciousness it need not reveal itself in the same way always; then there will be no problem in admitting the existence of consciousness in deep sleep.

Likewise, the whole world can be a form of manifestation of consciousness but the mode of its manifestation need not always be the same in all things. For example, the present-day conception of matter, according to which matter and energy are convertible terms, was not the conception of matter earlier. The *Sāṁkhya* concept of matter (*prakṛti*) is radically different from that of Cārvāka philosophy. However, we have to depend upon *Śruti* to know that all that is is a manifestation or self-expression of *Brahman* which is consciousness. We shall discuss this problem in more detail in the next chapter.

Brahman and Human Understanding

Now all this discussion about the nature of *Brahman* presupposes that (1) *Brahman* is the cause, both material and efficient, of the world; (2) *Brahman*'s nature is revealed either fully or partly in the world; and (3) man can either independently or on the authority of *Śruti* can comprehend the nature of *Brahman*. Unless these are critically discussed to test their validity our understanding of the nature of *Brahman* which is conceived in relation to the world will not be of much significance.

Man's understanding is shaped or formed by his experience of the world or empirical reality. The categories of his understanding are derived from or based on his empirical experience, and are valid in understating the empirical reality. Therefore man's understanding will be unfounded when he tries to know the nature of *Brahman*, which is not an empirical reality, in terms of his understanding which is formed on the basis of his empirical experience. How far man is justified in extending his understanding to know *Brahman* and if extended what will be its validity? If we accept that the world has a cause, and that cause is *Brahman* then and then only the various conceptions of *Brahman* can have some meaning and validity. We are going to discuss these problems in a separate chapter dealing with the reality and status of the world. However, if these presuppositions are proved baseless then the discussion based on them about *Brahman* would be invalid. *Brahman*'s being the origin of the world, its presence and revelation within the world and its various attributes are meaningful and valid only in terms of man's understanding which is formed on the basis of his empirical experience. And if these presuppositions are proved to be logically untenable all that we say about *Brahman* either by way of definition or by way of description cannot be true of *Brahman*. Thus we are to admit two forms (*rūpa*) of *Brahman*, one that is meaningful in relation to the world, and is intelligible in terms of man's understanding, and the other in which *Brahman* is sought to be known as it is in itself. As long as man tries to understand the nature of *Brahman* as if it is something other than himself, or as long as man's mind is active in knowing the nature of *Brahman* he cannot know whether his understanding of *Brahman* is valid objectively or not. All that he can know about *Brahman* either independently or in the light of *Śruti* is conditioned by the limitations of his understanding, and is valid and meaningful in relation to it. To conceive *Brahman* as the Lord of the world or Īśvara who is all-pervasive, omniscient and omnipotent is meaningful and intelligible only when the reality of the world is accepted, and is regarded as something caused. Only on this assumption or belief man tries to understand the ultimate cause of the world, which he identifies with *Brahman*, and accordingly conceives its nature. This belief is presupposed or is the basis for an enquiry into the nature of *Brahman*, and unless one tries to understand critically the validity of such beliefs one cannot say whether all the definitions of *Brahman*, which presuppose such beliefs, are objectively valid or not. Our understanding of *Brahman* is in relation to the world of empirical experience, and is conceived in relation to it, and is based on the belief that the world of our empirical experience is a dependent reality and is caused by *Brahman*. On the other hand, if the reality of the world of our empirical experience is not what we believe it to be, a created or dependent reality, all the definitions of *Brahman* involving causation will lose their meaningfulness and validity. As the various definitions of *Brahman* are formulated on the belief that the world is a created reality hey cannot be true of *Brahman* independently of its relation to the world. And when our beliefs about the world are proved baseless the definitions of *Brahman* which presuppose such beliefs will be invalid. In the absence of valid arguments to show that the world is a creation or a caused reality our understanding of *Brahman* as the cause of the world, will not be meaningful. However, until man transcends his empirical understanding, which is influenced or even conditioned by his beliefs about the world, the various conceptions of *Brahman* conceived in relation to the world would remain meaningful and valid. When man transcends his empirical understanding by freeing himself from all presuppositions and beliefs that condition his understanding, the various conceptions of *Brahman* will lose their meaningfulness and validity. This happens when *Brahman* is realised directly and immediately by being it. Then there would be no conception of *Brahman* or its definition. Then the various conceptions of *Brahman* based on man's empirical understanding, which is guided by the law of causation, cease to have any objective validity. Thus *Brahman* in itself is a matter of direct and immediate knowledge or realisation by being it, and till it is realised directly *Brahman* is viewed and conceived in relation to the world of empirical experience, and defined accordingly in different ways. The various conceptions of *Brahman* refer to *Brahman* as conditioned or determined by man's understanding, and when man becomes aware of this fact, he sees the justification in knowing *Brahman* as free from those limitations that are imposed on it by his understanding. Thus there is a philosophical justification for two forms of *Brahman*. While one is objective, the other is conditioned by various subjective factors. About *Brahman* in itself nothing can be said, and anything that is said about *Brahman* is said by way of superimposing on *Brahman* what is meaningful and valid to man's empirical understanding. Thus Śaṅkara makes a distinction between *Brahman* that is an object of direct knowledge, and *Brahman* which is an object of attainment.[32] Conception of *Brahman* as the object of ultimate attainment or the ultimate goal of one's life depends on what man thinks of himself which determines his thinking about his relation to *Brahman*. The objective knowledge of *Brahman* can alone dispel ignorance about the nature of *Brahman*, and it is not used for any other end. *Brahman*-knowledge is an end in itself.[33] Knowledge by its very nature cannot alter or modify the nature of reality. Objective knowledge can only reveal the true or objective nature of reality, and it has no other purpose to serve. It is an end in itself. Such knowledge does not serve any purpose of man except freeing him from ignorance about the true nature of reality. *Mokṣa* which refers to the state of objective knowledge of *Brahman* is the same as *Brahman*. *Brahman* and *mokṣa* are synonyms, as *Brahman* is not different from *Brahman*-knowledge, for *Brahman* is pure knowledge or pure consciousness. It is not an object of knowledge known to someone, or it is not knowledge in the ordinary sense. It is knowledge of *Brahman* by being *Brahman* which is pure knowledge. Pure knowledge or pure consciousness is not an object of knowledge. In being it one is not attaining anything new as it is one's being. Such knowledge cannot be expressed or stated in the form of a statement or proposition either scriptural or empirical. *Brahman* is not an object of knowledge, and therefore cannot be the content or meaning of a proposition. The best way of describing *Brahman* is to remain silent, silence born of direct and immediate realisation of *Brahman*. Anything that is said about such realisation is said by way of praise or glorification, but not to describe it.

References

1. *ṚVSaṁ*, 1.164.4.
2. *Ibid.*, 1.164.6.
3. *AitUpBh*, 1.1.2.

4. *BṛUp*, 2.5.15.
5. *BṛUpBh*, 4.3.20; 4.4.22; *AitUpBh*, 1.2.1.
6. *KaṭhaUpBh*, 2.3.5.
7. *RVSaṁ*, 3.41.3.
8. *Ibid.*, 6.51.8.
9. *Ibid.*, 10.114.8.
10. *BṛUp*, 1.6.1.
11. *Ibid.*, 2.5.1.
12. *Ibid.*, 3.7.15.
13. *ChāUp*, 5.11.1.
14. *BṛUp*, 3.4.1.
15. *SūBh*, 1.2.3.
16. *AitUpBh*, 3.1.3.
17. *TaitUpBh*, 2.6.1.
18. *KaṭhaUpBh*, 2.3.12.
19. *Ibid.*, 2.3.12.
20. *TaitUp*, 2.6.1.
21. *TaitUpBh*, 2.6.1.
22. *SūBh*, 3.2.21.
23. *ChāUpBh*, 6.2.1.
24. *SūBh*, 3.2.22; 2.2.31.
25. *Ibid.*, 1.1.4; 1.1.11.
26. *AitUpBh*, Introduction; *TaitUpBh*, 2.3.1.
27. *SūBh*, 1.1.2.
28. *Ibid.*, 2.1.11.
29. *Ibid.*, 1.2.7.
30. *ChāUp*, 7.24.1 and Śaṅkara's commentary on it.
31. *KaṭhaUpBh*, 2.3.12.
32. *Ibid.*, 1.2.16.
33. *BṛUpBh*, 1.4.2.

4

World

In this chapter we try to understand the reality of the world, and its relation to *Brahman*. For a proper understanding and appreciation of the concept of world, according to *Advaita*, it is desirable to have an understanding of the concept according to the *Veda* and the *Upaniṣads*. The object of our discussion of the concept of world, according to the *Veda* and the *Upaniṣads*, is not to trace the historical development of the concept within the Vedic tradition but to provide a significant background to Śaṅkara's philosophical analysis and understanding of the concept. This will help us in understanding the approach and analysis of Śaṅkara, and the philosophical problems he faces in understanding the nature and reality of the world.

Vedic Conception

The world is seen by the Vedic seers as an abode or dwelling place of the deities, who as varied manifestations of the Divine, reveal themselves in and through the diverse phenomena of the world. Each deity dwells within a phenomenon of the world, reveals itself within it, and forms the essence and unity of that phenomenon. The various deities that dwell within the various phenomena of the world constitute the essence or inner reality of the world, and therefore reveal themselves or the Divine as the inner unity of the world. As the abode of the Divine or the deities the world is the source of divine revelation to man. The world with all its richness and variety is the creative manifestation of the Divine, as each phenomenon of nature is a creative manifestation of a deity. And as all the deities are a manifestation of the Divine, the world in all its diversity and richness is a manifestation of the Divine. Being a manifestation of the Divine the world can reveal the Divine, its source, as its essence and unity. The world is the *kāvya* or creative expression of the Divine and its wisdom, or a manifestation of divine creativity.[1]

How the world came into existence, or the manner of its creation, and its relation to the Divine, its ultimate source, are the problems with which the Vedic seers are not generally concerned. Nevertheless, there is speculation in the *Veda* about the origin of the world, and the manner of its creation. We find some theories about the origin of the world in the *Veda* though the general attitude of the Vedic seers towards all cosmological theories is one of scepticism. "Who has seen the origin of the world? Who can tell it to us?"[2] There can be no clear and definite knowledge of the creation of the world as man's existence presupposes the existence of the world. Even the deities do not know the secret of creation as they also come into existence in the process of creation or self-manifestation of the Divine. The Sanskrit word for creation (*sṛṣṭi*) does not mean creation as it is understood in the context of Western religious traditions. It means a spontaneous outflow of divine creativity and wisdom, as *kāvya* is an outflow of *kavi*'s creativity and wisdom.

However, one thing is common to all the accounts of creation found in the *Veda*; the world has no existence independently of its source or the Divine. It is a manifestation of the Divine, and therefore the world depends for its existence on the Divine, and shares the nature of the Divine. Although the world is not the same as the Divine so that one who knows the world knows the Divine it is not at the same time completely different from the Divine. As the Divine is known through the world the world is not completely different from the Divine. As a creative manifestation of the Divine the world reveals the glory and splendour, and the creative wisdom of the Divine. And the Divine transcends its own glory or is something more than its expressed glory and wisdom.[3] The Divine reveals itself within the world but the world does not and cannot contain and exhaust the glory and wisdom of the Divine. The Divine transcends or exceeds (*ati*) the world. As expressed in the *Puruṣa Sūkta* only a part (*pāda*) of *puruṣa* is all this world while three-fourths of Him transcend the world. The world is an expression of divine glory (*mahimā*), and the Divine exceeds its own glory.[4] Nevertheless, all this is *puruṣa* though *puruṣa* is more than all this. When it is said that a part of *puruṣa* is all this it does not mean that *puruṣa* has parts, but the idea sought to be conveyed is that the infinite glory and splendour of *puruṣa* cannot be contained and exhausted by the world. *Puruṣa* is the world, and at the same time He transcends the world. The world is his manifestation or self-expression (*vyakta*). It is said in the *Veda* that the deities like Indra can become or assume several forms at will in terms of their creative wisdom or creative power (*māyā*), which is inherent within all the deities, and because of which they manifest themselves variously in the form of the world. In this sense the world of our empirical experience is real, but only as a manifestation of the Divine. It has no existence independently of *puruṣa*.

Upaniṣadic Conception

In the *Upaniṣads* we come across several theories of creation, and what is commonly asserted in all of them is that in respect of substance the world is not different from its ultimate source. In some of the theories the ultimate reality is conceived in personal terms. It is said that the reality after creating the world entered into it to the last detail. The *puruṣa* wanted to create, and so He created the world out of His own nature, and entered into it. He manifests Himself in the form of the world for His self-realisation. In all the analogies employed in the *Upaniṣads* to explain or understand the manner of world creation the reality or *Brahman* is seen to have become all that is or the world, or the world has come into existence out of the nature of *Brahman*. Whether it is the example of spider weaving a web out of itself, or herbs growing on earth, or hair from the living human beings, or sparks of fire emanating from fire, the world can have no reality apart from or independently of *Brahman*. It is *Brahman* that has become all or the world, or the world comes into existence out of *Brahman* as naturally or spontaneously as the growth of hair from the body of a living man, or a web from the body of a spider, or sparks from fire. The creation of the world is also likened to the breathing in man which is natural and spontaneous. Just as man breathes in and breathes out without any effort, the world comes into existence out of *Brahman* (*asyaiva tāni sarvāṇi niśvāsitāni*).[5] It is not therefore for the fulfilment of any purpose of *Brahman* the world is created or manifested. At the most we can say that the world is an outward or external manifestation or expression of all that is within *Brahman* or *ātman*. It is by way of self-expression or manifestation of *Brahman* the world is brought into existence. It is an expression (*vyakta*) of *Brahman*'s nature. Since the world is a manifestation of *Brahman*, by knowing *Brahman* the world or all that is is known. And the world differs from *Brahman* in terms of name and form only. A pot made of clay is clay only with the difference that the pot is known as pot on the basis of its form. The non-difference between *Brahman* and the world in respect of substance is asserted in the *Upaniṣads*. In the *Bṛhadāraṇyaka Upaniṣad* the creator is identified with the creation. "I indeed am the creation, for I projected all this. Therefore he is called creation (*aham vāva sṛṣṭirasmi*)."[6] This identification is possible as the world has no reality independently of *Brahman*, or without *Brahman* there can be no world, as without clay the pot made of clay is unthinkable. Because of the substantive unity of the world and *Brahman* the world is distinguished from *Brahman* only in terms of name and form.

Ontologically there is no difference between them as ontologically there is no reality other than *Brahman*. Though the world is not different from *Brahman* in substance it is nevertheless seen and conceived differently. Both the concepts, the world and *Brahman*, refer to the same reality, but have different meanings, or are different insofar as they are conceived and understood by man differently. The meaning of the one is not the same as the other. Thus the world without name and form is *Brahman* just as pot without the form of pot is clay only. What is ontologically real is *Brahman* only, but it is known differently as *Brahman* and world because man has two different conceptions of the same reality in terms of its manifestation. This ontological or substantive oneness of the world and *Brahman* is asserted in all the *Upaniṣads* though the manner of presenting it is not always the same in all the *Upaniṣads*. All this is *Brahman*, as it is born from *Brahman*, and will in the end be dissolved into *Brahman*; and before its dissolution it lives in *Brahman*. When understood in its substantive identity or without its name and form the world is nothing but *Brahman*, as Śaṅkara interprets later. The world and *Brahman* refer to two distinct concepts or have two distinct meanings or names but having the same reality as their referent.

Even though the world and *Brahman* refer to the same reality, while differing in terms of their meaning to man, the *Upaniṣads* do not directly negate or deny the process whereby *Brahman* has become the world. Two conceptions of the same reality are possible as the same reality has become the world, but because of it if we think that *Brahman* and world refer to two different realities we are wrong. And at the same time they are not one and the same. They are one insofar as they refer to the same reality, but mean differently as the concept of world has a meaning which is not the same as that of *Brahman*. In other words, though there are no two realities corresponding to the concepts of *Brahman* and world, the two concepts are not identical, and there is justification for the concept of world in terms of *Brahman*'s manifestation.

Whether the manifestation is real and objective or only illusory is not really a problem to the *Upaniṣads*. However, there are certain statements in the *Upaniṣads* in which multiplicity (*nānātva*) and difference (*bheda*) are denied, and Śaṅkara refers to these kind of statements when he seeks scriptural justification for his final view on the reality and status of the world. He constantly refers to two kinds of Upaniṣadic statements in which the reality of the world is both asserted and denied. He tries to build a logically consistent cosmology of the *Upaniṣads* on the basis of certain statements in which the world is seen as a manifestation of *Brahman*, differing from *Brahman* in terms of name, form and action, but denies ultimate validity to all this on the basis of certain other statements in which all difference and multiplicity are negated or denied. Whether it is possible to reconcile both the kinds of statements, without denying validity to either of them, depends upon the value one attaches to the logical requirements of interpretation. Whether Rāmānuja's interpretation in which both the types of statements are interpreted without rejecting validity to either of them at any level is philosophically or rationally adequate or not is a different problem. However, according to Śaṅkara, if one is to be logically consistent and coherent in his interpretation or understanding of the *Upaniṣads* both the kinds of statements cannot be reconciled or harmonised by giving equal importance and validity to both the kind of statements. Whether there is any real conflict among the various statements of *Śruti* about the reality of world, or is only apparent, or is a matter of perspective, or is due to the method of interpretation one adopts is a crucial problem. There would be no philosophical problem if both the types of statements are understood and interpreted from two different points of view, but then the problem would be whether the two different points of view can be reconciled and made valid from another point of view. Otherwise, how the statements asserting the origin of the world, and its reality can be reconciled with the statements in which the origin and reality of the world are denied? Whether both the positions can be sustained on the basis of *Brahman*'s nature is not a problem which we can resolve on the authority of *Śruti* as *Śruti* clearly maintains both the positions. It has not tried to reconcile them; it has simply presented both the positions.

If the *Upaniṣads* were not to deny multiplicity and difference, but only asserted the origin of the world from *Brahman* there would have been no problem of world in *Vedānta*. Or if they denied consistently any world process then also the problem of the world would not have been there. But the *Upaniṣads* asserted both, and both cannot be equally valid and true at the same time or from the same point of view. Now which kind of statements are to be given final validity is not a major problem as the statements that deny or negate the validity of other statements are finally valid. But as both kinds of statements are equally made by *Śruti*, or express the wisdom of *Śruti*, they enjoy the same authority, as otherwise we have to attribute imperfection and ignorance to *Śruti* which is not acceptable to any interpreter. We cannot say that some of the *Śruti* statements are false, and are therefore not authoritative, while some other statements are true and are therefore finally authoritative. *Śruti* statements are either true or false, but cannot be both. But if we admit that some of the *Śruti* statements are meaningful and true from one level of understanding or point of view, and the others from another level of understanding or point of view, both the kinds of statements can be reconciled without denying validity to either. That means both the kinds of statements cannot be true and meaningful from the same level of understanding or point of view. On the other hand, the reconciliation of both the kinds of statements, without denying validity to either of them, would be possible if we are prepared to admit some kind of difference or duality ultimately. But as we shall soon see the explanation of both oneness and difference in terms of one and the same reality is not logically possible.

Most of the problems which we face in Śaṅkara's interpretation of the Upaniṣadic philosophy are in the ultimate analysis related to the existence of the world and its explanation, as only while explaining the world and its reality he had to introduce the concept of *māyā* and the two levels of understanding and validity to the Upanisadic statements. All these are related directly or indirectly to the problem of the existence of the world, its nature and reality. Before we try to understand the philosophical position of Śaṅkara about the world we have to keep in mind one or two things. Apart from the minor works like *Vivekacūḍāmaṇi*, etc., in which Śaṅkara expressed his views freely, in all his major works, which are commentaries on texts, like *Vedānta Sūtras*, he had to comment upon or explain or elucidate the meaning of the texts. And these texts though they reflect a sort of unity in meaning and purpose contain within themselves statements which do not completely agree among themselves. They occasionally contradict each other, or at least do not agree with each other. It is possible to develop a system of thought basing mainly on some passages of the *Upaniṣads* which need not agree with other systems of thought as developed on the basis of some other Upaniṣadic statements. In all such interpretations the texts which are not completely amenable to one type of interpretation, or one system of thought are either made to lend support to one type of interpretation, or are regarded as secondary in importance and metaphorical in their meaning. These problems arise when one wants to identify what is central to the *Upaniṣads*, or what is the essential or cardinal teaching of the *Upaniṣads*, and justify it. In this process of determining the central philosophy of the *Vedānta* texts, all of which are not amenable to any one kind of interpretation, the importance and significance of some of the statements are reduced while some are given supreme importance and significance.

In the *Upaniṣads* there are several conceptions of reality as there are different theories of creation. For instance, in one it is said that *Brahman* wanted to create, and so created the world, and in another the creation is said to flow spontaneously from the nature of *Brahman* without any effort or desire on the part of *Brahman*. Similarly about the nature of *Brahman* also most of the time the *Upaniṣads* speak of *Brahman* in personal terms, and attribute to him all that is great. He is seen as the ultimate source or cause of the world, and therefore our knowledge of *Brahman* is logically linked to our knowledge of the world. In some of the statements all this is denied. How to develop a consistent and coherent system of thought on the basis of the *Upaniṣads*? Now, Śaṅkara while interpreting the texts of the *Upaniṣads* or the *Vedānta Sūtras*, for instance the *sutras* 1.1.4; 2.1.4, etc., appears to be in full agreement with the cosmological theories of the *Upaniṣads*, namely, that *Brahman* is the ultimate origin or cause of the world. He is both the material and efficient cause of the world; and the world comes into existence out of the twofold nature of *Brahman*. The twofold nature of *Brahman* is sufficient to explain the world in its material and spiritual aspects. In all such interpretations Śaṅkara seems to agree with the texts he interprets, and the texts speak of the world as a positive reality having its source in Brahman. Śaṅkara does not however admit that in the final analysis the world is real, and therefore requires explanation. All cosmological explanation in his philosophy is not an explanation of the world that is positively real but of the various views of the world. If we look at most of the Upaniṣadic statements about the world we may feel that Śaṅkara in his interpretation is not only not true to them but goes against them. But, on the other hand, if we think that his philosophy is true to those passages of the *Upaniṣads*, which are a few but are basic to the philosophy of the *Upaniṣads*, then his philosophical understanding of the *Upaniṣads* is true to the spirit of the *Upaniṣads*. Whatever may be the mode of creation of the world and its relation to *Brahman* in all the *Upaniṣads* the reality of the world is admitted. Otherwise the significance of the Upaniṣadic wisdom in asserting the essential oneness of all with *Brahman* will be meaningless. Since these statements are not plain tautologies there is justification in asserting the oneness of the world with *Brahman*. Can we then say that Śaṅkara has missed the basic spirit or wisdom of the *Upaniṣads* in denying reality to the world and to the individual self of man, or is it the case that in a more profound sense he agrees with the *Upaniṣads* so that his understanding of the *Upaniṣads* is completely true to them in spirit, if not in letter? In understanding the problem of the reality of the world, according to Śaṅkara, we should adopt his categories of understanding, and follow his approach to the problem instead of using our concepts and categories.

Śaṅkara on World

According to Śaṅkara, the world refers to our empirical knowledge and experience which are due to various sources of knowledge, including scriptures, and to the beliefs and doctrines which we inherit from tradition based either on *Śruti* or *Smṛti*. We normally believe in the existence of the world, the arena of our activities and experiences, and in God (Īśvara) its creator and destiny. Since we use these concepts we distinguish them and think that they refer to two distinct realities, however closely related they may be. So is the case with man's reality or self. These beliefs and concepts which form the world of our empirical understanding and experience help us in planning and leading a meaningful life. As we live by these beliefs, and they give meaning to our lives we are attached to them. As they sustain man's emotional and spiritual life he seldom tries to understand them critically or objectively, as in doing so he is afraid of losing the support which they lend to his life. Without them he thinks that his life will be a void or his day to day life will be meaningless. All these beliefs have pragmatic validity and justification, and without them man's life, especially his moral life, based on several distinctions will not be possible and meaningful. If reasoning is unfounded in transcendental matters practical life of man would have come to an end, as man's practical life is not simply based on his empirical knowledge and experience but relates itself to something that is non-empirical. Man is attached to the world of his beliefs, and considers it to be real as without it he thinks his empirical or practical life would not be meaningful, and even possible. Such beliefs may change from time to time, and from tradition to tradition but their validity lies in their practical efficiency to man. Without such beliefs human relations at all levels, and his conduct either social, moral or religious would not be possible. Man's beliefs about the reality of the world and its nature depend on his level of understanding, and in relation to his needs and aspirations. We have several beliefs about the world, and all those beliefs may not be valid and meaningful to all, but are meaningful and valid to some. Some of the beliefs which are not held by modern man, and are not meaningful and intelligible to him, were once held by people and were regarded as valid and meaningful. Every belief about the world is meaningful insofar as it is believed by some. Ordinary or unthinking people may believe in the objective validity of their beliefs, while the thinking people may consider them as having only practical or pragmatic validity. World is real to man as it has a meaning to him, and that meaning is interlinked with the meaning he gives to his own reality, or *vice-versa*. Can we say that all these views and beliefs about the world are objectively true and valid apart from the pragmatic validity they enjoy?

The world of which the most ingenious person cannot have an adequate conception or understanding is the totality of things seen and unseen (*dṛṣṭādṛṣṭa viṣaya samudāya*).[7] Though objectively the world is the same for all of us there are nevertheless several conceptions or views of it which are not valid and meaningful to all. According to *Vedānta*, the world consists of name, form and action, and the world consisting of names and forms is common to all, while the beliefs or views about its origin and destiny may vary from person to person, or from tradition to tradition. They are mostly inherited from one's tradition. While the world consisting of names and forms is the objective side of the world, and is common to all, actions which depend upon one's station in life and caste, and other social factors are not common to all. Depending upon one's understanding of oneself, and his place in the society one may act in a particular way. His actions, values and aspirations depend on these factors, for if one gives up one's particular social identity then actions, attitudes and values which are related to that identity automatically cease to be meaningful and valid. For him his world will not then consist of such actions, values, attitudes, religious beliefs and rites, etc. That is to say, the idea of world involves not only name and form, which are common to all, but also the beliefs, values and aspirations of people all of which are indicated by the term action in *Vedānta*, and these in turn depend upon the structure of the society in which one lives, and his place in it. One's world will thus be different from that of others, as the world of a man is largely his own creation or projection. Man is also a creator, and in his creativity he creates much of his world. All that a man creates, which includes values, meanings, beliefs, etc., has no objective validity though it is valid and meaningful to him. The moment one is freed from a particular social role or identity, or from a belief system or culture all the values and meanings and actions which are significant and valid from that position will no more be meaningful and valid to him. "The domain of ignorance is relative existence which consists of ends and means, and religious rites with five factors which again depend on the division of man into four castes."[8] "For a man who does not identify himself as a brāhmaṇa or a kṣatriya or the like the rites and their accessories which are the effects of that consciousness are dropped automatically, because of the giving up of that consciousness."[9] Each man's world is true to him as he lives in and by it. It has a pragmatic validity to a person, or valid and meaningful in relation to his conduct (*vyavahāra*) in the world. While an ignorant person attaches objective validity to his beliefs, as he thinks that all his beliefs about the world are true, a discerning one admits only conventional or practical validity to them. Thus much of the world has no objective reality or universal validity as it consists of much that is created by man.

But as pointed out earlier name and form which are common to all or have objective validity cannot be explained away. The objectivity of the world consists of name and form. On the other hand, the world of beliefs and views is both real and unreal. It is doubted by many sceptics. But the world consisting of name and form in terms of which it is differentiated into many is vouched by all the means of knowledge, and is experienced by all. All the means of knowledge, including scriptures, can operate only when there is difference, difference of at least subject and object. Every knowledge has an object of reference (*sannimittam*) or is of an object (*viṣaya*) which is different from the subject or knower. To know is a transitive verb, and requires an object of knowledge to operate on. There is no knowledge which is without an object (*nahi nirviṣayā prajñapti*),[10] whatever may be the status of the object. Simple awareness has no variety in itself, and therefore the variety experienced or known is due to differences in the objects known or experienced. If, for example, there is no wound or burn external to knower there would be no experience of pain, as knowledge or awareness is not itself painful. On the other hand, if pain belongs to knowledge itself it should be experienced whenever there is knowledge, which is not the case. Even when we doubt the reality of an external object, for it can be an imaginary object, as in the case of imagination or dream experience, the experience of it is real. Furthermore, man's actions, either good or bad, are not possible in the absence of differences, for man cannot act in the absence of differences. Duality or difference is a fact, and it does not require any proof at least at the empirical level, as duality is the basis of man's knowledge and conduct. "The scriptures seek to instruct man according to existing circumstances. They do not teach a man as soon as he is born either the duality or the unity of existence. Nor does duality require to be taught, and nobody thinks from the beginning that duality is false."[11]

Śaṅkara's criticism of *Vijñāñavāda* of Buddhism shows that his denial of what is empirically known and experienced is not based on some clever philosophical arguments. We give here one argument of Śaṅkara against *Vijñānavāda* to show how he is not against common sense and empirical experience. He argues that even if we somehow are able to prove the subjective origin of all our knowledge and experience, as *Vijñānavādins* tried to do, we cannot explain subjectively the very notion of externality. Unless the subject experiences things outside of itself it cannot have the notion of externality as opposed to internality or subjectivity. Even if we suppose that there are no objects external to the subject, and dismiss the reality of the external world as only seeming or apparent, even then the seeming externality of the world cannot be explained purely in terms of subject. Since Śaṅkara's criticism of *Vijñānavāda* is powerful, as he puts forth several arguments to reject it, we cannot say that Śaṅkara's position with regard to the existence of the world is similar to that of *Vijñānavāda*, and for the same reasons. The world is real as far as our empirical experience and knowledge are concerned, and as the existence of the world is a matter of experience, and is supported by all the means of valid knowledge, no amount of philosophical argumentation can disprove the existence of the world, and its diversity.

The *Śruti* also does not have authority to deny what is known through other means of knowledge, like sense perception and inference, and the world is an object of knowledge to the latter. The authority of *Śruti* as a source of valid knowledge is with regard to those things or reality which cannot be known through other means of knowledge. And if *Śruti* contradicts what is known through other means of knowledge then *Śruti* will lose its authority and validity. "The *Śruti* is not supposed to have authority in matters which are contradicted by other means of knowledge."[12] Even if hundreds of *Śruti* statements say that fire is not hot we have to disregard *Śruti* and accept the validity of perceptual knowledge. *Śruti* is a valid means of knowledge in trans-empirical matters or with regard to what is not known through other means of knowledge. Every means of knowledge is valid in respect of its object of knowledge, and other means of knowledge cannot be used to judge the validity of a knowledge obtained through some other means, for each means of knowledge can give us knowledge about those things that cannot be known by any other means of knowledge. For instance, what is known through the eyes, like colour, can only be known through eyes, and therefore no other sense-organ can be employed to judge the validity of the knowledge got through eyes. All the sense-organs cannot give us knowledge of the same thing, or quality of a thing. We cannot perceive sound by means of our eyes, and form and colour through our nose and ears. It is only when the same thing can be known through more than one means of knowledge, or is an object of different sources of knowledge, the problem of validating the knowledge got through one source of knowledge in terms of another source arises. On the basis of this principle reason and *Śruti*, and *Śruti* and sense-experience cannot contradict each other, for what is known through one is not known through the other sources of knowledge. Therefore there can be no contradiction between *Śruti* and other means of knowledge. Moreover, *Śruti* as a source of knowledge is only recollective or informative (*jñāpaka*) as it reveals the true nature of a reality which is known to all through all the sources of knowledge. Therefore the knowledge got through various means of knowledge is valid, and all the means of knowledge testify to the reality of the world of name and form. The various objects which constitute the world are known through sense-perception and inference, and we have no valid reasons to doubt their reality.

Whatever is experienced is real, and the various means of knowledge give us knowledge of the world of differences or multiplicity. When a thing is perceived it is to be accepted as real as the reality of what is perceived cannot be judged by other means. To deny the reality of what is actually perceived is absurd because it is actually observed. The possibility or impossibility of what is actually observed does not arise as these are to be decided on the ground of the operation or non-operation of the means of valid knowledge, but not on the basis of pre-conceived possibilities and impossibilities. "Whatever is apprehended by perception or some other means of knowledge is possible, and impossible is what is not so apprehended."[13] "If you deny an observed fact saying it is impossible you would be contradicting experience, a thing which nobody will allow. Nor is there any question of impossibility with regard to an observed fact because it has been actually observed."[14]

Even the metaphysical assumptions should be made in accordance with or consistent with the facts of experience, as otherwise one can make any number of assumptions, and there would be no way of judging their validity. Certain means of knowledge, like sense-perception and inference, are common to all, and they give us knowledge of the world of differences, and this knowledge is what is common to all of us. To deny validity to this knowledge is to do something which no man of sound common sense will approve. Even when it is attempted it only amounts to mere words having no basis in experience. The world or what is objectively there is common to all, common to those who accept the authority and validity of their own knowledge and experience, and to those who accept the reality of *Brahman* alone. Perfect or objective knowledge of *Brahman*, which is the sole object of *Śruti*, cannot alter the nature of reality nor can it deny reality to what is objectively real. It cannot create a reality which is not objectively real nor can it alter or modify or deny reality to what is objectively real. If knowledge can alter or destroy what is objectively real there would have been by now no world as many had realised *Brahman* or attained *Brahman* knowledge in the past.

Śruti Knowledge and Empirical Knowledge

Brahman is objectively real, and the purpose of *Śruti* is to give us objective or perfect knowledge of it. There are no two realities, one corresponding to our empirical knowledge, and the other represented by scriptural knowledge. The reality is one only without a second, and the same is the object of all the sources of knowledge, including *Śruti*. If one and the same reality is the object of both scriptural knowledge and empirical knowledge can there be any conflict between them? While perception, inference etc., or all the sources of empirical knowledge testify to the fact of difference, *Śruti* denies difference and asserts oneness; otherwise both of them reveal the same reality. To put it in Advaitic terminology, the reality is one only without a second, but we have two types of knowledge or experience of the same reality, one empirical (*vyavahāra*) and the other *pāramārthika*. Therefore the problem of the existence or reality of the world, or its non-existence or unreality is to be formulated differently as the problem of validity or otherwise of man's empirical knowledge of differences, for in the ultimate analysis the reality of the world of differences is only a matter of empirical experience. World refers to a type of experience (empirical experience), and therefore to judge the reality of the world is to judge the validity of man's empirical experience. We now consider some of the important reasons why *advaitins* think that the world of differences has no objective reality, but only refers to an experience. It is ordinarily believed that the world is a creation or is caused, and the cause is God (*Īśvara*) or *Brahman*. But when this belief is put to logical analysis and understanding it is found out to be a belief without any objective or logical basis, as it cannot be justified either in terms of the concept of *Brahman*, the supposed cause of the world, or on the basis of the nature of the world as something caused or created. In the writings of Śaṅkara we come across several arguments to prove the existence of *Brahman* and its nature on the basis of the world with the understanding that *Brahman* is the cause of the world, or the world is caused by *Brahman*. These arguments are almost similar to the arguments formulated to prove the existence of God in other traditions, with the exception of ontological argument. We find all other arguments like teleological, cosmological and moral arguments in the writings of Śaṅkara. What is common to all these arguments is some sort of causation on the part of *Brahman*. They start with the world, that is given to man's empirical experience, and basing on the law of causation try to trace its origin to *Brahman*. What is implicit in all such arguments is the belief that the world cannot exist by itself, and therefore must have a cause, and that cause is *Brahman*. But on a critical examination both the beliefs or assumptions are untenable logically. By definition *Brahman* is absolute or absolutely perfect. Is such a conception of *Brahman* logically compatible with the idea of cause? Causation involves a capacity to change on the part of the cause if the cause is conceived as matter, or a motive if it is conceived in personal terms. If the ultimate reality is matter, and is capable of change, which is not imposed on it from outside, then there can be no creation having a beginning, as capacity to change must be conceived as intrinsic to the cause. Otherwise we cannot explain why it activates itself at a certain point of time to create the world. Then the world cannot be substantively different from *Brahman*, its cause. At the most, the world will be a modified version of *Brahman* or a transformation of *Brahman*, its material cause. If *Brahman*, on the other hand, is spiritual or intelligent we have to explain the reason for him to create the world. And if we are to admit some reason for the creation of the world we have to admit some motive to *Brahman* in creating the world, and every motive or desire involves some lack or deficiency in *Brahman* to fulfil which or to overcome which he creates the world. No intelligent person acts without a purpose (*prayojana*), and if the creation is to serve a purpose of its creator it contradicts the eternal perfection (*nitya tṛptatvam*) of *Brahman*. To think of any lack or deficiency in *Brahman*, which alone can be the reason for *Brahman* to create the world, is to deny absolute perfection to *Brahman*. Only when we can think of some imperfection or want in *Brahman* then only we can think of

Brahman as the cause or explanation of the world. Furthermore, the law of causation, in whatever form it is conceived, is valid within the realm of man's empirical experience, and there is no logical justification or valid ground to extend it to *Brahman* which is not within the realm of man's empirical experience. How can we know and justify that the law of causation, which is valid within the realm of man's empirical experience, is also valid outside the realm of man's empirical experience? The laws that operate within the empirical realm, and are valid within it may not be valid transcendentally (*pāramārthika*). We have therefore no basis or justification for extending the laws of empirical reality to non-empirical reality. And if we extend them then they will have no foundation in experience, and consequently anything can be said about *Brahman*, as no justification is required then. Thus apart from common belief *Brahman* cannot be conceived as the cause of the world, or the existence of the world cannot be explained in terms of *Brahman*.

Can the world exist by itself, or is it uncaused? The world is not a caused reality as the ultimate constituents of the world, the bare simples, cannot be said to be caused or created, for we cannot prove the fact that they are caused or created. A composite reality can be said to be caused or created in the sense that its constituents or components are joined or assembled together to create the composite. But this is not true with regard to the simples which go to make up the composite. There is no reason to assert that they too are created or caused as we cannot prove that they cannot exist by themselves. They are uncaused, and are therefore ultimate. If we thus admit that creation is not a logically valid idea as we cannot prove the creation of the world either in terms of its own reality or in terms of *Brahman*, the supposed cause of it, then we have to accept either two independent realities, *Brahman* and world, which are in no way related to each other, or accept the reality of what is given to our empirical experience or the world only which is all that is. To accept the reality of God who is in no way related to the world of empirical experience, and whose existence is a matter of pure faith does not serve any philosophical purpose. On the other hand, the world as all that exists and uncaused is known to all as it is the object of all the means of knowledge. It does not require any explanation.

Now the difference between the empirical knowledge of man and the perfect or objective knowledge of *Śruti* is not about the existence or non-existence of the world or *Brahman*, but about the true or perfect nature of what is empirically experienced by all. The authority of *Śruti* is not to reveal the existence of a reality which cannot be known otherwise but to reveal the true or objective nature of what is known to all. "The texts cannot create anew since a text is not meant to reverse anything. It is concerned with revealing things as they are (*na hi vacanam vastūnā anyadhākaraṇam yadhā bhūtārdhavat dyotane*)".[15] And at the same time if the *Śruti* says the same thing about the reality as it is known to all then also it loses its authority and validity. The Śruti is authoritative, and its knowledge is valid or true over ordinary knowledge because it reveals the true nature of what is empirically known, or gives us perfect or objective (*vastu*) knowledge of the reality which is experienced by all commonly.

Our knowledge of what is there is not objective as it is not, in the first place, universal, for there are different views about it, and secondly, each view is in conflict with other views or even contradicted by other views. These views about what is there objectively go on changing, and are often modified and negated or sublated by other views. Thus we have several metaphysical, religious and popular views of the world. All these views cannot be true as they are about the same reality. There is no finality about these views. One view may appear to be final only till it is negated or contradicted by another. This charge can be levelled against *Śruti* also as several views are present within *Śruti*, and they are not mutually compatible. Because of this fact *Śruti* is amenable to different interpretations. How can we therefore say that *Śruti*-knowledge is objective? But the point we want to make or emphasise here is that *Śruti* does not talk of or give us knowledge of a reality which is other than or different from what is known to all. The same reality is the object of both *Śruti* knowledge and empirical knowledge of man. "Scriptural or empirical outlooks depend entirely on knowledge and ignorance."[16] "This unreal phenomenal existence created by differentiation is indeed a fact for those who do not believe in things as different from *Brahman* as well as for those who do believe."[17] All of us accept the existence of the phenomenal world though there is no agreement among us about the true nature of it. Though *Śruti* and ordinary knowledge have for their object the same reality the knowledge of it as presented in *Śruti* is not the same as ordinary knowledge of it.

The characteristic difference between ordinary knowledge or *avidyā* or *ajñāna* which does not mean the absence of knowledge but wrong knowledge, and scriptural knowledge is that while ordinary knowledge reveals the reality as full of differences, the scriptural knowledge reveals it as homogeneous, and without any kind of difference. The empirical knowledge of reality as consisting of differences and distinctions is the basis of man's empirical life. The world, according to *Advaita*, refers to the reality as known or experienced by man empirically, and the same is known as *Brahman* when it is seen objectively, or as it is in its true nature (*svena rūpeṇa*). This will clear a basic misunderstanding about *Advaita* that in denying reality to what is experienced by all it is denying objective reality to the world. What it emphatically denies is not a reality that exists objectively, but a knowledge or experience which according to it is based on ignorance (*avidyā* or *ajñāna*). The world of empirical knowledge and experience is real only as a matter of knowledge or experience, or it refers to an experience only, and when that experience or knowledge is sublated by scriptural knowledge no objectively existing reality is negated or rejected. In real terms the denial of reality to the world means the denial of reality to difference or duality but not the reality of something (world) that is objectively real. What is questioned and what is denied ultimately is the reality of difference either between man and the world, or world and God and man and God. If what exists objectively is *Brahman* and *Brahman* alone, and that is without any differences, either internal or external, but which are obvious to man's empirical experience, how to explain the differences which are experienced empirically, and are its very basis. Is the reality free from all differences as revealed by *Śruti* or is it full of differences as revealed to man on the basis of his empirical experience? Differences are real as they are experienced by man, and also form the very basis of his experience. Whether the objects of our empirical knowledge are real or not, knowledge itself cannot arise in the absence of difference between what is known or object and the knower or the subject. The very fact of knowledge proves the reality of difference as without an object the notion of subject is unintelligible, and *vice-versa*. Whether what we see or perceive is real or not the fact of seeing or perceiving presupposes the duality of seer and seen as otherwise seeing would be unintelligible. Knowledge also presupposes the knower and the known, and it does not matter whether the known is objectively real or illusory, as without some kind of object knowledge would not be possible.

Śaṅkara on Difference

Does Śaṅkara deny difference? According to *Advaita*, name, form and action constitute the world of differences, whether the differences are gross or subtle. Here we do not try to discuss the nature of general difference as between gold and clay or cow and horse in which the difference is not simply one of name and form as in the case of clay and the pot made of clay. According to Śaṅkara, there are no generic differences as all the differences are due to name and form only, and the reality is one, and is homogeneous in its nature. If the difference is generic it goes against the non-duality of reality as in the case of Sāṁkhya where *puruṣa* and *prakṛti* are generically different.

Difference in name and form does not vitiate the homogeneous nature of *Brahman*, as all the differences point to difference in form of the same reality, but not to difference in the nature of reality or different realities. Name is based on form as there can be no name without a form corresponding to it. Name is due to speech or language while form is something real. Name, form and action constitute the world. In the absence of a form a name has no meaning. For instance, the same water is known as sea, wave, foam, etc., because the same water has taken different forms, and therefore is known by different names, and all the names refer to the same reality, that is, water. But unless there is transformation of water into waves, foam etc., it cannot be distinguished in terms of various forms, and named differently. The *Upaniṣads* and Śaṅkara are justified, keeping in view the non-dual and homogeneous nature of *Brahman*, in reducing the world of experience to name, form and action. But can we say that name and form are unreal? If there are no names and forms the actions based on them will not be possible. For instance, men are differentiated into different castes, and each caste has its own functions, and is related to other castes, and if such differentiation is not done the caste distinctions and the resultant actions and relations will not be valid. The whole of empirical life is based on differences and distinctions made in terms of or on the basis of name and form. For instance, man attaches different values to gold, diamond and earth though all of them are nothing but earth and its different forms of manifestation. Or in the Hindu context the value attached to funeral fire is different from that attached to sacrificial fire. Here the distinction is not objective or ontological but is based on man's attitudes. There is no objective difference in the nature of both the fires.

Can we then say that from the standpoint of *Brahman* there is oneness or unity of all that is, though from the point of view of empirical experience differences in terms of name and form are also real? There is oneness in terms of *Brahman* which is ultimately real, and the differences, which are due to name and form, are not ultimately real, for when a thing loses its form it also loses its name. We may understand this with the help of an example. We call something a piece of cloth when threads are interwoven, and the cloth is real as it has a form different from that of threads, and serves a different purpose. But when the individual threads are separated the cloth will have no reality. Now it will be known as threads only. And when the threads are further analysed into fibre then the thread will lose its reality. It will have no form of thread and cannot therefore be called thread. And this process can be continued till nothing that has a specific form and hence a particular name are left. Thus names and forms are not ultimately real. All the differentiated world was *Brahman* only in the beginning, that is, before *Brahman* manifested itself into different forms. This will also be the case at the time of final dissolution (*pralaya*). It is only in between the two states the world as differentiated by name and form has existence, and is real. If this type of analysis is followed, and its validity accepted we have to admit the reality of the world of name and form as well as the reality of *Brahman*, as one without a second, before it manifests itself into name and form, or the world of differences. Then both of them will be real though from two different points of view. Thus the oneness of *Brahman* and the world of differences will both be real, just as motion and rest can be attributed to the same object at two different times. "Scriptures by giving examples of clay and gold are in favour of a *Brahman* capable of modification, and also from experience clay and gold undergo modification. Why not we therefore attribute both change and changelessness (*kūtastha*) to *Brahman* in two different states?"[18] On this analogy and explanation both *mokṣa* and empirical life are equally real and meaningful. While *mokṣa* refers to that state of realisation in which the oneness of *Brahman* is realised, the empirical life refers to the experience of differences based on name and form. Nevertheless, names and forms will have objective existence as they are true till such time a form is not destroyed along with its name. We may here say a particular form and the name related to it may come to an end, but some other form and hence some other name will come into existence. And if, we understand the meaning of form in the sense of concept, as pot which refers to a form is also at the same time a concept which includes all the pots, past, present and future, a concept is relatively more real than the individual members it represents. And if all the forms or concepts are present in *Brahman* potentially before they are manifested *Brahman* can be viewed as one without a second, and at the same time as the explanation of the differences. All the scriptural analogies like clay and its modified forms, sea and its modifications, etc., point to *Brahman* and its manifestation into various forms on which depend the meaning of various names. Śaṅkara at times seems to agree with this interpretation, as he maintains such a position while commenting upon the *Vedānta Sūtras* and the *Upaniṣads*. For instance, while interpreting the Upaniṣadic statement *sa imān lokān srjata* (He created these worlds), Śaṅkara says that just as wave and foam, which are nothing but sea water modified into wave and foam, the omniscient Being created the universe consisting of name and form which were one with itself before their manifestation. It is like an intelligent *māyāvī* who without any material adjuncts (*upādāna*) transforms himself as it were into a second person ascending into space. Similarly the omniscient Being, like a supreme magician, creates himself as another in the form of the universe (*ātmānameva ātmāntartvena jagadrūpeṇa nirmita*) for the sake of self-realisation (*ātma prabodha-nārtham*).[19] He entered into all beings and realised himself as 'I am *Brahman*' in and through the differentiated beings (*sākṣāt pratibudhyata*). Whenever he had to comment on the world-process statements affirming the creation of the world, either found in the *Upaniṣads* or in the *Vedānta Sūtras*, Śaṅkara was positive in his interpretation, and if one were to depend upon such explanations, which are plenty in his writings, Śaṅkara would appear to accept the reality of the world as consisting of names and forms. We need not repeat here all such statements and explanations.

However, he asserts that all such explanations are made or can be made only from the point of view of empirical experience, according to which, the world of name and form is real, and has its explanation in *Brahman*. But they can have only a means or instructional value as the real purpose of such explanations is to teach the oneness of *ātman* or *Brahman*, and beyond that they have no validity and meaningfulness. They are introduced to teach the oneness of *Brahman* but not to teach the reality of world process, and the objective reality of the world of differences. "Texts about origin, continuity and dissolution of the world are only to strengthen the idea of *Brahman* being a homogeneous unity and not to make us believe in the origin, etc., of the world as an actuality."[20] "The real object of the text is not to describe creation but to indicate that all the deities are but *virāj* as stated in the text, for manifested objects are not different from the manifestor."[21] All the texts dealing with creation are intended to make one realise the oneness of *ātman* (*ātma ekatva darśanam*). Such statements are the scriptural way of saying or showing that *ātman* is the oneness of all that is. The statements of creation or about the world do not contradict the statements dealing with the absolute oneness of *Brahman* or the statements of non-duality. They subserve the purpose of teaching the oneness of *Brahman* or its non-duality. Even if they contradict, it does not matter, "since the creation of the world and similar topics are not at all what the *Śruti* really wishes to teach. The welfare of man does not depend on them. Such statements are only subordinate members of passages teaching *Brahman* and its non-dual nature."[22] The statements of creation or the statements explaining the world process are secondary in their importance to statements dealing with *Brahman* and its non-duality. For example, numbers and sounds are taught with the help of certain marks or signs (which are conventional), and the intention is not to identify the marks or signs with the numbers and sounds, but with their help to teach numbers and sounds which can be represented by any signs. The marks or signs have only an instrumental value, and when once the nature of numbers and sounds is realised one can see that the marks or signs are not the numbers and sounds. Marks and signs have no reality of their own as any mark or sign can serve the purpose of representing the sounds and numbers.

According to Śaṅkara, the central concern of the *Upaniṣads* or their chief object is to make one realise the oneness of all that is or *Brahmán*, but not to explain the world process which does not serve the highest purpose of man. In realising *Brahman* or *ātman* one is freed from *ajñāna* and attains the highest end of life, but no such purpose is served by knowing the world and its creation. However, without taking into account the empirical fact of name and form or the differences the oneness of *Brahman* cannot be taught as if in a vacuum. All instruction is meaningful at empirical level only. Duality is a fact at one level of understanding or experience, and non-duality is a fact at another level. All are not convinced from the beginning of the reality of *advaita* and the unreality of *dvaita*. The starting point to establish the truth of *advaita* is the world of duality, or the world of name and form. On the other hand, if *advaita* though objectively true is self-evident to all as *dvaita* is, there will be no need to teach it, and criticise *dvaita*. Till *advaita* is realised directly and immediately *dvaita* is real and meaningful, and with the help of *dvaita* only, or from within the framework of *dvaita* only *advaita* is to be taught. If duality is not real empirically where is the need to teach its unreality; and also to whom it can be taught and by whom and with what means? The world of name and form, or the empirical experience of man is the basis for all of his actions and aspirations, and if however that is the ultimate reality man's dissatisfaction with it will have no meaning. And if, on the other hand, both are equally real we cannot say that the one who is having empirical knowledge and living in the world of differences and happy with it is ignorant, and what *Śruti* teaches is perfect knowledge. In other words, if both the knowledges are objectively true and valid there is no meaning in saying that one is the realm of *avidyā* and the other is the realm of *jñāna*. Then one knowledge cannot be negated or sublated by the other. And one who knows the world of differences cannot be blamed for having wrong knowledge, and should look to *Śruti* for attaining right knowledge. The scriptural knowledge can cancel or sublate empirical knowledge only if the latter is not objective or perfect. And if both the knowledges are true and objective one cannot be negated or sublated by the other, and one cannot be regarded as wrong knowledge or *ajñāna*.

Critique of the Theories of Creation

If the scriptural accounts or explanations of creation are taken in their primary or literal sense they come into conflict with or even contradict the texts dealing with *Brahman*. The very notion of creation will be unintelligible and logically untenable if we understand by *Brahman* the reality that is all-pervasive. Creation needs space in which it can come into existence, and this would be possible only if we assume that *Brahman* is not all-pervasive or there is some space in which *Brahman* is not present and in which the world can come into existence. Even the idea of all-pervasiveness of *Brahman* goes against the notion of *Brahman*. The idea that *Brahman* pervades all implies space in which *Brahman* can pervade without leaving any space unoccupied. Normally pervasion means something that is extended in space, and if *Brahman* is the only reality there is no sense in saying that it is all-pervasive. The idea that *Brahman* is all-pervasive involves the idea of all, and the concept of all refers to something other than *Brahman*. Light can pervade more space, and if there is to be nothing but light we cannot say that it pervades everywhere. Thus *Brahman* entering into all after creating all involves contradiction. This would be meaningful only if *Brahman* is conceived as a limited reality so that it can enter into another reality, as someone entering a room. On the other hand, if *Brahman* is the only reality there is no sense in saying that it entered into something or into itself. And if that other reality is also *Brahman* there is no point in saying that *Brahman* entered into itself or *Brahman*. Even then it involves the idea that *Brahman* became many in space and entered into them.

Such problems would equally crop up even when we try to understand the world as *Brahman*'s manifestation, for manifestation is possible or intelligible only when there is some space left for *Brahman* to manifest itself, or to bring into existence newer and newer forms of manifestation. On the other hand, if they are supposed to exist within *Brahman*, as *Brahman* does not exist in space, like earth or water, then some part of Brahman is to be replaced by some other part. Otherwise internal manifestation would not be possible. We may say that some parts of *Brahman* take on a different configuration to form a new form, but unless we admit some empty space within *Brahman* we cannot explain how and where the configuration can take place within *Brahman*. Or, if a new form has to come into existence it has to push aside some other part of *Brahman* so that it can come into existence. That means some change should take place either within or without *Brahman* which needs some scope or space in which it can take place. Now, external manifestation is ruled out as there is no space without or outside of *Brahman* as *Brahman* is not an entity within space. Equally any change within *Brahman* is meaningless as it involves some replacement within *Brahman*. However, all these ideas like internal, external, entering, pervading, etc., are perfectly intelligible and meaningful within the realm of empirical experience involving space and time. Within the empirical realm all things are limited by space and time, and therefore they can grow or change or evolve, enter, pervade, etc., either in space or in time. Space limits all things. and it allows scope for them to grow or expand as space means basically such scope (*avakāśa*). One can move in space, change or grow in space, enter into one space from another space. Similarly, all types of causation are possible and meaningful within the empirical realm in which time is a basic factor. When these categories which are perfectly intelligible within the realm of empirical experience are applied or extended to *Brahman*, which is not a reality in space and time, they end up in contradictions and absurdities.

Thus the *Śruti* statements about creation contradict the statements about Brahman, and both cannot be reconciled if they are given the same kind of validity. Therefore both the kinds of statements cannot be accepted as equally authoritative and basic to *Śruti* because when logically analysed they contradict each other. As long as the world of name and form or the empirical reality is experienced *Brahman* remains as an idea but not a reality that is directly known, and when *Brahman* is directly realised the world simply ceases to be, like the illusory snake. Both are not known or experienced simultaneously as it is impossible to experience change and changelessness, mortality and immortality, oneness and difference simultaneously. Light and darkness cannot be experienced at the same time and in the same place. There cannot be two different and opposing experiences of the same reality at the same time. Here we have to depend on the authority of those who have realised *Brahman* directly and immediately or *Śruti*, as *Śruti*, according to Śaṅkara, expresses such experiences, to know that the world of name and form ceases to be the moment Brahman is directly realised.[23] This is the real justification or basis or authority for denying objective reality to the world of differences. Even otherwise the world consisting of names and forms does not have a nature or essence which is its own so that it can have objective reality, and can endure for ever. If the world has a nature (*svabhāva*) or essence it is *Brahman* only, just as a pot cannot have a nature or essence of its own which is not at the same time that of clay. The substance of clay is the only substance, and a pot is only a modification in form of that substance. Reality or existence belongs to clay only, and only metaphorically we can say that pot exists as apart from clay pot cannot have existence.

Reality of Name and Form

We now discuss the reality of name and form. Name and form are experienced, and that experience is real, and it would not be possible if name and form do not have some kind of reality. Śaṅkara maintains that name and form which constitute the world are not different from *Brahman*. Before we discuss this problem we have to note that most of the problems concerning the nature and existence of the world arise because we try to understand the nature and meaning of manifestation of *Brahman* on the analogy of manifestation of a material reality. All the scriptural analogies given to explain or elucidate the relation between *Brahman* and the world, like sea water and wave, clay and pot, gold and golden objects refer to the manifestation or modification of a material reality, and the mode of manifestation of a material reality is quite different from the mode of manifestation of a spiritual reality. What would be the nature and mode of manifestation in the case of a spiritual reality, and how are we to conceive the relation between a spiritual reality and its manifesations? There are certain analogies given in the *Upaniṣads* which are not taken from the material realm but from the world of living beings, like the spider weaving a web, hair growing from a living human being, and more significantly the process of breathing to understand the nature of relation between *Brahman* and its manifestation or the world. It is said in the *Bṛhadāraṇyaka Upaniṣad* that the scriptures and all the beings emanate from *Brahman* as naturally as breathing in man without any effort. The whole creation or all that is proceeds from *Brahman* like its breathing (*ayam ca lokaḥ parāśca lokaḥ sarvāṇi ca bhūtāni asyaivatāni sarvāṇi niśvāsitāni*).[24] This world, the other world, and all the beings are like the breath of *Brahman*. With the help of these examples or on their analogy the spontaneity of manifestation of *Brahman* is stressed in the *Upaniṣads*. In this process we cannot attribute any motive to *Brahman* for manifesting itself into the world of name and form as it takes place as spontaneously as breathing in man. It is not an act which involves motive, purpose, etc. The manifestation of name and form is due to the very nature (*svabhāva*) of *Brahman*, and Śaṅkara along with the *Upaniṣads* likens the manifestation of the name and form to the breathing of *Brahman*. "It is the name and form in all their states, gross or subtle, or the various stages of their grossness and subtleness that constitute the phenomenal existence. Hence name is compared to breath. By this is implied that form too is like breath."[25] Just as breathing is not different from the person who breathes, the names and forms are not different from *Brahman*. "Name and form are one with *Brahman*."[26] Name and form are identical with *Brahman* in a deeper sense, and are also distinct from it in a particular sense. Name and form are one with *Brahman* as without *Brahman* there can be no name and form, and at the same time they are distinct from *Brahman* in the sense that they differentiate *Brahman* into many. Śaṅkara in his attempts to explain the non-difference of name and form from *Brahman* adduces the examples of the sun and light and a gem and its lustre. Though language creates the illusion that the sun is different from light, and a gem from its lustre, as when we say the light of the sun or the lustre of a gem, in reality the light is not different from the sun. It is not an attribute of the sun as the sun is nothing but light; they are not different. But still we talk of the light of the sun as if they are different. We cannot think of the sun without light or the sun not shining at times. It would be meaningful to talk of the sun and light if the sun were to shine at times. If that is the case how is it meaningful to separate them in the first place? It is only when the sun is different from light, which can be known only when the sun even for a moment can exist without light, we can talk of light being the property of the sun. But that is not the case. But as we use language in which the sun is differentiated from light, as when we say that the sun shines, we think they are two, but in reality they are not two, or are not different. The light of the sun is not different from the sun.

Brahman and World

Can we then identify the world with *Brahman*? They cannot be identified as the concepts of world and *Brahman* have two different and distinct meanings. Furthermore, it is only when the separate existence of the world is admitted its oneness or identity with *Brahman* can be asserted meaningfully. If there is a world, and is different from *Brahman* then only some relation either of identity or identity in difference, or simple difference can be maintained between the two. It is only when we think that the sun is different from light then only it is meaningful to assert any relation between them. But as the difference between the two is only a creation of language there is no point in trying to think of any relation between the two, as in reality there are no two things, the sun and light. The sun's nature is light and yet we say the sun shines (*nitya prakāśa svarūpo'pi san savitā prakāśate*). It is like saying that the hill stands or sits firm (*śaila tiṣṭhati*), or the head of Rāhu, or the body of an idol.[27] Rāhu is nothing but head only, and an idol is nothing but body only. Nevertheless, it is the mode of speech that creates the illusion of Rāhu as something more than head, and an idol as something more than body. It is therefore meaningful to assert that they are not two or are non-different. The difference is a creation of language, but not objective.

It is the belief of people, either inherited from tradition or generated by the scriptures, that the world is different from *Brahman*, and therefore the assertion that they are not two, or are not different is significant and valid. In reality or ontologically there are no two realities of *Brahman* and world, and therefore there is no point in establishing any relation between them. But as people believe in their difference their non-difference is to be asserted, and in so asserting we are not admitting two different realities of world and *Brahman*. As in reality there is no world different from *Brahman*, either in denying reality to it or in asserting its non-difference from *Brahman*, the intention is to correct an illusion that they are different, but not to admit or assert any kind of relation between them. There is a valid reason why *Brahman* cannot be identified with the world though in reality there is no world different from *Brahman*. It is one thing to say that the world is *Brahman*, and quite another to say that *Brahman* is the world. It is like the difference between saying that a pot is clay and clay is pot. A pot is nothing but clay with a form, and for that reason clay cannot be identified with pot as clay is more than a pot. Even if we can exhaustively know all the manifestations of clay and identify them with clay, we cannot say with any definiteness the possible forms of manifestation of clay in future, and therefore to identify clay with its various manifestations is invalid, whereas the manifestations of clay can be identified with clay as then we will not be limiting the nature of clay. We can consider one more example to elucidate this point. Factually one who rules the whole earth is also the ruler of a particular country, but for that reason the sovereignty of the ruler cannot be identified with the rulership of a country as it limits the sovereignty of the ruler. As the ruler of all earth he is also the ruler of all the countries. However, we will be limiting his power if we identify his rulership with this or that country though as a matter of fact he is the ruler of every country. This is the significance of the negative description or *neti, neti* adopted in the *Upaniṣads* to describe *Brahman*. Thus even if it is possible to identify *Brahman* with all the names and forms which are manifested and known so far, we will not be exhausting all the names and forms which *Brahman* may give rise to in future. "The complete revealing of names and forms cannot be accomplished by anything else but *Brahman*."[28] This we shall discuss fully in the next chapter.

As long as *Brahman* is not realised in its true or objective nature the world is seen as the sum total of all the things known empirically and scripturally, and when *Brahman* is realised the world is seen as not different from *Brahman* (*jagadātmā bhāvena paramārtha svarūpeṇa nirupyamāṇam nānā-vastvantara bhūtam bhavati*). However, when seen as *ātman* (*ātmabhāvena*) the non-dual reality does not continue to be known as many, as manyness has no existence, just as the illusory snake has no existence apart from rope. And to see the clayness of pots they need not be destroyed and reduced to clay. One can see or know the oneness of substance of the various pots without literally reducing them to clay. The world of name and form is not destroyed when *Brahman* is directly and immediately realised. As anything that has objective existence cannot be destroyed in knowing its nature objectively or truly, in knowing the true or objective nature of the world (as *Brahman*) it is not destroyed, as otherwise the world of name and form would not have been now as several in the past had realised *Brahman*. The disappearance of the world after *Brahman* realisation is not like the melting of *ghī* or butter, but like the disappearance of an illusory snake. "What is meant by annihilation or disappearance of the world after *Brahman* realisation? Is it like the melting of the solidity of butter when in contact with fire or like the removal of the error of double moon? If it is like the melting of the solidity of butter in coming into contact with fire the scriptures expect something impossible to achieve, for no man can actually annihilate the whole existing world with all its animated bodies and its elementary substances, like earth, air, water, etc. And if it were possible the first realised person would have accomplished it, and there would have been no world now."[29] "Even if hundreds of *Śruti* statements say realise *Brahman* and dissolve the world nothing will happen."[30] The same idea is presented by Śaṅkara in a different way. *Paurāṇikas* or those who accept the authority of *Smṛti* literature accept the idea of final dissolution of the world (*pralaya*) in which all the differences are dissolved into their material cause, and remain unexpressed and undifferentiated, as if in the form of a seed, whereas the supreme dissolution of the world, according to *Advaita*, takes place when direct knowledge of *Brahman* arises or when *Brahman* is realised directly.[31] In that state there is no literal merging or dissolution of the world of differences, as the world of differences is in the first place due to ignorance only; and when ignorance is destroyed differences created by it too disappear, and the world is seen as non-different from *Brahman*. And that is *advaita*.

From the standpoint of ignorance (*ajñāna*) the differences created by name and form are seen as different from *Brahman*, or the world of name and form is seen as having an existence of its own. And with the destruction of *ajñāna* all its creation also comes to an end, and the reality, which is one only without a second, is seen in its true or objective nature. One has to realise that the various views of the world have no objective validity, or there are no different realities corresponding to several concepts of the world which are believed by different people on the basis or authority of popular or religious traditions. All the views of the world are in the final analysis constructions of human mind, and *Brahman* is the objective or ontological basis of all construction or imagination (*kalpanā*). When the objective basis of all construction is directly known or seen in its complete objectivity, which means to stop viewing it in terms of one's inherited beliefs and concepts, the various views automatically drop, or are seen as illusory, or having no objective validity. They are only views believed in by man. Till man attains objective knowledge of *Brahman* the various beliefs about the world, and man's attachement to them for existential and pragmatic reasons will continue to be meaningful and valid. Since man holds several views about the world there is no justification for admitting objective validity to them all. But man on his own gives them up the moment he comes to know the reality directly and objectively. Most of the views about the world which people believed in for a long time are given up in the light of scientific knowledge about the world. But before that they were taken to be valid, and people planned and organised their lives accordingly.

Such views are due to or are based on *avidyā* or *māyā* which is neither completely objective nor completely subjective; it involves both the elements. The views are about the reality that is objectively there, and yet in knowing it man is influenced by his own subjective factors. As the subjective factors vary from person to person, or from tradition to tradition, we find several views or conceptions of the world. In the final analysis all the theories and doctrines of the world are views only, partly objective and partly subjective. They are not completely objective nor completely subjective. In denying objective validity to such views, as historically man had discarded several such views of the world, the world or what is there objectively is not affected. Only man's attitudes and his life patterns are affected. Thus in denying objective reality to the world, Śaṅkara is only denying objective validity to the various views of the world, or the various explanations of it. It is almost axiomatic with *advaita* that what is there objectively cannot be explained away or destroyed by means of knowledge, including scriptural knowledge, and what is not there objectively cannot be brought into existence, even by the scriptures. *Advaita* stands for knowledge, and it is not the object or end of knowledge either to bring into existence what is not objectively there or to remove or destroy what is objectively there. Its object is to reveal the true or objective nature of a thing or reality, and what it can remove or destroy is ignorance or wrong knowledge and its projections which do not have any objectivity. If there is to be an objectively existing reality corresponding to our various views of the world not even hundred scriptures can alter or destroy it. But when we talk of the world we are really talking about our views about the world, which are many, as apart from the views we hold about the world we do not know what the world is in its objectivity, and therefore in denying objective validity to the views or conceptions of the world nothing that is objectively real is denied. Only subjective views born of man's ignorance are denied, and thereby man is freed from the burden of his own ignorance and its consequences.

All that is said above can be significant and valid only from the standpoint of objective or perfect knowledge of the world. Before attaining objective or perfect knowledge of the world one cannot know whether any or all the views about the world are true or false. In our empirical usage the concepts true and real are relative. For instance, water of a river is real when compared to mirage water, or mirage water is unreal when compared to river water. If there is no mirage water there is no significance in asserting that river water is real. Similarly, in relation to an illusory object only we can say some other object is real. If there is nothing that is objectively real we cannot say whether something is real or unreal. Real is meaningful as distinguished from what is unreal. If there is not the possibility of something being unreal the assertion of its reality is not meaningful. Therefore the reality of the world, or the validity of the various views about the world is judged from the standpoint of what is objectively real, and so long as man has not attained objective knowledge of what is there he will have no basis and justification for judging whether the world of his experience and conception is real or illusory. It is only from the standpoint of *Brahman*-knowledge the world is judged as illusory. "This apparent world whose existence is generated by all the means of knowledge cannot be denied unless someone should find out some new truth (*ayam sarva pramāṇa siddha loka vyavahāra anya tattvam anadhigamya sakhyate apāhatum*). A general principle is proved by the absence of a contrary instance."[32] "This phenomenal existence created by differentiation is indeed a fact for those who do not believe in things different from *Brahman* as well as for those who do believe. We do not maintain the existence of things different from *Brahman* in the state when the highest truth is definitely known (*avadhāraṇā*), nor do we deny the validity for the ignorant of actions with their factors and results while the relative world of name and form exists."[33] It is only when both the experiences or knowledges are of the same reality then only it is possible to judge the objective validity of one experience in terms of the other. Now, in the case of what is there or the world there are two knowledges, one empirical and the other scriptural. As pointed out earlier, when we talk of world we mean by it a type of experience, or knowledge, or a view or conception. And the real object of man's empirical experience is *Brahman* though as experience it is different from *brahmānubhava* or *Brahman*-experience, or *Brahman*-knowledge is the knowledge of the world in its complete objectivity. Thus we have two knowledges or experiences of what is there objectively. The empirical experience in which one experiences the world of differences, and *brahmānubhava* in which one realises *Brahman* directly are not different and unrelated having two different objects for themselves. They are of one and the same reality. Though as experiences they differ they have the same reality as their object, that is to say, one and the same reality is known or experienced differently. When there can be more than one experience of one and the same reality the problem arises as to which experience is true and objective. How to decide the validity or truth of an experience? Normally false views or wrong knowledge disappear on their own when the right knowledge is attained. No further effort is required to destroy or negate a false view or knowledge. Though every experience, as pointed out earlier, has an objective reference in most cases subjective factors influence the nature of object experienced. And in knowing the nature of reality objectively or truly (*vasturūpeṇa*), as completely objective knowledge is what is meant by perfect knowledge (*samyak jñāna*), the other knowledge which is also of the same reality, but as influenced by ignorance, is automatically sublated. In other words, when *Brahman* is known in its true or objective nature the empirical experience of differences comes to an end on its own as it is not completely objective in its character. Therefore in denying reality to the world of differences what is really denied is objective validity to an experience, and that is done on the basis of *brahmānubhava* or objectively valid experience of what is there. When an experience or knowledge is completely objective it cannot be sublated, and what can be sublated cannot be true or objective. And when there is no objective reality corresponding to the various conceptions of the world the denial of objective validity to those conceptions does not amount to denial of an objectively existing reality. "Scriptural or empirical outlooks depend entirely on knowledge and ignorance. In fact all schools of thought must admit the existence or non-existence of the phenomenal world according as it is viewed from the relative and absolute standpoints."[34]

This gives rise to a problem which is very much significant in this context. If the empirical experience and *brahmānubhava* refer to the same reality can we say that what is known as world is in reality the same as *Brahman*, or is *Brahman* seen as the world during empirical experience? If *Brahman* is pure consciousness, even when it is experienced as world, it should not lose its essential nature and appear as if it is matter, the opposite of consciousness. To this it may be said that the real nature of the world is consciousness though the manner of its manifestation in the case of the world is different from the manner of its manifestation in man. Even in man consciousness does not manifest itself always in the same manner. It does not manifest itself in the states of swoon and deep sleep as it manifests itself during waking experience, and for that reason man may appear to be devoid of consciousness in the states of swoon and deep sleep. Therefore one may say that the world is consciousness though the manner of its manifestation is not the same as that in man during his waking experience. What objection can we then have in identifying the world with *Brahman* if the world in its true nature is *Brahman*? Otherwise, how to explain that the real object of empirical experience is *Brahman*, but not the world? If this is admitted we have to accept that the true nature of the world is consciousness though we fail to recognise it because of our limited capacity and knowledge. The latter view depends for its validity on the former, that is, if what is known as the world is in reality *Brahman* then world must share the essential nature of *Brahman*, as *Brahman* in all circumstances cannot be devoid of its essential nature. Why cannot we therefore say that the world is *Brahman*, though we cannot say that *Brahman* is world, for that would limit *Brahman* to the world as discussed earlier. Here the crucial point is that the moment the true nature of Brahmā is realised it is no more experienced as the world. In other words, the empirical experience of which the world of differences is the object comes to an end the moment *Brahman* is directly realised. In knowing the true or objective nature of *Brahman* which was seen wrongly as world, the experience of the world comes to an end. When the rope is seen as rope it is no longer seen as snake, and the snake ceases to have any kind of existence. The snake and rope can be identified or related only when the two are objectively real, or can exist at the same time, or if the knowledge of snake survives the knowledge of rope. When the rope is seen as rope there remains no snake so as to be identified or related in any manner with rope. When the reality which was seen or known as the world due to ignorance is known in its complete objectivity the world experience comes to an end. Then *Brahman* alone remains. It is not therefore possible or meaningful to relate an unreal or illusory reality with what is real. The world experience can at the most remain in memory as it belongs to a past experience. As there are no two realities, the world and *Brahman*, but only two experiences, one true and objective and the other illusory and wrong, there is no justification in saying that the world is the same as *Brahman*. At the most one can say that what was experienced as world during the state of ignorance is not really world with all that it means, but something else or *Brahman*. Or what had been experienced as world of differences is really *Brahman* without any differences, and in so realising the world of empirical experience will not be there to be related with *Brahman*.

Furthermore, to identify the world with *Brahman* is semantically meaningless. The concept of world has its own meaning, and the concept of *Brahman* has an altogether different meaning, and therefore both cannot be identified. If they can be identified than anything can be identified with any other thing, as if all the words can mean all the things. The world as world or what it means to us cannot be the same as *Brahman* with its meaning as the ultimate source of the world. No one with any sense of linguistic propriety can attempt to identify the world with *Brahman* as both the words or concepts have their own meanings which are different.

Thus if the world is unreal or illusory there is no point in trying to know whether it is physical or spiritual or seemingly spiritual. When we say 'this is world' or 'this is *Brahman*' the reality that is denoted by 'this' and whose true or objective nature is not yet known is determined or interpreted as world or *Brahman*, and therefore what is objectively true of 'this' cannot be true of the latter, world and *Brahman*, as both can be wrong interpretations of 'this'. A wrong perception or experience does not have any objective validity; its validity is dependent upon its being perceived or experienced in a particular way. Therefore we cannot identify the real nature of what is denoted by 'this' with any of its interpretations. At the most we can say that the world which is a wrong experience or view of reality points to reality as its objective basis or substratum, and therefore what is objectively true of reality cannot be true of its wrong experience. And if a wrong experience or knowledge of the reality can share the nature of reality it cannot then be wrong knowledge or experience. The world is a wrong knowledge or experience of *Brahman* as in it *Brahman* is not known as it is but as something else. If the world and *Brahman* share the same nature then the knowledge of the world cannot be regarded as wrong knowledge or ignorance.

Māyā

The world, according to Śaṅkara, is a matter of experience or a view or a conception, and there can be several views or conceptions of the world. As all of us do not have the same view or conception of the world, or entertain the same view of it, for what is valid and meaningful to one person or community of persons at one time and place is not valid and meaningful to another person or community of persons at another time and place, no view or conception of the world is objectively valid. Thus the world we talk about is not an objectively existing reality. But all the views and conceptions are possible because there is some objectively existing reality behind them, or as their basis. When that reality is known directly and immediately in its true or objective nature the various views of it are found to be wrong, and cease to be objectively valid. As views they do not have any reality corresponding to them so that when the views are destroyed or come to an end on their own when perfect knowledge of reality arises nothing that is objectively real is destroyed. When all the views superimposed on the reality are negated or denied, or ignorance, the basic reason for their existence, is destroyed, reality reveals itself in its true or objective nature. To know it, on the other hand, as the world or as God or *Īśvara* is to superimpose on it our conceptions of it, and identify it with what we think of it which is due to *māyā* or *māyā* itself. In all this nothing that is objectively real is affected or what is not objectively real is created. But man sees or knows the reality in its true or objective nature, and is freed from *māyā* or *ajñāna*, the source of all mental construction or imagination, or the source of all the views and conceptions of the reality which present the reality as what it is not.

References

1. *Ṛ̣VSaṁ*, 10.55.5.
2. *Ibid.*, 1.164.4.
3. *Ibid.*, 10.90 (*puruṣa sūkta*)
4. *Ibid.*, 10.90.

5. *BṛUp*, 2.4.10; 4.5.11.
6. *Ibid.*, 1.4.5.
7. *TaitUpBh*, 2.8.5.
8. *BṛUpBh*, 2.4.1. introduction.
9. *Ibid.*, 2.4.1.
10. *MāKāBh*, 4.24.
11. *BṛUpBh*, 5.1.1.
12. *Ibid.*, 3.3.1 introduction.
13. *SūBh*, 2.2.28.
14. *BṛUpBh*, 1.4.10.
15. *PrUpBh*, 6.2.
16. *BṛUpBh*, 3.5.1.
17. *Ibid.*, 3.5.1.
18. *SūBh*, 2.1.14.
19. *AitUpBh*, 2.1.1 introduction.
20. *BṛUpBh*, 2.1.20.
21. *Ibid.*, 1.4.6.
22. *SūBh*, 1.4.14; ***see also*** *AitUpBh*, 2.1.1 introduction.
23. *AitUpBh*, introduction to chapter 1; ***see also*** *TaitUpBh*, 2.3.1.
24. *BṛUpBh*, 4.5.11.
25. *Ibid.*, 2.4.10.
26. *AitUpBh*, 1.1.2.
27. *SūBh*, 2.3.29.; 2.3.29; *MāKāBh*, 4.98.
28. *Ibid.*, 1.3.41.
29. *SūBh*, 3.2.11.
30. *Ibid.*, 3.2.11.
31. *BṛUpBh*, 2.4.12.
32. *SūBh*, 2.2.31.
33. *BṛUpBh*, 3.5.1.
34. *Ibid.*, 3.5.1.

5

Advaita

THE *Upaniṣads* are mostly concerned with understanding the nature of *Brahman* or *ātman*, the reality of the world and its origin, and the reality or self of man, and its destiny or its relation to *Brahman*. All the examples given and the evidence and arguments adduced in the *Upaniṣads* to explain their basic teaching presuppose the reality of the world, and *Brahman* or *ātman*, the essence and unity of the world. In most of the statements which are clear, unambiguous and definite in their meaning, the *Upaniṣads* assert *Brahman* or *ātman* as the essence and unity of all that is. It is the truth of truth (empirical truth) or the ultimate ground and explanation of all that is empirically experienced. The fundamental teaching of the *Upaniṣads* as expressed in such statements like 'I am *Brahman*', 'you are That', 'all is *Brahman*' is intelligible only when the reality of all, including the individual self, is accepted, as otherwise there is no point in asserting the oneness of all with *Brahman* or *Brahman* as the inner unity of all that is. If *Brahman* is the only reality, and there is no reality besides it the teaching of the *Upaniṣads* would have no significance, and even basis and justification. Unless the reality of what is empirically known and experienced by all is accepted it would not be meaningful to assert *Brahman* as its ultimate ground and explanation. And the fact that the teaching of the *Upaniṣads* is intended for someone, and is about *Brahman* or *ātman* shows that duality is admitted by the *Upaniṣads*.

This would have represented the final teaching of the *Upaniṣads*, and enjoyed ultimate authority had they not denied validity to all such statements involving duality. If the Upaniṣadic statements like "there is no manyness or multiplicity anywhere (*neha nānāsti kiñcana*)",[1] "One who sees differences or multiplicity does not know the truth",[2] which contradict or negate much of its own teaching involving difference or duality, are to be given greater or basic importance and final validity it would be difficult or rather impossible to reconcile or harmonise both the types of statements. When the *Upaniṣads* assert both duality and non-duality, but deny validity to the statements expressing duality or difference, the statements denying duality enjoy final authority, and are to be taken as expressing the basic teaching of the *Upaniṣads*. What was asserted by the *Upaniṣads* in certain contexts was later denied by them, and therefore the statements denying or negating duality are more authoritative and basic than the statements denied. Why then they have admitted in the first place duality or difference if the chief object of the *Upaniṣads* is to assert non-duality, and deny reality to duality? What is the purpose or intention of the *Upaniṣads* in admitting duality or difference, which is evident to all and does not therefore require any instruction, or the authority of the *Upaniṣads*, if it is to be denied ultimately is a problem with which Śaṅkara is mainly concerned while interpreting the philosophy of the *Upaniṣads*. If both the types of statements are to be accepted as equally authoritative and valid, as both of them are made by *Śruti*, one has to reconcile them, and establish harmony between them without denying validity to either of them. Do they have the same kind of validity or are they both equally true? This problem was felt not only by Śaṅkara but by all the *vedāntins*, and each attempted to reconcile both types of statements in his own characteristic way. For instance, Rāmānuja tried to reconcile both the types of statements without denying validity to either of them though, according to him, some statements are more significant than others. To him both are equally meaningful, and are true finally. How are we to judge the adequacy or soundness of any method of reconciliation between duality and non-duality? We are not here concerned with the different methods of reconciliation but with the method adopted by Śaṅkara. And the validity of a method of reconciliation does not depend on whether somehow the duality and non-duality can be reconciled or not, but on the logical soundness and adequacy of the method itself. Both duality and non-duality or difference and non-difference are admitted in the *Upaniṣads*. However, duality is more meaningful and intelligible to man's rational understanding, and is supported by all the means of valid knowledge, whereas non-duality has no proof, and cannot be supported either by human reason or by the various means of knowledge. Duality does not require any proof, and no one doubts the reality of difference or duality as it is experienced by all, and therefore *Śruti* is not required to establish the reality of duality or difference. Therefore in asserting duality *Śruti* is not revealing anything new or what is not known otherwise. Non-duality, which is not evident to man, and is not intelligible to his rational understanding is to be known in the light of *Śruti*, or the real purpose of *Śruti* is to reveal non-duality as *Śruti* is not authoritative in matters which can be known through other means of knowledge, like sense perception and inference. Inferential reasoning which is based on sens-perception is more nearer to man's understanding than *Śruti* which when talks of non-duality goes against reason, and comes into conflict with what is known through various means of valid knowledge. The authority of *Śruti* lies in its capacity to reveal the truth which cannot be known otherwise. Whether the two truths which man comes to know, one through his own experience and knowledge and the other through *Śruti*, are equally valid and true or not can be decided in one or two ways. If the object of knowledge in the case of both empirical knowledge and scriptural knowledge is one and the same then reconciliation between them would be impossible as there can be no two different knowledges, especially when they contradict each other, of the same objectively existent reality. Either of them must be true and the other false. Or we have to assume that the reality appears in one way to man's ordinary or empirical knowledge and quite differently to the seers of the *Upaniṣads*. But this position cannot be justified logically as then we have to admit that the reality is devoid of essence or nature of its own. If *Śruti*, on the other hand, talks of a reality which is other than and different from the reality which is known to man empirically then there can be no contradiction between what is revealed by *Śruti* and what is known to man, because what is revealed by *Śruti* is a reality different from what is known to man. In that case there is no problem of reconciliation between the two. But *Śruti* nowhere says that the reality it talks about is otherwise unknown to man. The object of *Śruti* knowledge is the same as the object of man's empirical knowledge and experience. Even when it talks of duality and non-duality it is not talking about two different realities but of two different knowledges or experiences of one and the same reality. What it denies is not the reality of what is experienced by man unaided by *Śruti*, but the truth or validity of his empirical experience. In other words, it denies truth to dualistic experience or the experience of differences. When *Śruti* talks of duality and non-duality, or asserts differences and denies them it is all the while referring to the same reality. It is not referring to two different realities, one corresponding to the empirical knowledge of man, and the other to the knowledge of which it (*Śruti*) is the source. In other words, when it talks of two forms of *Brahman* it is not asserting two realities but two kinds of knowledge of *Brahman*, and both the knowledges cannot be equally true of *Brahman*. And when the true or objective (*vastu*) knowledge of *Brahman* arises the other knowledge is known to be false, and ceases to be true on its own. The two knowledges are: The empirical knowledge of differences got through the various means of knowledge, tradition and rational understanding of man, and the other which is based on or inspired by *Śruti*. The former knowledge is not perfect or objectively true as in it the human imagination or mental construction (*kalpanā*) plays a significant role, or is mixed up with subjective factors. Though its object is *Brahman* in the absence of an objective knowledge of *Brahman* man's imagination or subjectivity plays an active role in knowing it. The subjective factors differ from person to person, or from one system of metaphysics to other systems of metaphysics, or from one religious tradition to other religious traditions. Empirical knowledge or knowledge based on ignorance does not refer to any one knowledge or understanding of reality, but refers to any knowledge in which the knower is active or his mind plays an active and significant role. Because of the play of human mind and its constructions the reality is not known in its complete objectivity or in its true nature to man's empirical knowledge, whereas the other knowledge (*pāramārthika*) reveals *Brahman* in its complete objectivity or as unmixed by human imagination or mental construction. *Pāramārthika* means the supreme or ultimate meaning, which is universal, whereas in ordinary meaning of things subjective factors play a role, and therefore cannot be completely objective, and true to all.

Validity of Knowledge

When there are two kinds of knowledge of the same reality, one empirical (*laukika*) and the other *pāramārthika*, how to decide the truth or validity of one over the other? Since both the kinds of knowledge are not possible at the same time in the same person we cannot say that both are equally true. Logically also it is not possible for anyone to experience the same reality in two or more different ways at the same time. If it is to be the case one experience or knowledge cannot negate the other or invalidate the other. Every knowledge or experience is valid *per se*. The truth or falsity of an experience can be judged only in the light of another experience. So long as the scientific knowledge of the world was not available to man his ordinary knowledge was not judged wrong. Only in the light of scientific knowledge man is able to know and judge the validity of his ordinary knowledge. A knowledge or an experience is accepted by man as true as long as there is no other knowledge or experience which comes into conflict with it, and proves it to be wrong. But the latter can also be found out to be untrue in the light of another knowledge. This goes on till man attains a knowledge which cannot be sublated or negated. When the true knowledge arises the false knowledge automatically ceases to be valid or is corrected as no knowledge lacks some objective element. It is only in relation to scriptural knowledge man comes to doubt the validity of his empirical knowledge, that is to say, only in comparison to *Śruti* knowledge we can know that our ordinary or empirical knowledge of reality is not objectively true or valid. *Śruti* knowledge can also be sublated in terms of or on the basis of a higher knowledge. Then *Śruti* also ceases to be valid, or its authority comes to an end. *Pāramārthika* knowledge refers to that knowledge which is ultimate in the sense that it cannot be further sublated or negated. It is therefore supreme or ultimate.

Śruti knowledge is meant to correct the ordinary knowledge, or remove or cure the error in ordinary knowledge, but is not supposed to give us knowledge of a reality which is not known to man through his empirical experience. Both are knowledges, and true or objective knowledge removes or destroys wrong knowledge in the sense that it helps man to see the reality truly or objectively. *Śruti* need not do anything more to remove the wrong knowledge than revealing the true or objective nature of reality. Thus the chief purpose of *Śruti* is to correct an error or remove ignorance but not to reveal the reality as if for the first time, as the reality is known to man through his empirical experience though wrongly. It is only when both the knowledges are somehow equally true the problem of their reconciliation arises.

Reconciliation of Two Standpoints

Several *vedāntins* have attempted to reconcile and integrate both without denying validity or truth to either in terms of a conception of reality which can explain both difference and non-difference, or change and changelessness. If *Brahman* is somehow the source of both the kinds of knowledge then *Brahman*'s nature must be such as to give rise to both the types of knowledge. Some of the *vedāntins* favour the doctrine of unity or oneness in difference, according to which, both unity and differences are equally true and meaningful, and refer to the same reality. Oneness and difference are both true, as *Brahman* is both or both are the states or forms of *Brahman*, and are intrinsic to the nature of *Brahman*. Most of the Upaniṣadic statements speak of *Brahman* as the essence and unity of all that is (*ekatva*). Unity is the unity of differences, for when there are no differences there will be no unity either. Unity is the unity of different things. One cannot talk meaningfully of unity without admitting differences. However, unity is meaningful and valid only if the differences do not pertain to substance. A horse and cow cannot have unity, whereas a pot and another pot made of clay can find their unity in clay. When the same reality has become many it is the common substance of all, and therefore in one sense, or from one point of view it is one, and in another sense, or from another point of view it is many. Thus oneness and manyness can both be true of the same reality. According to this view, ignorance means either not seeing the unity but only differences, or not recognising the differences but only unity. Thus attempts are made to reconcile both the kinds of *Śruti* statements in terms of the nature of *Brahman*, that is, by conceiving the nature of *Brahman* in such a way that it can be the reconciliation of both oneness and difference.

The other way of looking at the problem is to explain the two knowledges or the conflict between them not in terms of *Brahman*'s nature but in terms of man's understanding. If we think that corresponding to man's understanding and conceptual thinking there is a reality then that reality will have no coherence and identity as there can be several, and at time, mutually contradictory conceptions of reality. If one system of metaphysics is true and objectively valid then the other systems of metaphysics cannot be true and objectively valid. The various systems of metaphysics, dualistic, nihilistic, etc., cannot be reconciled and integrated ontologically or in terms of reality. The different systems of metaphysics like that of the *Upaniṣads*, Buddhist, Jaina, *Sāṁkhya*, *Vaiśeṣika*, Cārvāka, etc., cannot be reconciled ontologically, unless we are prepared to admit that reality can become several things to several people, or the reality has no identifiable essence of its own. This will lead to scepticism. All the conflicting conceptions of reality, which cannot be true universally, as they are not objectively valid point to the active play of human mind in their formation. Therefore their explanation is not intelligible in terms of the nature of reality, but in terms of human understanding.

This problem assumes a different significance when we accept the authority of *Śruti* as *Śruti* also propounds several conceptions of *Brahman*. *Śruti* presents several conceptions of reality, and all cannot be equally true. They may be due to differences in the levels of human understanding in apprehending the subtle nature of *Brahman*, or are intended by *Śruti* for those with varying levels of understanding and spiritual maturity in grasping the subtle nature of *Brahman*. Since *Śruti* is intended to teach man about the nature of *Brahman* it takes into consideration the levels of understanding and spiritual growth of man before it teaches. Much of the Upaniṣadic teaching has only instructional value, or is intended to teach man the final truth gradually or by stages. In this connection we can refer to the story of Indra and Virocana mentioned in the *Chāndogya Upaniṣad*, and the several dialogues between Yājñavalkya and others as mentioned in the *Bṛhadāraṇyaka Upaniṣad*. We cannot therefore say that every conception of *Brahman* as found in the *Upaniṣads* is equally true and valid. *Śruti* talks in terms of duality or difference not because it accepts duality as ultimately true but with its help to teach *advaita* which it accepts as final truth. *Advaita* is to be taught with the help of the categories of human understanding, which are based on man's empirical experience, and are valid within the framework of man's empirical experience and understanding, as otherwise no instruction about *advaita* is possible. These are the categories which are intelligible to man's empirical understanding, and without employing them *advaita* cannot be communicated. The various categories of human understanding like individual and universal, cause and effect, one and many, unity and difference which are meaningful and valid within the realm of man's empirical experience and understanding, however, lose their intelligibility and validity in relation to *Brahman* which is non-empirical and non-dual. If the real intention of the *Upaniṣads* is to teach *advaita*, and if that is their ultimate and basic position, all their teaching involving duality is to be taken metaphorically or only as a means (*upāya*) to teach *advaita* which when realised directly is the negation of all their dualistic teaching. *Advaita* cannot be taught otherwise. It can somehow be shown, and the ultimate object of all the *Upaniṣads* is to make one realise directly for oneself the truth of *advaita* without saying anything about *advaita* directly which is not possible.

Śruti statements are not to be taken literally as they then lead to contradiction. They are not intended to describe *Brahman* in a straightforward way, as we can describe an object of empirical experience, but to direct our attention to the truth of *advaita*. And when *advaita* is realised directly with the help of *Śruti* or in its light, *Śruti* loses its authority and validity, and this would not be possible if the *Śruti* statements are literally true. This is the position of *Śruti* itself. All instruction, including that of *Śruti*, is dualistic or involves duality, but the real purpose of *Śruti* is not to teach duality which is evident to all. When non-duality is realised directly the duality, and the instruction based on duality cease to be valid. What then is the role of duality in revealing non-duality? Can we say that non-duality reveals itself in and through duality, or somehow duality can reveal non-duality before it is proved to be unreal or illusory? Śaṅkara admits means or instructional value to duality, and the dualistic teaching of *Śruti*. It is a means to realise *advaita*, which ultimately means the negation of duality, as otherwise it is not possible to communicate the truth of *advaita*. The ultimate reality or *Brahman*, as pure consciousness, is self-evident and self-revealed by its very nature, and therefore no instruction is required to know its existence and nature. All instruction is meant to remove wrong knowledge about *Brahman*, and *Brahman* is revealed in and through the empirical experience of duality or differences. In the rope-snake example whether one sees rope as snake or as something else one is really in cognitive contact with rope only. The real object of our empirical experience is *Brahman* only but not a different reality though it is experienced in the form of world. This seeing of *Brahman* as what it is not or as world of differences is to be corrected so that *Brahman* is revealed in its true or objective nature. Since man's empirical knowledge and understanding are conditioned by duality and the categories it gives rise to man is to be taught the true nature of *Brahman* in terms of the categories which shape or form his empirical understanding, and are intelligible to him. Otherwise, any instruction or talk about non-duality will be utterly unintelligible to man's understanding. Man's understanding till *Brahman* is directly realised is conditioned by the categories of empirical experience, and they are to be resorted to if the error of duality is to be corrected as we have no other means to achieve that. Śaṅkara explains this with the help of a significant example. If one who is riding a horse is to correct its path or change its direction he can do so only with the help of the horse.[3] Some other means is not used for that purpose. It is like pointing out the errors in the use of language with the help of language itself, or like using a thorn to remove another thorn stuck into one's body. And when once the thorn is removed with the help of another thorn both are discarded. *Śruti* can communicate or teach the truth with the help of concepts and categories involving duality but it is not the intention of *Śruti* to teach us duality, which requires no teaching, but to overcome duality. Scriptural knowledge, which is also a mode of dualistic knowledge, is intended to correct the basic error of duality on which is based the empirical experience of differences, and when once it is achieved the scriptural knowledge along with empirical knowledge of duality gets itself dissolved on its own, and the real nature of *Brahman* which is revealed all the while is revealed as it were for the first time. We shall discuss these in the next chapter on *advaita* and language to show how language creates differences and distinctions while expressing the truth of *advaita*. And how to use language meaningfully to express *advaita*, or what would be the function of language in communicating the truth of *advaita*?

The method of reconciling *Śruti* statements asserting and denying duality, according to Śaṅkara, consists in superimposing duality or the categories and concepts involving duality on *Brahman*, which is non-dual, purely for the practical purpose of teaching *Brahman* or non-duality, and then in negating them all. Differences are tentatively admitted as without them nothing can be said about *Brahman*, and *Brahman*-knowledge cannot be communicated. But when the purpose is accomplished, that is, when a person in the course of his *sādhanā* comes to realise *advaita* directly *Śruti* denies reality to all kinds of duality which in the first place it has superimposed on *Brahman*. Thus there will be no problem of reconciling both the kinds of *Śruti* statements if we recognise the methodological value and validity of the dualistic statements of *Śruti*, or their means or instructional value.

But how can one have the conception of duality or difference if in reality there is no duality? Even to imagine duality which is superimposed on non-dual *Brahman* there must be some basis in reality, as imagination, according to Śaṅkara, is not completely unrelated to what man experiences. The imagination may be unreal but the images are not unreal as they are derived from experience. Only the way they are related and organised may not be true to objective experience. This we shall discuss later. *Advaita* by its very definition lacks proof, and is beyond all means of knowledge. It is equally beyond all description. Proof, meaning and description are intelligible only in the realm of dualistic experience as all of them are possible in the realm of duality. They involve duality. They are possible when the basic distinction of subject and object is accepted as without such a distinction no proof is possible and meaningful. All the means of knowledge and all types of proof and description in language involve duality, and are possible only in the realm of duality. The various categories of understanding, like unity and difference, cause and effect, without which nothing can be said about *Brahman* are intelligible within the realm of empirical experience of differences, and non-dual experience is the negation or end of empirical experience. Therefore the various categories of understanding, the various means of knowledge and language without which there can be no empirical experience and its description and communication are meaningless in relation to *advaita* as they are not simply possible when the empirical experience comes to an end in realising *advaita*. And we cannot say anything about *advaita* while remaining within the realm of empirical experience without using the empirical categories. Any attempt therefore to explain or elucidate or simply talk of *advaita* involves the use of empirical categories of understanding and language which are based on the empirical experience of differences and distinctions, and are meant to describe and communicate such experience. This situation can be avoided to an extent if we realise that all we can say about *advaita* can only be true metaphorically but not literally. Metaphors and paradoxes have a communicative value, and they are more effective in communicating the truth which is not given to man's empirical knowledge and understanding. The language in relation to *advaita* is not therefore descriptive but indicative or pointive. It serves its purpose by directing our attention to the truth of *advaita*. The *Upaniṣads*, and the various commentaries on them are meant to point to the truth and meaningfulness of *advaita* without making it the object of their direct description. One has to be spiritually sensitive and pure to see through the scriptures and realise the truth for oneself which is intended by them. On the other hand, when they are taken to be literally true one ends up in distorting the intended meaning of the scriptures, and creates certain logical problems which are difficult to surmount. What we therefore intend to do in the following is to point to the possibility and meaningfulness of *advaita*, but not to prove it.

Advaita is not an empirical truth, and therefore no proposition, including those of the scriptures, can hold and express it. *Advaita* is unthinkable (*acintya*), as thinking involves empirical categories and concepts which are formed on the basis of dualistic experience, and are intelligible within the realm of dualistic experience. Thinking involves an object and a subject, and these are possible within the realm of empirical experience. When there is no knowledge or understanding in the ordinary sense description also is not possible. What is not knowable and thinkable as an object cannot also be described and communicated in language. However, when *advaita*, which transcends all the empirical distinctions and relations, is realised directly it will have its profound significance to man. The way of knowing it or rather its realisation is not the ordinary or empirical way of knowing involving subject-object distinction, but by being it. Such realisation, which is direct and immediate, cannot be conceptualised and communicated in the ordinary ways. Paradoxically its real communication is through silence, silence born of real enlightenment or realisation, and is more profound than verbal communication.

Meaning of Advaita (1)

We can understand the meaning of *advaita* in three distinct ways, or the concept of *advaita* can be interpreted in three different ways. And all of them will help us in comprehending the meaning and validity of *advaita*. The *Upaniṣads* represent all the three meanings of *advaita* which are fully developed by Śaṅkara in his writings. The object of this chapter is to elucidate the concept of *advaita* or the three ways of understanding its meaning with a view to showing the profundity of it, and also to an extent its intelligibility to man's rational understanding. All the three meanings or conceptions of *advaita* supplement each other, enrich each other and help us in grasping the concept more clearly and comprehensively.

The *Upaniṣads* assert in clear terms that *Brahman* is the reality of all that is, including man, and it is one only without a second (*advitīyam*). It is all or the inner reality of all that is, and the knowledge involving duality or difference is *avidyā* or *ajñāna* or wrong knowledge, and the one who sees duality or difference does not know the truth.

As discussed fully in the second chapter, *Brahman* is not a speculative idea or an abstract metaphysical entity meant to explain the world. It is that which is known directly and immediately by being it. That is to say, it is not an object of knowledge or of thought. There are several conceptions of *Brahman* in the *Upaniṣads* in which it is identified with *prāṇa*, with the sun, with matter, etc., but all of them are ultimately discarded by the *Upaniṣads* as they are mostly speculative in character. They do not give us direct and immediate knowledge of *Brahman* which alone can fulfil man's existence by dispelling ignorance or wrong knowledge. The Upaniṣadic enquiry into the nature of *Brahman* presupposes the existence of the world, and the person who undertakes such an enquiry. *Brahman* is conceived as that reality by knowing or in knowing which all that is is known. It is the ultimate explanation of all that is without leaving anything unexplained. It is the truth of truth, or the truth of what is empirically known and experienced. It is the reality which comprehends everything, and what comprehends all by being present within all and sustaining all is the essence of all. It is their nature (*svabhāva*) or reality (*svarūpa*) or simply *ātman* of all. It is that because of which not only things exist but that by which they are what they are. It is their *ātman* or essence or the real or true nature of all that exists. *Ātman* is used in the sense of essence, and *Brahman* is that essence. And therefore to know *Brahman* is to know the essence or *ātman*, or the true nature of all. In the process of knowing the essence or *ātman* of all that is one's understanding or knowledge of one's own reality or essence is of great help and significance. An enquiry into the nature of *Brahman* can start either with the reality of man or with the reality of the world, but man's knowledge of the essence of a thing or phenomenon other than his own will be indirect or inferential. Man cannot know the essence of fire or water or earth or any other phenomenon as directly and immediately as he can of his own essence or self. He can know the nature of his own essence or inner reality directly without any mediation, and such knowledge is clear and definite. It is free from doubt and error. And since the same reality is present within all as their essence human reality or the reality of oneself is the best point to start with in knowing the reality of *Brahman*. Man can know his own reality directly and immediately as he is a self-conscious being. Thus though ontologically *Brahman* is the same as *ātman*, and refers to the all encompassing inner reality or essence of all that is, in order of knowledge of *Brahman* man's knowledge of himself as *ātman* is of utmost significance to man as it is the direct and immediate revelation of *Brahman* to him. Though in the order of existence or ontologically *ātman* is *Brahman* or *Brahman* is *ātman* in the order of knowledge *ātman*, as the essence or self of man, is the direct source of *Brahman* knowledge. Therefore the enquiry undertaken into the nature of self in the *Upaniṣads* is different in its purpose and significance from the enquiry into the nature of self undertaken in other systems of philosophy. The object of the Upaniṣadic enquiry into the nature of self is not just to know the reality of man but to know the nature of *Brahman*. On the other hand, if the object of the Upaniṣadic enquiry into the nature of self is to know man and his reality it cannot lead to or culminate in the realisation of *Brahman*, the reality of all. "Otherwise the individual self as circumscribed by one's own body will alone be perceived as it is by the Sāṁkhya and others; and in that case the specific statement 'it is non-dual' made by the *Upaniṣads* will have no distinctness, for then there will be no difference from the philosophy of Sāṁkhya and others."[4] The Upaniṣadic intention is clearly stated in the *Chāndogya Upaniṣad* in which the self of man is identified with *Brahman* by stating clearly that the indwelling essence of all or *ātman* is also the self (*ātman*) of man. "That which is (this) subtle essence (of all) is *ātman*, that is all, that is truth; that is *ātman* and thou art That O Śvetaketu." (*sā yā eṣa animā etat ātmā idam sarvam tat satyam sa ātmā tat tvam asi śvetaketo*).[5] In the *Māṇḍukya Upaniṣad* after identifying *Brahman* with *ātman*, and *ātman* with the self of man, the three different states of man's experience, waking, dream and deep sleep, are identified with the cosmic states of *Brahman*.[6]

The essence of man or his self (*ātman*) is identified with consciousness because it is the only reality in man which does not change along with the changes in his body and mind. At times things may change even in their essence, but consciousness, the *ātman* of man does not change (*svarūpa vyabhicāriṣu padārtheṣu caitanya avyabhicārāt*).[7] It comprehends all that a man knows and experiences, and there can be no doubt or error about its existence or nature. "Mistakes may be made concerning what lies outside our minds. But the conscious subject never has any doubt whether it is itself or only like itself or similar to itself."[8] If consciousness is *ātman* it is the reality or essence of all or the *ātman* of all. Everything else in man is conditioned or determined by several factors while consciousness is absolute or unconditioned. It is invariably present in all knowledge and experience, and while the latter go on changing depending upon the objects known or experienced consciousness remains unchanged. The objects of knowledge change accounting for the richness and variety in knowledge, but awareness as such does not change along with the change in the objects of knowledge. Though consciousness by its very nature is self-revealed, its revelation at the level of empirical or dualistic experience is dependent upon the experience of objects. During the waking and dream states consciousness reveals itself while revealing objects. At this level consciousness means consciousness of something as it reveals itself while revealing objects of knowledge. All knowledge at the empirical level is knowledge of some knowable (*sannimittam*), and in the absencc of the latter the former cannot also be maintained.

Nature of Consciousness

At the empirical level consciousness is identified by several philosophers either with the knower or with the knowledge, and as these are not possible without a knowable they cannot think of pure consciousness or consciousness as such (*cinmātra*) as it reveals always itself in and through the acts of knowing or experiencing or thinking something. And independently of these acts it is not intelligible to talk of consciousness. Accordingly they try to define consciousness or self as that which knows, experiences, reflects, thinks, etc., and all these are attributed to self. Even Śaṅkara admits that at the level of dualistic or empirical experience consciousness or *ātman* is known indirectly or inferentially as that which knows, thinks, etc. Can we then say that knowing, thinking, etc., in and through which consciousness reveals itself at the level of dualistic or empirical experience constitutes the nature of consciousness? Is consciousness in itself or as free from those functions a myth as it is highly unintelligible? Now those who think about consciousness admit the duality of subject and object, and identify consciousness with the subject of knowledge. The subject of knowledge is not only distinct from the object of knowledge but there is also opposition between them, as what is an object of knowledge cannot be the subject of knowledge, and *vice-versa*. If the subject is not different from the object of knowledge no knowledge is possible. If the objects perceived belong to subject it cannot know them. If, for instance, pain belongs to subject of experience it cannot experience pain, and pain will not be contingent. And if pain belongs to the subject it cannot experience pleasure, and if consciousness is green or black or finite or mortal it cannot be aware of other colours and qualities. Now, according to Śaṅkara, the knower is also an object of knowledge. Ordinarily, we think that in self-consciousness the self or consciousness becomes an object to itself or knows itself. But on a closer examination we come to know that in the act of self-consciousness, in which we think the knowing self becomes an object to itself, the object is not self or consciousness but an idea or image of self which is given as an object to consciousness. In every act of self-knowledge one comes to know oneself as this or that, and without an idea or image of oneself being the object of consciousness there can be no self-knowledge or self-consciousness. Moreover, we not only know objects but we are also aware of the fact that we know something. We not only think of something but we are also conscious of the fact of thinking. Thus not only the knowable is an object of consciousness but the fact of knowing also. Just as the objects, which are known through various senses and mind, are given to consciousness as objects of knowledge the functions of the senses and the mind are also given to consciousness as objects. Seeing is not seen by the eyes, and thinking is not an object of mind, as the object of thought is, but seeing and thinking are objects to consciousness, as one knows one is seeing or knowing or thinking, etc. Knowledge and ignorance, though they are different, are nevertheless cognitive functions, and both are objects to consciousness, for hey can be described and communicated. One is aware of one's knowledge and ignorance as one is aware of one's body and other objects. This shows that the knower is also an object to consciousness, and therefore it cannot be identified with consciousness. "Difference of knowledge from *ātman* is perceived, and the enlightened people communicate the knowledge of self to others and others grasp it. Accordingly knowledge and ignorance are to be ranked with name and form (which are known). They are not the attributes of *ātman*."[9] The fact that one knows that one is ignorant, or can describe and communicate his knowledge to others shows that ignorance and knowledge are also objects of awareness. Furthermore, the notion of subject or self or soul is not intelligible without body and mind, as the notion of self involves the functions of one's body and the characteristics of one's mind, and all these are objects to consciousness. "The aggregate of the body and mind, etc. is substantially indistinguishable from sound, and it too is equally a knowable. It cannot therefore be the real knower."[10]

While certain things are objects of sense-perception some are objects of mind. The colour, shape, sound, etc., are perceived by the senses, and pain, pleasure, thinking, reflection, etc., are objects of mind, whereas consciousness is not an object at all either to senses or to mind. At the empirical level it is to be inferred as that to which all are given as objects, or because of which objects are known. The self or *jīva* which is the knower, thinker, etc., is an object of knowledge, as there is knowledge of it which can be communicated to others, while consciousness is not an object of knowledge by its very nature. Therefore the ordinary notion of self of which there can be some knowledge belongs to the object realm, and consciousness cannot be an object either to itself or to some other consciousness. What we know as subject or self which is intelligible in relation to objects of knowledge, and is also known in relation to them is equally an object to consciousness, and therefore consciousness cannot be understood and defined in terms of a subject or knower.

Is consciousness conscious of itself? This problem would arise if we can think of consciousness as not being consciousness at times, or lapsing itself into states of unconsciousness. As one may not be aware of himself while he is lost in the knowledge of objects, there is sense in saying that one occasionally becomes conscious of himself. Consciousness of oneself (as subject) and consciousness of objects are not simultaneous, just as no two cognitions are simultaneous. When one is conscious of something other than oneself, one is not conscious of himself, and when one is conscious of himself in the act of self-reflection one is not conscious of objects. That means, self-consciousness alternates with object-consciousness. Thus being conscious of oneself is meaningful as he is not always conscious of himself, but consciousness cannot be unconsciousness at any time, and if it becomes really unconsciousness then that fact cannot be known, and if it is known it shows the presence of consciousness. Therefore there is no point in stating that consciousness is conscious of itself, and even if it is asserted it is superfluous.

Consciousness is presupposed in the very act of self-consciousness, and the consciousness which is presupposed in all that is known or experienced cannot be an object of consciousness, and if it were to become an object of consciousness we would have to deny inwardness to man, and admit another consciousness to which it can become an object. Is it meaningful to think that fire, in the absence of fuel to burn, burns itself, or in the absence of objects to illumine light illumines itself? Fire burning itself or light illumining itself are meaningless expressions as burning is fire and illumination is light. And even when it is asserted it states nothing. Similarly consciousness is not required to be conscious of itself as it is consciousness. Even if we assert that consciousness is conscious of itself we will not be saying anything significant. However, these problems arise as we tend to identify consciousness with subject or self or soul. Only if consciousness is the same as self or subject the problem of its being aware of itself in addition to its being aware of objects arises as the self or subject is conceived as having certain qualities in addition to consciousness, or when self is conceived as a spiritual substance having consciousness as its essential attribute. Thus there is a difference between self being conscious and self being consciousness. If the self is a conscious being possessing certain other qualities it can be aware of its own qualities, but if self is consciousness there is no problem of its being aware of itself. Unless we admit that the self has some content other than being simple awareness or consciousness there is no meaning in saying that consciousness is aware of itself, and anything that is regarded as the content of self will be an object to consciousness, and cannot therefore belong to consciousness, and affect it.

It is the major contention of Śaṅkara that anything that is given to consciousness as an object (*viṣaya*) cannot belong to consciousness, because of the opposition between consciousness and the objects of consciousness. Anything that is known or being aware of cannot belong to awareness as in being known or being aware of the object is something different from and other than consciousness. Unless something is different from and other than consciousness it cannot be the object of consciousness. Anything that is illumined is not light. Therefore to characterise consciousness as this or that is not justified as this or that are given to consciousness as objects, and cannot therefore belong to consciousness. All that can be known, or can be thought of or conceived cannot belong to consciousness, and affect it because in all these consciousness is presupposed. Just as seeing cannot be an object of seeing, hearing an object of hearing, consciousness by being the very source or basis of knowing, experiencing, thinking, etc., cannot be an object of them. By its very nature consciousness cannot be an object of knowledge, and anything that is said about it or attributed to it cannot belong to it, as all that can be said about it is an object to it, and is therefore something other than itself. It is only to an object of knowledge something can be predicted. Even to say that consciousness is immortal, birthless, infinite, etc., is to transpose or transfer those attributes which legitimately belong to an object of knowledge or thought, and can be true or false about an object of knowledge or thought, to something which is not an object either of knowledge or of thought. When no attribute can belong to consciousness, and when no notion or idea can be true of it because all of them are given to it as objects, nothing can condition or determine consciousness. It is unconditioned and indeterminate. It is absolute in every sense of the term, and though not an object of knowledge or of thought it is eternally self-revealed. It is known by being it which amounts to saying that consciousness is the very being of *ātman*. When the realisation that *ātman* or consciousness is not an object of knowledge or experience takes place enquiry into the nature of *ātman*, as if it is an object of enquiry, stops or comes to an end. One realises then that *ātman* is not an object to be known or experienced, but the true nature of himself, and that is a matter of being oneself in one's own true nature. It is the true nature of one who wants to know, or the knower.

As pointed out earlier, the various functions like knowing, thinking, etc., attributed to self cannot belong to consciousness, for all these functions are given as objects to consciousness. On the other hand, if they belong to consciousness, or are intrinsic to it, it should never be without them. But it remains in itself or as free from all these functions during deep sleep. These functions can be attributed to consciousness only metaphorically or indirectly as consciousness is presupposed by these functions, and without it they cannot operate. Śaṅkara tries to explain this with the help of an example. Normally we attribute the functions of going or cutting, etc., to the agent, though in reality he is not the goer or cutter. Going and cutting are not the nature of an agent but nevertheless he is identified with these functions as when we say one is going or cutting.[11] Going is not the nature of one who goes nor cutting that of one who cuts. They involve certain instruments, and are basically the functions of the instruments. The act of cutting is a function of the instrument but as the agent is associated with the act he is wrongly identified with the act, and is called a cutter. An agent by himself cannot do these functions. Similarly, because of its association with the mind and the senses consciousness is identified with the functions of mind and senses. Thinking, seeing, etc., are the functions of the mind or of the senses as the mind or the eyes are active in thinking and seeing, but consciousness which is present equally in all these acts cannot be said to act. Consciousness which is essential for these acts to take place is not an agent of the acts, just as light which is essential for perceiving objects is not an agent of perception. Consciousness by its very presence or existence enables the mind and the senses to function without itself being active. At the most, we can say that the agent in all the actions is not consciousness but ego which is not the same as consciousness. Therefore even when the mind and the senses are not active, or when there is no thinking or perception consciousness is present, as in deep sleep. Since it does not act it is not affected by the various acts of the mind and the senses. In this sense consciousness is known as witness (*sākṣī*) which however depends for its intelligibility and meaning on dualistic experience. In the absence of acts or functions of the mind and the senses *ātman* cannot be called witness. In itself consciousness is neither a witness nor a knower, and such state of its true nature reveals itself in deep sleep, and in the final or fourth state of direct realisation. In deep sleep consciousness remains in itself or in its true nature. We present here some of the basic arguments to show that consciousness in itself is present during deep sleep. The basic reason why we fail to recognise consciousness in deep sleep is not because of its absence, but because of our inability to recognise its presence. This is because we understand or define consciousness on the basis of dualistic experience of waking and dream states in which it is known as that which reveals something, or is known while revealing something. In other words, the mode of revelation of consciousness during the waking and dream states is different from the mode of its revelation during deep sleep. During waking and dream states it reveals itself while revealing objects, and when this mode of revelation is absent during deep sleep we construe its absence. This is not however to admit that consciousness reveals itself in two different ways during waking state and deep sleep. The way we know or recognise consciousness during waking and dream states is conditioned as we think of consciousness and define it as that which reveals objects, and when this condition is not fulfilled during deep sleep we construe its absence. Our understanding of the nature of consciousness which is conditioned by our dualistic experience in which it is known in one way prevents us from recognising its presence during deep sleep. The way in which we know consciousness during waking state is not possible during deep sleep. As pointed out earlier, consciousness which cannot be defined in terms of any characteristics or functions is yet wrongly identified and defined during dualistic experience as having certain characteristics and functions, and when those characteristics and functions are absent during deep sleep we construe its non-existence. But if we admit that in the first place our definition or understanding of consciousness is not really true of it then we need not search for those defining characteristics during deep sleep to know whether consciousness is present or not. For example, if we define light as that which illumines objects of knowledge we may fail to see it in the absence of objects to be illumined. Here our definition or understanding of light is wrong. It can exist without there being objects to be illumined, but if we accept the definition of light as that which illumines objects, and when there are no objects to be illumined, we may conclude the absence of light. Likewise, if we identify consciousness as that which reveals objects or the functions of the mind and the senses, we see its non-existence in the absence of objects, and the functions of the mind and the senses. Consciousness is present during deep sleep but its existence cannot be known or recognised in the way it is known during the waking and dream states of experience.

During dualistic experience it seems to depend for its revelation on the existence of things other than itself. As this condition is not fulfilled during deep sleep we think of its non-existence. We may consider two more examples of Śaṅkara in this connection. Eyes can see colours, but in darkness the eyes fail to perceive colours, and this is not due to the non-existence of eyes but due to darkness. Fire is known to us when it burns something, and when there is nothing to burn fire does not cease to be, but exists in itself. Furthermore, consciousness cannot be known in the manner things are known. It is its own revelation, or strictly speaking its revelation is meaningless as there is no other consciousness to which it can reveal itself. The other argument is that the denial of consciousness during deep sleep proves its existence. To say that there is no consciousness during deep sleep proves its existence, as how anyone can dispute that consciousness which denies consciousness during deep sleep. We may here point out that the denial of consciousness during deep sleep is not done during deep sleep but after it is over, or when one is awake. That means, the denial of consciousness during deep sleep is strictly speaking inferential, as the characteristics or functions which we attribute to consciousness during waking state are not found during deep sleep. But this cannot be valid as we argued earlier. The so-called characteristics of consciousness known during waking state are not really the characteristics of consciousness. Pure consciousness reveals itself during the fourth or final state (*turīya*), and that is the real evidence to know its non-dual nature. All the arguments and evidence presented here are only to show that the idea of pure consciousness is not absurd or utterly meaningless, or to show its reality which a discerning person can know, not because of these arguments but in the light of these arguments. All our attempts in this chapter are not directed towards proving *advaita*, which is impossible, but are intended to make it meaningful and intelligible to our dualistic consciousness and understanding.

Though consciousness which reveals itself during dualistic experience and during deep sleep and *turīya* is one and the same the ways in which it is known are different. In the former its nature is conditioned as it were by our ways of knowing it, and in the latter it is known in its unconditioned nature or as unaffected by our empirical ways of knowing it. Consciousness though is known in relation to a body or person it is not personal; it does not belong to a person or an individual. Though it is revealed within a body it is not limited by any body. The fact that all that can be known and thought of cannot belong to consciousness shows that it transcends all the concepts and ideas.

Even if we admit that consciousness is absolute or it is *Brahman* or *ātman* yet it does not mean the negation or denial of duality. Though during deep sleep and *turīya* it reveals itself in its true nature as absolute or unconditioned, yet during waking and dream states its revelation is presupposed by duality. If man does not have the states of waking and dreaming but only deep sleep and *turīya* the problem of duality would not have arisen. Much of man's life consists of waking and dream experiences. If deep sleep and *turīya* are the only states no instruction about *advaita* and the denial of *dvaita* are necessary, and all the proofs and evidence to establish one and deny the other will not be required. All philosophising about *advaita* takes place during waking state of duality. And even when it is established that consciousness is absolute or unconditioned it does not mean the negation of duality. Then there would be no difference between the *Sāṁkhya* concept of *puruṣa* and the advaitic view of consciousness. Here we have to accept the authority of *Śruti* which says that what is experienced during waking state as something different from and other than *ātman* is in reality *ātman* only. *Turīya* in which non-dual nature of *Brahman* is realised is equally present throughout the waking and dream states though we do not realise that.

Turīya and its Validity

How to know or establish that the real nature of *Brahman* is that which is revealed during *turīya* but not what is revealed during waking and dream states? On the other hand, if we take the nature of *ātman* as what is revealed during waking experience then what is revealed during other states is to be considered as something illusory. Why should we accept that the non-dual nature of *Brahman* as revealed during *turīya* is the objective or true nature of *Brahman*, and judge the waking experience of duality as something based on ignorance? The basic reason for accepting the finality of *turīya* is not only that there is no lapse or return from that state, when once it is realised, to a state of ignorance or duality, but most importantly that state is a state of cessation of all desires and imperfections. When man's quest to know more and more, and to seek explanation of all, which characterise his existence in the state of duality, come to an end with the realisation of *advaita*, the desire to know or seek further explanation comes to an end. *Turīya* is the end of all desires and quest as it is a state in which all desires and quest to know and explain are supremely fulfilled. It is a state of desirelessness, or fulfilment of man's quest to know the truth. When there is a desire to know more and more man achieves progress in knowledge, whereas all the desires of man are fulfilled when the desire to know the truth is ultimately satisfied by realising the truth directly by being it. Any state of desire is a state of imperfection, as desires are born when man feels the lack of something, or when he feels some imperfection which he wants to overcome by realising a state of perfection. And such seeking comes to an end in realising that or in being that which is absolute perfection or *ānanda*. The state of desirelessness attained by realising that which is the ultimate quest of man is the final state of perfection in comparison to which the state of desires is imperfect. Since *turīya* is that state of desirelessness or perfection or *ānanda* it is final and absolute. It is the state in which the desire to know is absolutely fulfilled. It is the end of all knowledge, *vedānta*.[12]

But how to explain the duality experienced during waking and dream states if *turīya* is the final truth, and is non-dual? If *turīya* is final and ontological as the state of *turīya* or *mokṣa* is the same as *Brahman* or *ātman* — all these terms are synonyms — it is present throughout man's experience whether he knows it or not. *Brahman* is the real object of experience during waking state also, though as an experience it is different from *turīya*. The duality that is experienced during waking state is not true of reality, or it is not ontological or objective. It is not that that *Brahman* has become dual or many during waking state, and it is experienced in its non-dual nature during *turīya*. If differences are intrinsic to the nature of *Brahman* it cannot be without differences at any time of its existence, as what is natural or essential to a thing cannot be destroyed. If *turīya* is final or ultimate state of realisation, and in it *Brahman* is realised in its non-dual nature, or if *turīya* is *Brahman* the duality experienced during waking state cannot be real and objective. It can have only psychological validity. If *Brahman* is the object of knowledge or experience of both waking and *turīya* states, though experienced differently, both cannot be true objectively, and if *turīya* reveals *Brahman* in its objective nature waking experience cannot be true objectively. The difference between *turīya* and waking experience, according to *Śaṅkara*, is one of knowledge and ignorance or one of perfect or objective knowledge and imperfect or partly objective knowledge. The difference is not due to any change in the nature of reality experienced, but is in the nature of experiencing. Therefore what is known wrongly during waking state is realised during *turīya* perfectly or in its complete objectivity. Or the ignorance that causes waking experience is completely overcome during *turīya*. This, according to Śaṅkara, is the purport of the basic Upaniṣadic statements like 'I am *Brahman*' or 'you are That' or 'all is *Brahman*'. The true or objective reality of man is *Brahman* only, but wrongly known as *jīva* or self, and what is wrongly seen or known as the world of differences is in reality or objectively the same as what is known rightly or objectively as *Brahman* during *turīya*. While in the empirical experience the reality is not known in its complete objectivity, due to the play of subjective factors or ignorance, in *turīya* due to the absence of ignorance the reality is experienced objectively. This is what the Upaniṣadic statements like 'I am *Brahman*', 'you are That', 'all is *Brahman*' intend to assert. In these statements the terms 'I', 'you' and 'all' belong to the realm of empirical experience or knowledge, while 'Brahman' or 'That' refer to the reality that is not empirically known. Therefore there can be no identity between 'I' and '*Brahman*' or 'you' and 'That' or 'all' and '*Brahman*' in their direct sense as they mean different things, or have different meanings. There can be no identity between them as far as their direct meanings are concerned. Moreover, while one is known empirically the other is not known empirically. How can we identify 'I' or 'you' or 'all' which are empirically known with '*Brahman*' or 'That' which is not known empirically? Nevertheless, they are identified in the *Upaniṣads*, and the identity or oneness cannot be meaningful and valid at the empirical level. It is only during the state of *turīya* one comes to know the identity between them, as one comes to know then that what was known as 'I' or 'all' is in reality the same as what is indicated by the terms '*Brahman*' and 'That'. While in empirical experience the 'I' and 'all' are known directly, *Brahman* is known indirectly, or it is an idea only, whereas in *turīya Brahman* is known directly and immediately by the same person who had experienced *Brahman* as 'I' or 'all'. Therefore he can know their oneness or identity. What was known as 'I' or 'all' during empirical experience is known as '*Brahman*' during *turīya*. Therefore when the factors that cause empirical experience of duality are overcome, as in *turīya*, the reality that was experienced as world during empirical experience, due to certain subjective factors, is realised in its true or objective nature during *turīya* due to the absence of those factors that cause empirical experience. Thus the same reality is referred to by different terms meaning thereby the objective oneness or identity of the reality referred to by different terms. This realisation comes when what is seen wrongly is seen perfectly or objectively. Thus non-duality or *advaita* means the oneness or identity of the reality that is empirically experienced and the reality that is known during *turīya* or as *turīya*. The reality that is empirically experienced is not different from the reality that is known during *turīya* or as *turīya*.

Meaning of Advaita (2)

The concept of *advaita* can have a different meaning or can be interpreted differently. While in the statements 'I am *Brahman*' and 'you are That' the *Upaniṣads* assert the non-difference between the self of man and *ātman* or *Brahman*, in the statements like 'all is *Brahman*' or 'I am the creation' (*ahameva sṛṣṭirasmi*) the non-difference between all or world and *Brahman* is asserted. Before we discuss the non-difference or non-duality of *Brahman* and all or world we should understand the concept of difference (*bheda* or *bhinna*). Things are different in several ways, or there are several kinds of difference. The difference between a horse and a cow, or gold and copper is one of kind. Horse and cow belong to two different kinds of species, and gold and copper belong to two different kinds of substance. The difference between sea-water and wave, or between milk and butter, or clay and pot made of clay is not one of kind or substance but of form. And the difference between a tree and its branches is one of whole and part, and the difference between an illusory snake and a real rope is one of illusion. There is also another kind of difference which is modal, that is, the difference between a snake that is straight and one that is coiled. A coiled posture of a snake is different from the snake when it is straight. In the case of golden ornaments and copper ornaments the difference is substantive, though there is similarity in form and name. We call a golden ring a ring and a copper ring also a ring. Thus as far as form and name are concerned they are identical but as substances they are different. In the case of sea-water and wave, or the clay and clay-pot, the difference is not one of substance but of form and name. In the case of a snake in its coiled position and straight position the difference is one of mode. The *Upaniṣads* while explaining the difference between *Brahman* and the world prefer the examples of clay and clay-pot and sea-water and wave in which the difference is due to form and name. Clay and sea-water differ from pot and wave only in form, as otherwise they are the same reality. All these types of change and difference are discussed by Śaṅkara. He also discusses another kind of difference which is purely nominal or verbal, that is, the difference between the sun and sunlight, and a gem and its lusture. However, all these examples or analogies are taken from the material realm, and in understanding *Brahman*, which is consciousness, and its change or manifestation we have to be careful in adopting the analogies taken from the material or physical world. In addition to these analogies we find both in the *Upaniṣads* and in the writings of Śaṅkara examples illustrating functional difference. The same person is known differently as father, teacher, etc., depending upon the functions he performs. The same psyche (*citta*) or intelligence is known differently as mind (*manas*), intellect (*buddhi*), heart (*hṛdaya*) depending upon the functions it performs. The same psyche or intelligence is known as mind when it does certain jobs like co-ordinating, remembering, etc., and is known as intellect or *buddhi* when it discerns, discriminates and judges. Thus the same reality can be differentiated and known by several names according to its various functions, and even qualities. There is still a different kind of difference. The same sound produced by an instrument is differentiated into different notes. These are the kinds of difference which are real, and are meaningful in the world of empirical experience.

In the spiritual realm things manifest themselves differently. For instance, the power of intelligence is put to several uses, and accordingly it is known differently, and yet much of its power may remain unmanifested at any given time. All that the human spirit is capable of accomplishing may not be known at any given time, but its diverse expressions, which take different forms, are the expressions of the same spirit, and find their oneness in it. And these creative expressions of the spirit are spontaneous as they express the spirit or manifest it as spontaneously as the shining of the sun. At times, language creates difference when in reality there is none. When we use such expressions like 'Rāhu's head' and 'body of a stone image' they may create the illusion of difference. The expression 'Rāhu's head' may make one think that Rāhu (a planet) is different from his head while in reality Rāhu is head only. Similarly, the expression 'body of a stone image' may give rise to the illusion that the image is more than body, whereas it is nothing but body.[13] When we say 'the sun shines' language creates a distinction between the sun and light, while in reality they are not different, as the sun is light only. In other words when we say that the sun shines we think the sun is different from his light, and therefore try to relate the two. In these cases the differences are created by language; they are only nominal. Likewise, if the *Śruti* statements are interpreted in their literal sense they may seem to assert or uphold duality or difference. For instance, we significantly use the world 'village' in three different senses, one to mean its inhabitants as when we say 'the village has come', secondly to mean the habitat when we say 'the village is deserted', and thirdly in both the senses as when we say 'one must not enter the village'.[14]

At times, difference in name or difference in form may create the illusion of real difference if understood in one sense, while they can also show the oneness if understood differently. Śaṅkara's basic contention is that the differences are due to name and form only, but are not objectively real, and on the other if the differences are taken to be real because of the difference in name and form it is wrong knowledge. Human creations which are an expression of man's creative intelligence are designated differently, but the separate names given to the creations do not mean real difference, and to realise their oneness all the thoughts and creations need not be reduced to intelligence or destroyed. To see the oneness of all that is made of clay the clay objects need not be literally reduced to clay. One can see their oneness by seeing the clay in them, or by knowing that the difference between different clay objects is a matter of form and name.

But our knowledge of pot is not the same as our knowledge of clay. Our knowledge of certain expressions of man is not the same as our knowledge of the person. Clay is known through its varied forms, and a person is known through his varied expressions. And for that reason both are not identical in one sense, and are one in another sense. If we take the analogy of sound produced by a musical instrument, which is differentiated into various notes, there is no difference between the general sound and the sound differentiated into various notes, as the latter cannot exist without the former. It is the general sound which is differentiated into various notes, which are included within the general sound, and cannot exist without it.

Non-difference

Ātman or consciousness, which is absolute, expresses itself variously (*vyakrīyate*), and there is no limit to its expressions. Its self-expressions, which are not different from itself, are given various names, and these names and forms constitute the world or all (*sarvam*). The self-expression of *ātman*, which is as natural and spontaneous as breathing in man, is differentiated in terms of forms and names which may appear as different from *ātman*. However, in all the examples given above like the clay and its various modifications, or the general sound and its differentiation into various notes, the various forms of their manifestation can be differentiated in terms of space and time. But in the case of *ātman*, as it is the only reality, its differentiation in space or in time by way of self-expression or manifestation will not be meaningful. It would be possible and meaningful only when we can think of *ātman* as a reality limited in space and time. The differentiation of *ātman* or *Brahman* in terms of its self-expression will be meaningful only when we can differentiate one expression from another either in terms of space or in terms of time. But this is not meaningful as *Brahman* is not a reality that exists in space or in time. The self-expression of *Brahman* does not take place in some space which is devoid of *Brahman*. It is meaningful to talk of movement in space but not the movement of space as there is no other space in which space can move. If *Brahman* is all that is, its movement, as any notion of change involves movement, is impossible. Movement or change requires space, and there is no space either within or without *Brahman*. How to understand then the idea of self-expression or manifestation of *Brahman* or *ātman*? This problem arises basically when we differentiate *ātman* from its expression or manifestation, and think that the self-expression of *ātman* is different from *ātman*, and somehow both can exist as pot and clay. In the case of general sound and the individual notes they do not occupy different spaces, and also cannot exist separately. Similarly, *ātman* and its self-expression that seemingly constitutes all or the world are not different in any sense as they do not occupy different spaces. They occupy the same space, and live the same life but are somehow differentiated or distinguished which is mainly due to the form of expression in language. On the other hand, if the distinction is taken to be one of real difference, as if *ātman* is one thing and its expression another, the problem of their relation arises. But the distinction is the creation of language. When the language developed on the basis of our experience of the world of duality or differences is employed to express non-duality it creates the problem, especially when it is taken and interpreted literally.

The various expressions of *ātman* constitute *ātman* as they are not different from *ātman*. *Ātman* cannot be known apart from its expressions, and the expressions cannot exist without *ātman*. They are non-different (*abhinna*) or one is not different from the other (*na-anya*). Nevertheless, the various self-expressions of *ātman* cannot be identified with *ātman* as *ātman* is infinitely more than its expressions. It is all its expressions, and at the same time more than all its expressions. Its expressions forming its nature are co-extensive with itself, and therefore to determine *ātman* in terms of any of its expressions is to determine or limit *ātman*'s nature. The nature of a thing cannot condition or determine the thing. It is only the limited or imperfect knowledge or ignorance of man which tries to determine the nature of *ātman* in terms of certain of its self-expressions, or in terms of certain names and forms. In terms of name and form only man tries to determine the nature of *ātman* in that he creates a distinction between *ātman* and *anātman*. Or because of his selective approach, guided by his empirical values, man tries to identify *ātman* with this or that definition of *ātman*, and to that extent he excludes from *ātman* something, or discriminates *ātman* from what is not *ātman* (*anātman*). In this process he creates all the differences. He differentiates *ātman* from himself and from the world, and thinks that all these differences, which are his own creation, are real. Howsoever comprehensive a definition of *Brahman* may be something is excluded from *Brahman*, or *Brahman* is defined as distinguished from something which is not *Brahman*. While a quality distinguishes a thing from its own species, a definition distinguishes the thing defined from something else. Otherwise a definition is not meaningful. But there is nothing different from *Brahman* from which it can be distinguished. Thus all the definitions of *Brahman* share this limitation, and cannot therefore be true of *Brahman*. In view of this the best possible definition or description of *Brahman* as attempted in the *Upaniṣads* is *via negativa*. The repetition of the term *neti* is intended, according to Śaṅkara, to include within the scope of negation all that can be thought of *Brahman*, both physical and non-physical characteristics (*neti neti bhūtarāśim vāsanārāśim; ādhidaivata ādhyātma tajjinita meva ca vāsanā lakṣaṇa rūpam*).[15] The range of negation is all inclusive. At the same time the object of negation or negative description of *Brahman* is to make one realise that *Brahman* is all or there is nothing which is other than and different from *Brahman*. This is a methodological device to make one realise ultimately the all inclusive or integral (*pūrṇa*) nature of *Brahman*. If, for instance, *Brahman* is defined in terms of this or that characteristic a doubt may arise whether something else is *Brahman* or not, and to obviate such doubts, which at the conceptual level cannot be avoided, the method of attribution (*āropa* or *adhyāropa*) and negation (*apavāda*) is adopted. This is fully explained in the *Bṛhadāraṇyaka Upaniṣad.*[16] When *ātman*, depending upon its various functions or the forms of its self-expression, is known differently such as mind, speech, thought, etc., someone may identify *ātman* with mind or speech or its other self-expressions and think that *ātman* is speech or mind only. In this sense one's knowledge of *ātman* is incomplete (*akṛstna* or *asamastha*). But we cannot identify *ātman* with more and more of its expressions or all of its expressions, for though the term 'all' seems to be all inclusive it is yet limited in relation to *ātman*, as at any given time of its expression the meaning of 'all' is limited. For example, when one asks his wife to cook all the rice, the 'all' refers to all the rice available in the house but not to all the rice available in the world. But *ātman* is all, if by 'all' we do not understand that which is limited in space and time. "When name and form existing latently in the *ātman* are expressed they get evolved, while retaining their intrinsic nature under all circumstances in time and space that are indistinguishable from *Brahman*."[17] "Then that evolution of name and form is the appearance of *Brahman* as many. In no other sense we can explain difference, for there is no non-*ātman* in the past, present or future which is different from *ātman*, and separated from it by time and space."[18] *Ātman* does not become something other than itself, like the birth of a son (*arthāntara*), in the process of its self-expression. It is because of *ātman* that name and form have their being under all circumstances, but *ātman* does not consist of them. However, they are essentially *Brahman* or are not different from *Brahman* since they cease to exist when *Brahman* is eliminated.

With the help of an illustration provided by Śaṅkara we can understand how any identification of *Brahman* with this or that of its expressions leads to distortion of its true nature, and limit its completeness. A ruler of earth may be called the ruler of a particular country, although he is at the same time the ruler of the whole earth. Factually he can be said to be the ruler of a country, as the country is included in the empire, but thereby his rulership gets limited.[19] The all-pervading space may be said to occupy a particular place, and this is true from a particular point of view, as space is present there also. *Brahman* is all as everything that is an expression of *Brahman* is *Brahman* but it is more than all its expressions. Clay is more than all the pots made of clay though it is in all the pots. Thus as in reality the 'all' is not different from *Brahman*, the meaning of 'all is *Brahman*' is not different in its intended meaning from that of 'I am *Brahman*'. The intention of the statement is not to identify all (*sarvam*) as if it is something different from *Brahman* with *Brahman*, but to show that both the terms *sarvam* and *Brahman* refer to the same reality, though by themselves they mean two different things. However, *sarvam* and *Brahman* are related by different thinkers in different ways as creator-created, one-many, being-becoming, unity in difference, and therefore the object of the statement 'all is *Brahman*' is to show that what is referred to by 'all' and what is referred to by *Brahman* is one and the same reality; they are non-different. There is no 'all' which exists independently of *Brahman* so that it can be identified with *Brahman*. "The statement of co-ordination made in the statement 'all is *Brahman*' aims at destroying the world, but in no way at intimating that *Brahman* is multiform in nature. When the differences created by ignorance are destroyed the universe remains one without a second (*bheda bhāva pranisite idamekam advaitam*)."[20]

But how can one know that something is the manifestation or expression of *Brahman*? To see something or all as an expression of *Brahman Brahman* is to be known first. Unless one knows what *Brahman* is one cannot know whether something is the manifestation of *Brahman*. But to know *Brahman* is not to know it as something, as there is nothing other than or different from *Brahman*. Therefore to realise *Brahman* is to see it as all. Realisation of *Brahman*, and the realisation that *Brahman* is all are not different. They are one and the same. The moment *Brahman* is realised there remains no individual separate from *Brahman* who can identify *Brahman* with all. And *Brahman* is not something that can be distinguished from some other thing in knowing it so that what is so distinguished from *Brahman* is later identified with it. Furthermore, in realising *Brahman* one does not see anything as other than and different from *Brahman*, and therefore there does not exist something different from *Brahman* which is to be identified with *Brahman*. In realising *Brahman* the reality of something which till then seemed to be different from *Brahman* ceases to be different from *Brahman*, and when it ceases to be something different from *Brahman* the problem of identifying it with *Brahman* does not arise. Since the existence of all or the world is in the first place created by wrong knowledge or ignorance its oneness with or its non-difference from *Brahman* is effected by knowledge. When the ontological oneness of all with *Brahman* is realised the 'all' is as it were dissolved into *Brahman* as in reality there is no world or all different from *Brahman*. While people relying on popular tradition (*purāṇa*) believe in the real origination of the world they also believe that it will be literally dissolved into *Brahman* at the time of final dissolution (*pralaya*) whereas, according to *advaita*, as there is no real origin of the world there is no real dissolution of the world also. Dissolution of the world of names and forms is the same as the destruction of ignorance, and that is the final (*atyanta*) or extreme dissolution of the world (*yat sarvam avidyā āropitam tat sarvam paramārthto brahma, na tu yad brahma tat sarvamiti*).[21] There is no real origin of the world, and therefore the dissolution of the world is also not real. Both take place in the imagination (*kalpanā*) of man, or both are his mental constructions, and therefore they do not affect *Brahman*. "The *Paurāṇikas* hold that the dissolution is natural (*svābhāvika*) while that which is consciously (*buddhipūrvaka*) effected by the knowers of *Brahman* through their knowledge of *Brahman* is called extreme dissolution which happens through the cessation of ignorance."[22] The world in its true or objective nature at any time is not different from *Brahman*, which is *prajñā*, and so there is no point in saying that it becomes one with *Brahman* at the time of dissolution. Thus the point of emphasis in all this discussion is to show that in reality the world of empirical experience, which is valid as experience only, is never different from *Brahman*, but ignorance makes one think that what is empirically experienced is different from *Brahman*, and therefore when ignorance is destroyed they are not seen as different. And along with ignorance the so-called world of differences, its projection, is also destroyed (*prajñāna ghane brahmaṇi paramārtha viveka jñānena pravilāpa*). All is merged as it were into *Brahman* which is pure intelligence through discriminative knowledge of truth.

It is only when the world exists differently from *Brahman* its oneness or identity with *Brahman* can be established or proved. Then it would be like the identity of a tree which is one as tree, and yet full of differences like branches, leaves, etc., which are nevertheless sustained by the same sap. The identity or oneness of the tree is due to the oneness of sap which sustains all the parts of the tree. Likewise, if it is supposed that *Brahman* is the essence and sustaining unity of all that is, we have to admit a reality which forms the outer aspect or the body of the world of which *Brahman* can be the *ātman* or essence. Though for the sake of instruction *Brahman* is identified as the essence of all or the inner unity of all it is also in reality the outer aspect as well. If *Brahman* is the essence as well as the outer form or body of the world there is no meaning in conceiving *Brahman* as the unity in difference. This would be meaningful if something other than *Brahman* is the source of the outer form or body of the world, and *Brahman* is the source of its inner unity. If *Brahman* is all ontologically there is no point in saying that it is the inner reality or *ātman* of all. And if the all or the world, which seems to exist from the point of view of empirical experience, is really *Brahman*, or when *Brahman* is the true or objective nature of the world, the world as world will have no existence. The same reality cannot be known as world and *Brahman* at the same time. That is to say, the moment the world is seen in its ontological or objective nature as *Brahman* the world as world ceases to be. On the other hand, as long as the world is seen as world *Brahman* is not realised, and when *Brahman* is realised the world is not experienced. Therefore both the experiences cannot be valid simultaneously. When the real object, that is, rope is seen as snake rope is not seen, and when the rope is seen as rope snake disappears, as the rope has not become snake, in any manner. Though we may be right in saying that what was seen as snake is in reality rope only we will be wrong in identifying the snake with rope as both are not real in the same sense, and the reality of one disappears in realising the reality of the other. Also conceptually the rope cannot be snake as they have two different meanings. So also the world as world having its own meaning and value cannot be identified with *Brahman* having a different meaning and value. However, when the reality that is indicated by both the concepts, or the reality that is the ontological basis of both the concepts is realised directly both the concepts will have only conceptual validity. "When name and form are tested from the standpoint of the highest reality they cease to be separate entities."[23] When the reality is stripped off both the meanings or concepts, *Brahman* and world, imposed on it because of wrong knowledge, it cannot be identified either as *Brahman*, the cause of the world, or as world caused by *Brahman*. When it cannot be identified either as *Brahman* or as world there is no meaning in asserting any relation between them. The reality which is conceived differently, or which is the ontological basis of different conceptions, is beyond those concepts, and its direct realisation is not possible until the conceptions with which it is wrongly identified are not transcended. *Brahman* which transcends all our conceptions cannot be known in terms of any concept, and cannot therefore be the identity of certain concepts. The concept of *Brahman* as the ultimate source or origin of the world is different from the concept of world which is created, finite and imperfect. And in realising *Brahman* directly one transcends the various conceptions of it, or becomes free from them. Then the concepts are seen only as concepts having no objective validity, and therefore the question of identifying them does not arise. The problem of identity or any other type of relation between the world and *Brahman* is meaningful only at the conceptual level, as at the level of direct realisation, in which both the concepts are transcended, the problem of identity or any other possible relation between them will not be there. "The aggregate of names and so on can be viewed as of the nature of *Brahman* only insofar as the individual character of those effects of *Brahman* is not sublated, and when their (individual) character is sublated how can they be viewed as symbols of *Brahman*, and how can *ātman* be apprehended in them?"[24] "Self is also a symbol, and other things like mind, sun, etc., are also symbols. One is not identical with the other, as one golden object is not identical with another golden object. And when *Brahman* is seen the so-called individual effects cease to be individual effects."[25]

Meaning of Advaita (3)

The above discussion will take us to the third meaning of *advaita*, that is, *advaita* as the negation or denial of all duality. As we have seen in the earlier discussion *advaita* does not mean establishing identity either between the self of man and *Brahman*, or between the world and *Brahman*. "We do not maintain the existence of things different from *Brahman* in the state when the highest truth is definitely known. Nor do we deny the validity for the ignorant of actions with their factors and results, while the relative world of name and form exists. The world is a fact for both."[26] "Whenever we deny something as unreal we do so with reference to something real."[27] "This apparent world whose existence is established and proved by all the means of knowledge cannot be denied unless someone should find out some new truth, for a general principle is proved in the absence of a contrary instance."[28]

Advaita has no proof; and nothing can be said about it which can be completely meaningful and intelligible to man's empirical understanding. All the sources of valid knowledge and man's rational understanding prove the reality of duality or difference. Duality is their presupposition as well as their object. No source of knowledge and man's understanding can function without the duality of subject and object. Subject-object or knower-known distinction is an empirically valid fact, and is presupposed by all the activities of man and his empirical knowledge and experience. Empirical life of man is not possible without duality, and his values, aspirations and hopes presuppose a world of duality in which he wants to achieve something and avoid some other thing. He adopts various means to achieve various ends. Human thought also is not possible in the absence of differences. Duality is so obvious it requires no proof or evidence as proof and evidence are meant to prove something to someone. The whole phenomenal world is an expansion of duality, or it is dualistic. Duality is the basis not only of man's secular or empirical life but also of his spiritual or religious life which is based on *Śruti* or some other sacred tradition. The very purpose of *Śruti* is to teach man about the nature of ultimate reality, the realisation of which is regarded as the highest end of human life, thereby presupposing the duality between man and ultimate reality, and between itself and man. It has to use language to communicate truth, and language can function only when there is duality.

Advaita cannot be an object of knowledge or of thought or of language. The validity and meaningfulness of all the categories of human understanding like substance, attribute, etc., and the operation of all the means of knowledge are possible within the realm of duality. As non-duality is the negation of all duality all the categories of understanding will have no relevance and application in relation to it. As it is the end of all duality it is also beyond all the categories of human understanding. Therefore the meaning of *advaita* cannot be grasped in terms of them. And what is beyond the categories of his understanding is something utterly unintelligible to man, as man's understanding simply cannot operate in the absence of duality or difference. Any attempt therefore to make *advaita* intelligible to man's understanding involves the employment of categories, and some referencc to his life and thought. And since *advaita* is not intelligible in terms of any categories or concepts, as it is the end of all dùality, there can be no positive teaching about *advaita*. Thus there can be no philosophy of *advaita*, or *advaita* is not a philosophical position or a metaphysical doctrine which can either be proved or disapproved. Within the realm of duality something can be proved or disapproved, or something can be asserted or denied. If *advaita* is a philosophical position or a metaphysical doctrine, which it is not, its validity or otherwise would be meaningful. Intelligibility or unintelligibility of *advaita* would be relevant only if it is something about which there can be some positive definition or understanding. We may however say so many things about *advaita*, either by way of approval or praise or by way of criticism, but all this would be relevant and significant only if *advaita* means a metaphysical doctrine or a system of thought. Strictly speaking all such judgements are beside the point, or are highly irrelevant in relation to *advaita*. To accept or reject any of the judgements or criticisms about *advaita* is to miss it, or it is only by misunderstanding *advaita* one can indulge in such things. *Advaita* is beyond all empirical or worldly dealings. It is the end or negation of all that is empirically valid and meaningful, and yet it is the only significant thing which man can aspire for and realise. *Advaita* is beyond all that is empirically intelligible and meaningful (*sarva vyavahārātīta*). It is the end of the worldly or empirical life of man, and all that is meaningful and valuable in relation to it (*prapañca upaśamana*). It is the end of all worldly life and values (*avasāna*).[29]

Advaita is basically a matter of direct realisation or experience but not of understanding. All the problems about *advaita* arise when it is taken to be a metaphysical doctrine, or a system of thought, or a philosophical position, or a sort of theology. Only when it is so all the criticisms against it or the various arguments in support of it would be significant and valid. And if *advaita* is a metaphysical doctrine it cannot be defended against those attacks and criticisms based either on reason or on common human experience. But *advaita* is the nature of reality or *Brahman*, and that is a matter of direct and immediate realisation. An experience has its own logic and justification, and is not open to philosophical criticism. If the experience is a caused one it can at the best have an explanation. Rational justification or criticism have nothing to do with an experience, and more so when the experience is natural and uncaused. Rational justification or criticism are valid and significant in relation to something that is based on reason. An argument can be rational or irrational but not so a fact of experience. Every experience is valid *per se*, and its objectivity or truth is to be judged in terms of its being cancelled or negated by another experience. An illusory experience is valid as experience though the object of such an experience has no objective validity. We are however not concerned here with the problems related to the validity of an experience. The direct realisation of *advaita* is a fact, as it has been realised by many, and can be realised by all as *Brahman* is an objectively existing reality, and is the true nature of oneself. And the Upaniṣadic statements about it are an attempt to describe it in language which by its very structure fails to describe it, and tends to make it dualistic. Therefore its description in the *Upaniṣads* cannot be literally true of it; at the most it can point to it. The whole attempt of Śaṅkara is to direct our attention to that experience or realisation, and to show its possibility or to make it intelligible and meaningful, as far as possible, within the limits of human understanding.

Critique of Duality

If *advaita* is basically a matter of direct realisation, and is the true or objective nature of reality then all the dualistic doctrines and systems of thought are false or illusory ultimately or when *advaita* is directly realised. *Advaita* and *dvaita* refer to two different experiences though having the same reality as their object. And both cannot be true of reality as one is the negation of the other. The advaitic realisation or experience is the highest as it cannot be sublated by any other experience, and is free from all illusion, or any trace of mental construction or imagination. It is the highest in the sense that when once it is realised it is the end of all quest, or its culmination. It leaves no scope for any doubt as it is direct and unmediated. It is the end of all quest and desires as it is the state of absolute perfection and bliss. However, all this is meaningful only by way of praise of *advaita*, and is not meant to characterise it or describe it. The dualistic experience of man though remains valid and meaningful till non-duality is directly realised it has no objective or ontological validity. It has only psychological validity, and is significant as long as it is experienced. And so long as duality is experienced and believed to be true non-duality, though objective, is not realised or known in the true sense of the term. *Advaita* being the very nature of *Brahman* is eternally self-revealed but is not realised as it were due to wrong knowledge or ignorance. While *advaita* is completely objective, dualistic experience involves the play of subjective factors or the active functioning of mind. Though it is a knowledge of *Brahman*, as *Brahman* is the only objectively existing reality, it is not perfect or objective. If *Brahman* is completely unknown to man at the empirical level its realisation by the liberated can be doubted. If *Brahman* is not known to ignorant people but is known only to the enlightened then faith will be the only means of knowing *Brahman*, and we cannot judge whether what is known only through faith is really objective or not. "If the ignorant man fails to reach *Brahman* though it is the common source of all then the attainment of *Brahman* by an enlightened person may as well be doubted."[30] It is both known and unknown at the empirical level in the sense that though it is known by all, as it is the real object of empirical experience and knowledge, yet it is not known in its complete objectivity.

In the absence of perfect knowledge of *Brahman* its nature is variously conceived by different people according to the differences in subjective factors. When the true nature of a thing is not known definitely man is free to impose on it his own understanding of it. Because such an understanding or imagination is significant and satisfying to man, either existentially or pragmatically, man identifies the nature of reality with what he thinks of it. Or technically he identifies the reality with his conception of it, or he superimposes his own understanding of reality on the reality, and thinks that the reality is what he conceives it to be. This may not be done by each person individually. It is done by some and others accept it. Thus different traditions, either religious or metaphysical, superimpose their different conceptions on reality, and consider it to be in accordance with their conceptions. Man's understanding of reality is thus conditioned by what he superimposes on it, and seldom man tries to know the nature of reality directly or independently of his conceptions of it. Ordinarily man is not prepared or willing to give up such conceptions to realise the truth directly for oneself. And from the point of view of such a conditioned understanding *advaita* may not be meaningful as it denies objective validity to such conceptions of reality. Since *advaita* does not serve the religious or metaphysical needs and aspirations of man or rather regards them as born of ignorance, he may see in *advaita* the negation or denial of all that is meaningful and valuable to him. "The knowledge of the supreme *Brahman* is never utilised for attaining human ends (*tad vijñānasya kecit puruṣārtha sādhane aviniyogāt*)."[31] As the end of all dualistic knowledge and experience *advaita* is the end of all human actions with their factors and results, while its realisation is an end in itself. It does not serve any purpose of man as in its realisation there remains no end or purpose or desire to be attained or fulfilled. The process of conceiving the nature of *Brahman*, which may differ from person to person, and within the life of a person from time to time, and from tradition to tradition goes on till *Brahman*'s true nature is ascertained, and is known definitely by direct realisation of it. Because of this process *Brahman*'s nature is conceived variously by different people, and we find several conceptions of *Brahman* or several views of it (*ekam sarvopādhi bheda bhinnam sarvai prāṇibhiḥ tārkikaica sarva prakāreṇa jñāyate vikalpyate anekadā*).[32] All these views may be meaningful and valid to those who hold them, and provide support (*ālambana*), either mental or spiritual, to them, but not to others. Thus *Brahman* is conceived variously as *puruṣa*, Prajāpati, *Īśvara*, etc., by different people, and accordingly they conceive different goals to their lives. In this context it is important to note the observation of Śaṅkara that the supreme *Brahman*, which is beyond all conceptions, is a matter of direct knowledge, while *Brahman* conceived variously by people is a matter of attainment (*paramcet jñātavyam aparam cet prāptavyam*).[33]

Now all the conceptions of *Brahman*, either formulated by different philosophers or as found in different scriptures, cannot be true of *Brahman* as they do not agree among themselves, and even contradict each other. No one view can therefore be objectively valid. They are mostly influenced by subjective factors or ignorance, and hence have their appeal and validity to some, but not to all. "Truth is that which does not change along with its conceptions or understanding (*yat viṣaya buddhir na vyabhicarati sat*)".[34] As long as man is attached to these views and doctrines, and his understanding is conditioned by them, he cannot see the truth of *advaita* or rather refuses to see it as his attachment to his views, which provide support to his life, prevents him from seeing the truth in its complete objectivity, or realising *advaita*.

As *advaita* is the true or objective nature of *Brahman*, which is eternally self-revealed, no effort is required to see it or realise it. Whether one recognises it or not *Brahman* is the object of all his knowledge and experience, but attachment to his views and conceptions prevents him from seeing it. All effort is therefore required to get rid of wrong knowledge of *Brahman*. Thus the main object of *Vedānta*, and the writings of Śaṅkara is to remove or dispel ignorance or wrong knowledge of *Brahman* but not to reveal *Brahman*. When the wrong knowledge of *Brahman* is destroyed the perfect knowledge of *Brahman*, which is self-revealing all the time by its very nature, is realised as it were for the first time, and that state is known as *mokṣa* or *advaita* or *brahmānubhava*.

To realise *advaita* or *Brahman* is to overcome or become free from ignorance, the source of all duality (*sarvasya avidyā parikalpitasya dvaitasya avasāna bhūtam advaitam brahma pratiṣṭha*).[35] The end of duality that is the creation of *avidyā* or ignorance is *advaita*, and it is the same as *Brahman*. The world of empirical experience is an expansion of duality or difference, and its extinction is the same as *mokṣa* or *advaita* (*prapañca dvaita bheda vistāraḥ tasyopaśame ātmasiddhiḥ* or *dvaitopaśame advaita siddhiḥ*). All duality is empirical or mental, and *advaita* is objective or supreme truth (*māyāmātram idam dvaitam advaitam paramārdhataḥ*). *Advaita* is freedom from all conceptions and views which involve difference or duality. To remain in the state of freedom from all duality is *advaita* (*dvaita prapañca upaśame svasthata advaita bhāvaḥ*).[36]

Since ignorance or its projection or *dvaita* prevents one from realising *advaita* to realise *advaita* is to criticise and negate duality. *Advaita* is primarily a critique of *dvaita*. Śaṅkara in his writings criticised all the systems of metaphysics available in his time, whether they are based on *Śruti* or on reason, and also those which are based on the personal realisation of the Buddha and Mahāvīra, namely, Buddhism and Jainism. All these systems are avowedly dualistic as they are about the nature of reality as known or experienced and propounded by someone. Of course, *Śruti* and the various systems of thought based on it are also dualistic. But while the systems of metaphysics based either on reason or on personal realisation of someone are completely dualistic, the *Śruti* at least, according to Śaṅkara, is not so as the real purport of *Śruti* is *advaita*, or the real intention of *Śruti* is to teach *advaita* though from the point of view of empirical understanding *Śruti* may appear to uphold *dvaita*. While all other systems of metaphysics accept and uphold *dvaita*, both at the empirical and *pāramārthika* levels, and are therefore out and out dualistic, *Śruti* admits the validity of *dvaita*, only at the level of empirical experience. Duality is admitted by the *Śruti* and by Śaṅkara only as a methodological device or requirement to teach *advaita*, and it is rejected the moment it serves the purpose of making one realise *advaita* directly. "Duality is created again and again for instruction, and for establishing *advaita* or the unity of *ātman* and all that is, and therefore it is negated again and again."[37]

Criticism and negation of *dvaita* are not done primarily on logical grounds or on the basis of reason only. One system of metaphysics can be criticised on the basis of another system, as the presuppositions and logic of one may not be the same as those of the other, and therefore may not be valid from the point of view of the one or the other. Thus the *Vaiśeṣikas* can criticise *Sāṁkhya*, and the Buddhists the philosophy of the *Upaniṣads*. Or as in the case of *Mādhyamika* philosophy of Nāgārjuna each system of metaphysics can be criticised in terms of its own inner logic by pointing out to its own incoherence and inner contradictions. But the Advaitic criticism of all dualistic systems of metaphysics is not to win a victory over them but to show how any system of dualistic metaphysics, or a system of metaphysics based on duality or difference is not objectively valid or true. The truth or validity or otherwise of a metaphysical system is to be judged in terms of its objective validity or experience. While purely speculative systems of metaphysics can be criticised on the basis of logical reasoning, a system of thought which is inspired by or based on some personal realisation or experience can be questioned and criticised in terms of another experience. But why or how to accept the ultimacy and objectivity of any one experience over other experiences? As pointed out earlier, *advaita* is ultimately a matter of direct realisation, but not a well constructed system of metaphysical thought free from all logical problems. An experience is valid *per se*, and therefore the truth of an experience cannot be judged by that of another. Then how to accept the finality of advaitic realisation or *brahmānubhava*? The non-dualistic realisation or *brahmānubhava* is accepted as final or supreme because it is natural or uncaused. As it is natural or uncaused it does not have its explanation in anything else. When an experience, on the other hand, can be shown to have been caused or as having an explanation it cannot be natural and objective, for when the factors that cause it are withdrawn the experience comes to an end. Those factors and conditions that produce an experience are the reasons for its validity, and also are its explanation. Since that is not the case with *advaita* or *brahmānubhava* its negation or sublation is not possible. It has no explanation as it is uncaused. It is free from all disputes and contradictions (*avivāda* and *aviruddha*). While dualistic systems of metaphysics find in *advaita* their opposition, *advaita* is not in conflict with any system of thought as it is the unity or oneness of all. It sees the same reality as being the basis of all systems of thought. Śaṅkara says the different limbs of one's body are not in conflict with each other as they constitute the same person. *Advaita* which sees the same reality being presented in those systems of thought, though wrongly, has no reason to come into conflict with them, or find any contradiction between itself and other systems of thought. An illusory snake does not come into conflict with a real rope, nor does it contradict the rope, as both are not equally real, but nevertheless one who sees snake is in cognitive contact with rope only, or rope is the reality that is perceived as snake. As with the realisation of *advaita* the duality ceases to be real there will be no scope for any conflict between the two. There can be no relation between what is real and what is illusory, let alone contradiction or conflict. This, on the other hand, would be possible if *advaita* is a system of thought contending with other systems of thought for truth and validity. As *advaita* is not basically a system of metaphysical thought there is no problem of its coming into conflict with other systems of metaphysical thought, be they dualistic or monistic. Monism as a metaphysical doctrine can come into conflict with non-monistic doctrines. But *advaita* cannot be classified into any type of metaphysics as it is not basically a system of metaphysical thought trying to establish or prove a doctrine. It is the end of all views and doctrines. It means ultimately *brahmānubhava* or direct realisation of truth in which all mental construction and thought come to an end, or are transcended. Even otherwise as *advaita* comprehends all by realising the non-difference between mind and its varied constructions and projections and *ātman* it does not see any difference anywhere. When *Brahman* is all, there is no basis for any conflict as nothing is excluded from *Brahman*, or nothing is seen as different from *Brahman*.

The differences are admitted by *advaita* only as a means to teach *advaita*. They have only instructional or means (*upāya*) value, whereas dualists admit ontological reality to differences. The Advaitic criticism of *dvaita* is not therefore to win a metaphysical victory over dualistic metaphysics, but to show how they are all wrong views of the same reality, or to show how what is really *advaita* is wrongly seen as *dvaita* by them. In other words, the criticism of *dvaita* is intended to show that the basis of duality when analysed logically ceases to be the real ground or basis for *dvaita*. *Advaita* being natural or being the nature of reality has no explanation, whereas *dvaita* which is mostly psychological can have an explanation. What cannot be analysed and explained further is ultimately real, and what is caused and can have an explanation cannot be the absolute truth. Since duality can be explained, as it is due to certain factors, it is not ultimately true or valid as when the factors of its explanation are absent it comes to an end. The ultimate explanation of duality is wrong knowledge or ignorance (*avidyā* or *ajñāna* or *māyā*) as in its absence duality is not experienced. Perception of rope as snake has an explanation but not the perception of rope as rope. Moon is perceived double, and when the reason for seeing the moon as double is known and removed the double moon phenomenon ceases to be. Duality is experienced due to ignorance or mind, and therefore the object of *advaita* as a philosophy is to clear the wrong knowledge or ignorance. *Advaita*, which means perfect knowledge of *Brahman*, does not materially affect anything because knowledge is not known to effect any change in the nature of reality. Knowledge does not create or alter or destroy anything. It can only remove wrong knowledge or ignorance, and enables one to see things as they are, whereas wrong knowledge or the absence of perfect knowledge of reality can distort the nature of reality, and present it as what it is not. The latter involves the active functioning of mind, which prevents one from seeing things as they are, as the mind projects its own construction or imagination on to the reality so that reality is not known in its true or objective nature.

As long as non-duality is not directly realised duality cannot be shown to be an illusion, even by hundreds of scriptures, and when *advaita* is realised directly duality on its own ceases to be true. This is a fact of realisation, and that is the real basis and justification for *advaita* to criticise and reject *dvaita*. Without direct realisation of *advaita* any amount of argumentation will be of no avail in refuting duality, which is also a matter of experience.

Duality, Mind and Māyā

If *Advaita* is objective and ontological duality needs explanation, as both cannot be true of the same reality. What Śaṅkara attempted in his writings is to show the ultimate unreality of duality by analysing the concept of duality, and tracing its ultimate source to *māyā*. Duality is equated with *māyā* or *māyā* is equated with duality as *māyā* is the explanation of duality. But *māyā* has no explanation as it also refers to an experience. We shall here discuss the nature of *māyā* mainly with a view to understanding the problem of duality. *Māyā* is the general explanation of duality while itself lacks any explanation. If *māyā* can be explained or if it is completely intelligible to man's understanding it ceases to be *māyā*, as *māyā* means or points to the limits of human understanding in relation to *Brahman*. While *advaita* does not pose any problem to those who have realised it directly, it is full of problems to those who want to understand it rationally. The statement that "*ātman* is known to those who think that it is not known, and unknown to those who think they know it", is of profound significance in this context.[38] Those who want to know it as an object of knowledge cannot know it, and is known to those who after realising the futility of attaining knowledge of it, in the ordinary sense of knowledge, turn their attention away from object-knowledge, and realise it for themselves by being it, which they are already, as *ātman* is that inner reality in man which cannot be known as an object (*viṣaya*).

Human failure to attain definite knowledge of *Brahman* or *ātman* may either end up in scepticism or nihilism. Or it may lead one to give up the search for truth or conceptual knowledge of reality. It is not easy to have faith in the authority and validity of scriptural knowledge, and man's quest to know the nature of reality is natural. And unless one realises the futility and impossibility of gaining definite knowledge of reality metaphysically one cannot turn one's attention away from metaphysical understanding of reality, and look for the knowledge of reality elsewhere. At the most, metaphysical understanding or enquiry can point to the possibility of *Brahman*'s existence as the ultimate ground and explanation of all that is, or to existence as such. But about its true nature, and the way it is related to the world of manifestation it cannot give us certain knowledge. Nevertheless, man has faith in his rational understanding, and its capacity to unravel the secrets of the world. Reason is nearer to man when compared to *Śruti*, as reasoning tries to understand the unknown, or what is not directly given to human knowledge on the basis of what is directly given or known. Although the object of *Śruti* is also to reveal the true nature of what is given and known to man empirically, it is not an extension of empirical knowledge, nor is it based on it, as it is in the case of reasoning. *Māyā* or *ajñāna* includes rational understanding of man also. *Māyā* as *ajñāna* is a cognitive activity of man, and stands for a kind of *prajñā* or knowledge (*prajñā vacano māyā śabdaḥ*).[39] Both knowledge and ignorance are the functions of the same, that is, human mind or intellect. *Ajñāna* is not the opposite of *jñāna*, as cognition is involved in both. Both are cognitions and reveal the reality. While the one reveals the nature of reality truly or objectively the other distorts the nature of reality while revealing it. Further, while knowledge is definite and beyond doubt, *ajñāna* leaves scope for doubt or is not free from doubt. While *jñāna* in relation to *Brahman* reveals *Brahman* perfectly or completely, *ajñāna* while revealing *Brahman* creates distinctions in it as it is not able to reveal *Brahman* in its fullness or in its all-comprehensive nature. Nevertheless, both reveal *Brahman*. There is a growth or development in man's knowledge of reality in which it grows to perfection and becomes more and more clear, definite and comprehensive, and each preceding knowledge though at that level appears to be true and objective is seen to be imperfect or incomplete or not completely objective, from the point of view of the succeeding state of knowledge. The various conceptions of *Brahman* found in the *Śruti* as well as those developed by different philosophers indicate growth in human understanding of reality. This is also due largely to individual differences or differences in the levels of human understanding in apprehending subtle things. One can grasp the truth and appreciate it when it is presented to him according to the level of his understanding. All may not have the same level of understanding as what one considers to be valid and meaningful someone else may consider to be invalid and meaningless. *Advaita* recognises the diferences in the levels of human understanding. In the course of man's growth in understanding he constantly overcomes his imperfect knowledge and understanding. What was once regarded as perfect knowledge may be later seen as imperfect knowledge. Thus in its growth knowledge tends to be more and more objective by overcoming subjective factors, and to that extent becomes more and more comprehensive in the sense that it sees reality not as fragmented by concepts but in its wholeness or fullness. In terms of his level of understanding and maturity man may conceive *Brahman* as *virāj*, Prajāpati, *puruṣa* ,etc., and understand their significance in relation to what is opposed to them. All these concepts aim at unifying human experience. But while they unify some phenomena they exclude some other phenomena. All these concepts are evolved to unify nature but differ in the levels of unity they achieve. In this process of seeing the unity of all that is the concept of *Īśvara* is more comprehensive, as the concept of *Īśvara* comprehends the whole creation as its ultimate source. Even if we admit that all these concepts are really about the same reality, though differing in their meaning and significance, as concepts they are distinguished or differentiated from one another, and to that extent they fail to represent the oneness of all that is. This is because of the very nature of human mind or intellect, and the manner of its functioning. Though in its range mind is all comprehending yet because of the manner of its operation through concepts it fails to see the unity underlying all the concepts, especially the unity of those that are opposed to each other. Though it tries to overcome the opposition among concepts by constructing more and more unifying concepts yet it cannot overcome certain basic differences, such as between the knower and the known, ruler and ruled, cause and effect which are its very basis, and without which it cannot operate. Mind as mind can operate only when something is given to it as an object of conception or understanding. And following its own categories like substance, attribute, cause and effect, without which it cannot function, it tries to understand and define the nature of reality in terms of these categories, and in doing so it determines the nature of reality. It cannot think or conceive a reality as devoid of these characteristics or a reality which transcends them. And also in its attempts to comprehend reality it tries to determine it by excluding something or some phenomena from the reality. Thus even the highest possible conception of *Brahman* like *sat*, *cit* and *ānanda* or *satyam*, *jñānam* and *anantam* excludes something from *Brahman*, that is, one who conceives *Brahman* as an object of thought excludes the reality of oneself from such conception. It is not possible for mind to overcome the difference between itself and the object of its conception or understanding, as mind cannot function in the absence of the difference between itself and the object of its understanding or conception. To negate this difference or transcend it so as to realise *Brahman* as non-dual is not possible for mind, as then it has to negate itself.

Ordinarily, man is pragmatic (*vyavahāra*) in his approach and understanding, and therefore may exclude from the conception of reality what is not significant to him pragmatically or existentially. Even the higher values of man like *mokṣa* are pragmatic, though in a higher sense. In being guided by the higher values, like *mokṣa*, in understanding the nature of reality or *Brahman* man tends to exclude from *Brahman* something like evil as man cannot see any value in evil. Śaṅkara often says that the ultimate object of *Vedānta* is *mokṣa*, but *mokṣa* is not a value to be pursued, though to an empirical understanding it is a value to be pursued and achieved. It is a fact as it is the same as *Brahman*. *Mokṣa* is regarded as a value from he standpoint of an individual, or from the standpoint of ignorance which is pragmatic. Scriptural knowledge is superior to empirical knowledge of man, but scriptural knowledge is also inferior to direct realisation of *Brahman*. Any knowledge which is based on the duality of knower and known is ignorance, and *Brahman* is realised directly when this difference is transcended. When *Brahman* is realised directly there remains no distinction between the one who realises and the object of realisation. It is *Brahman* without a second, and its nature is pure knowledge or *prajñā*. But in expressing such realisation in language we say that it is the realisation of someone as otherwise it cannot be expressed in language. This kind of talk which cannot be avoided as long as we want to communicate the nature of *Brahman* in language, is however meaningful and valid only in the state of ignorance in which one thinks of realising *Brahman* with the removal of ignorance. But in reality *Brahman* realises itself, which is redundant or meaningless, as *Brahman* is never without its self-realisation as it is pure knowledge or *prajñā*. Thus even if mind tries to overcome the duality of itself and its object it cannot do so as duality is the basis of its existence, and without it it ceases to be or will have no existence. Even when an enlightened mind cannot overcome duality in expressing non-duality, the ordinary mind which believes in the reality of duality cannot avoid it.

Mind and the ways of its functioning create the illusion of an individual self or *jīva* to which everything is given as an object of knowledge or understanding. It is the individual who imagines or conceives reality as an object characterised by certain qualities to the exclusion of some other. As long as mind is active, or the reality of the individual self is not seen as having no objective reality dualistic experience continues to be true and meaningful, and *Brahman* or non-duality is not realised. Non-duality as the very nature of reality is not realised directly so long as the mind is active, or the reality of the individual self is not seen as an illusion. And the moment non-duality is realised mind ceases to be along with the notion of an individual self. Therefore both duality and non-duality cannot be true at the same time, and non-duality cannot be known or conceived by man remaining within the sphere of duality. And to realise non-duality is to transcend mind and its projections, not in the sense of stilling the mind as in the case of Yoga, but by realising its oneness with *ātman* or its non-difference from *ātman*. It is only by believing in the existence of mind as something different from *ātman*, and by believing in its creations one believes in duality. Mind is a functional reality, and depending upon its various functions it is known variously as *citta*, *buddhi*, *manas*, etc., and when it has no function to perform there is no existence of mind or it simply ceases to be; and that state is *advaita*.

As Śaṅkara does not believe in the (Patañjali) Yogic concept of mind and its extinction through the practice of Yoga, the stillness of mind achieved in the state of *samādhi* is not the same as the realisation of non-duality. Since *advaita* follows the method of *jñāna* to realise *Brahman*, and its non-duality, it is not to stop literally the creativity of mind, which, according to Śaṅkara, is rather impossible like the stopping the waves of sea, but to see non-duality in all its creations. The differences it seemingly creates are not differences as they are not different from *ātman*. They are its spontaneous self-expression. When the mental creations are seen as pointing to duality or difference mind becomes a source of duality and bondage, but when one sees in all the creations of mind the spontaneous self-expression of *Brahman* or *ātman*, but as differentiated by name and form, one realises *advaita* without literally stopping the creations of mind. One need not reduce literally all the objects of clay to clay to realise their oneness in clay. So also the mind and its creations need not be stopped literally to realise non-duality. All that is differentiated in terms of concepts, or on the basis of name and form, which to a non-discriminating person mean duality, is really non-dual if one sees all as the self-expression of *Brahman* or as *Brahman*. Thus while mind and its creations, name and form, may create differences in reality to an unenlightened person, all that is is but a self-expression of *Brahman*, which as its nature, is not different from *Brahman* to a *brahma-jñānī*. The sun and sun-light are not two as one cannot be conceived and known without the other. It is only our manner of understanding and its expression in language which create the distinction between the sun and light, while in reality they are not two. Thus to overcome duality, which is not really there, or is not objective and ontological as ordinary people think, but nevertheless seems to be real because of mind and its functioning, by realising the non-difference between *Brahman* and all (*abhinna* or *ananya*) is *advaita*.

Māyā is ultimately identified by Śaṅkara with mind or even with sense-knowledge.[40] Mind exists as long as it functions or has scope for its activity, and ceases to be when it has no functions to perform. *Māyā* also means hypocrisy or inconsistency in one's behaviour and speech. It also means a sense of mystery. In the Vedic sense it stands for the dynamic wisdom or power of the deities whereby they manifest themselves variously. It refers to the activity of mind whereby the duality is created in terms of its conceptual activity. It creates differences and distinctions which are not really there or are not objective, and makes one believe in their reality. Instead of realising that all the concepts or forms express the same reality, without there being any change in the nature of reality, when the differences in forms of self-expression of *Brahman* are seen as different from *Brahman* duality is experienced. And *advaita* means the denial of such duality or differences as in reality there is non-difference between *Brahman* and its self-expression, or all that is. All that is is the nature or *svabhāva* of *Brahman*.

Finally, *advaita* as direct and immediate realisation of *Brahman* in which all that is, including the reality of oneself, is realised as non-different from *Brahman* refers to a state of supreme equality (*paramam sāmyam*) peace and bliss, which are different from what they mean in a dualistic framework. Ordinarily equality means equality in respect of certain qualities, or character, or essence, etc., but supreme equality that is *advaita* means the absolute oneness of all or the absence of difference.

References

1. *KaṭhaUp*, 2.1.11; *BṛUp*, 4.4.19.
2. *Ibid.*, 2.1.10.
3. *ChāUpBh*, 6.2.1.
4. *MāUpBh*, 3.
5. *ChāUp*, 6.2.3.
6. *MāUp*, 2-5.
7. *PrUpBh*, 6.2.
8. *SūBh*, 2.2.25.
9. *TaitUpBh*, 2.8.5.
10. *KaṭhaUpBh*, 2.1.3.
11. *SūBh*, 2.3.40.
12. *BṛUpBh*, 2.3.6.
13. *SūBh*, 2.3.29.
14. *Ibid.*, 3.2.22; *BṛUpBh*, 1.4.7.
15. *BṛUpBh*, 2.3.6.
16. *BGBh*, 13.13; *BṛUpBh*, 4.4.25; *MāKāBh*, 3.26.
17. *TaitUpBh*, 2.6.1.
18. *Ibid.*, 2.6.1.
19. *SūBh*, 1.2.7.
20. *BṛUpBh*, 2.4.12.
21. *SūBh*, 1.3.1. and Bhāmati on it.
22. *BṛUpBh*, 2.4.11.
23. *Ibid.*, 3.5.1.
24. *SūBh*, 4.1.4.

25. *Ibid.*, 4.1.4.
26. *BṛUpBh*, 3.5.1.
27. *SūBh*, 3.2.22; 2.2.31.
28. *Ibid.*, 2.2.31.
29. *MāUpBh*, 3 and 7; *TaitUpBh*, 2.5.1 introduction.
30. *TaitUpBh*, 2.6.1.
31. *BṛUpBh*, 1.4.10.
32. *AitUpBh*, 3.1.3.
33. *KaṭhaUpBh*, 1.12.16.
34. *BGBh*, 2.16.
35. *TaitUpBh*, 2.5.1.
36. *MāUpBh*, introduction.
37. *MāKāBh*, 3.26; *BṛUpBh*, 2.1.20.
38. *KenaUpBh*, 2.3.
39. *MāKāBh*, 3.24; *PrUpBh*, 1.16.
40. *KaṭhaUpBh*, 2.3.16; *KaṭhaUpBh*, 2.32; ***see also*** *Vivekacūḍāmaṇi* verses 169 and 180.

6

Advaita and Language

THE *Upaniṣads* are the primary source of *advaita*. It is mainly by way of interpreting the *Upaniṣads*, and the *Vedānta Sūtras* based on them Śaṅkara developed the philosophy of *Advaita*. And the same texts gave rise to different interpretations by different thinkers. In all this different interpreters have tried to understand and determine the meaning of the texts differently. It is not easy to decide which of the various interpretations is true to the texts interpreted, or represent the philosophy of the *Upaniṣads* as every interpretation claims to represent truly the philosophy of the *Upaniṣads*. In the case of ancient texts like the *Upaniṣads* we cannot compare the various interpretations with what may be regarded as the true or original meaning of the *Upaniṣads* as the true or original meaning of the *Upaniṣads* is again a matter of interpretation. And at the same time all the interpretations cannot be equally true of the *Upaniṣads*.

Scriptural Interpretation

How to interpret the *Upaniṣads* or how to understand and determine the meaning of the Upaniṣadic language? We are not going to discuss the various theories of meaning developed in the Indian tradition as that is not our concern in this chapter. Our object in this chapter is to understand whether *advaita* could be the true import of the *Upaniṣads*, and the various problems such an understanding gives rise to. Each interpreter of the *Upaniṣads* has faced such problems, and tried in his own characteristic manner to evolve the rules or guiding principles for interpreting the texts of the *Upaniṣads*. Their concern however with the language of the *Upaniṣads* is not just to formulate rules for interpreting the *Upaniṣads* but to justify ultimately their respective philosophical positions with regard to the *Upaniṣads*. And both are not unrelated, and the rules of interpretation are not completely arbitrary. When one grasps the meaning of the *Upaniṣads* as a whole, which involves more than understanding the language of the *Upaniṣads*, one tries to interpret the various texts and sentences of the *Upaniṣads* in the light of that meaning or vision. Such a meaning or vision is conveyed by the texts themselves, and therefore the texts are interpreted to justify or confirm the vision, or in accordance with the vision. As Śaṅkara puts it, the *Upaniṣad* primarily means the knowledge of the highest (*parā vidyā*) or *Brahman*-realisation, and since that is expressed through the language of the *Upaniṣads*, the assemblage of words (*śabda rāśi*) is also known commonly as *Upaniṣad*.[1] The language of the *Upaniṣads* tries to express *Brahman*-knowledge or realisation, and therefore in knowing the meaning of the *Upaniṣads* direct realisation of *Brahman* is of utmost significance. The sole purpose of all the *Upaniṣads* is to express in language *Brahman*-knowledge and make one realise it directly for oneself (*avagati niṣṭa*). All other things mentioned in the *Upaniṣads* have no independent purpose but to help in expressing or communicating *Brahman*-knowledge. As *Brahman*-knowledge is the sole object of all the *Upaniṣads* it constitutes the unity of their meaning which the various texts and sentences of the *Upaniṣads* try to express. They persuade man gently, like a friend, to realise the truth for himself, and as the purpose of the *Upaniṣads* is to help man to realise the truth directly for himself they take into consideration the varying levels or capacities of peoples' understanding in instructing them about the nature of *Brahman*. Thus though the *Upaniṣads* seem to talk of various things other than *Brahman* or *ātman*, like the theories of creation, their real purpose is to teach man the nature of *Brahman* or the oneness of all that is. This Śaṅkara tries to explain with the help of an example. The meaning of the statement 'one is going to cook food' is unitary though it involves various discrete acts like collecting firewood, buying provisions, etc., which can be expressed independently. One who wants to cook food collects firewood, buys provisions, etc., and each is an independent act by itself, and can be expressed independently like 'one is gathering firewood'. But the one who is doing all those things like gathering firewood, etc., sees the same purpose in all the discrete acts. In the process of cooking food each discrete act has its own meaning, which can be expressed independently, but that is not the meaning intended by the one who wants to cook food. He expresses all these discrete acts by the same sentence 'I am going to cook food' as for him the purpose or meaning of all the various discrete acts is the same, that is, to cook food.[2] And unless we know the purpose of all the discrete acts we will not be knowing the meaning of the various acts expressed independently.

The meaning of the *Upaniṣads* cannot therefore be arrived at by summating the meaning of various individual texts and sentences. It is not the case that while interpreting the *Upaniṣads* the meaning of each text or sentence is first determined and ascertained independently of other texts and sentences, and then all these meanings are summated to know the meaning of the *Upaniṣads*. The Upaniṣadic texts and sentences do not convey their meaning in isolation but in relation to other texts and sentences. The meaning of each text or sentence is to be understood and ascertained in the total context of the Upaniṣadic vision. The total meaning of the *Upaniṣads* helps in understanding the meaning of the individual texts and sentences, as the individual texts and sentences are the means of expressing or conveying the total or central meaning of the *Upaniṣads*. Thus each interpreter in understanding or arriving at the meaning of each text or sentence refers constantly to other texts and sentences as all of them are integrally related to each other in revealing their meaning. There is unity of meaning in all the *Upaniṣads*, and different interpreters have tried to grasp and establish that meaning. Through various examples, analogies and stories, and through various dialogues and arguments the *Upaniṣads* seek to express the same truth, that is, the oneness of all that is there. However, the meaning of the *Upaniṣads* cannot be ascertained and known apart from the various texts and sentences, but when once it is grasped it helps in discerning the meaning of the individual texts and sentences. In knowing the meaning of the *Upaniṣads* some of the sentences may be of crucial importance, but nevertheless the texts and sentences can convey the meaning of the *Upaniṣads* in unison. But different interpreters have tried to point out to certain passages in refuting other interpretations. This is true with all the interpreters. But the point we want to emphasise here is that an interpretation gains its validity and meaningfulness not on the basis of anyone sentence or text in isolation. If a particular interpretation is meaningful it helps in understanding the meaning of the individual texts and sentences, but not the other way round. Most of the interpreters of the *Upaniṣads*, who are opposed to Śaṅkara's interpretation of them, point out to some of the Upaniṣadic passages which according to them cannot go with Śaṅkara's interpretation. But they forget that the same is the case with their interpretations also. It is the total meaning or vision of the Upaniṣads, which is conveyed or expressed by means of all the texts and sentences in unison, and when it is grasped it helps one in discerning the meaning of the individual texts and sentences, though each text or sentence may seem to have its own meaning.

All this is meaningful as the object of the Upaniṣadic knowledge is not something that is unknown to man otherwise. The *Śruti* in revealing the nature of *Brahman* does not point to something completely unknown to man but to the true or objective nature of one's own reality which is not unknown to anyone. Therefore perfect knowledge of one's own reality gained with the help of *Śruti* will help one in knowing the true meaning of the *Upaniṣads*. On the other hand, if *Śruti* is the only source of knowledge of the reality it speaks about our attitude to *Śruti* would be completely different. The *Śruti* itself admits *anubhava* or direct realisation of *Brahman* or *ātman* as a source of knowledge of *Brahman*. The parable of one who lost his way to his own place is significant in this context. One who has lost his way to his own place can be guided by others as he can know and judge for himself whether he is being guided rightly or wrongly as he knows the place. Therefore in interpreting the *Śruti* one need not depend entirely on the words of *Śruti* in knowing the meaning of *Śruti*. One's own direct realisation of truth is highly valuable in discerning the meaning of the *Upaniṣads*. We have already discussed the problem of validity or objectivity of experience in the previous chapter.

Meaning of Upaniṣads

The differences in understanding the meaning of the *Upaniṣads* by different people are largely due to differences in the levels of their understanding and realisation. The same text may be understood differently by different people according to the level of their understanding, and for which the text is not responsible. For instance, those who are given to sensuous ways of understanding, and are attached to sense-knowledge and accept the reality that is known through the senses only may not recognise the *Upaniṣads* as having any truth or significance. In other words, those who do not see the validity of *Brahman* realisation as the highest possible state of man's realisation may not see anything significant and meaningful in the *Upaniṣads*. They may interpret the *Upaniṣads* differently or in a naturalistic way. Even those who recognise the authority of the *Upaniṣads* may understand the meaning of the *Upaniṣads* according to the varying levels or capacities of their understanding (*vijñāna kauśala tāratamya bheda*). As what *Śruti* teaches is not self-evident to all — and if it is self-evident then there is no need for *Śruti* — the role of man's understanding in interpreting *Śruti* cannot be denied. The understanding of the meaning of a text or language is in accordance with the quality and purity of one's understanding (*svacitta guṇadoṣa vasādevahi śabdārtha avadhāraṇam*).[3] According to Śaṅkara even the Śruti recognises the reality of human differences in understanding the nature of *Brahman*, and accordingly adjusts or arranges its teaching to help people with different levels of understanding.

Does this mean that the *Upaniṣads* have no definite meaning which can be universally valid? If the meaning of the *Upaniṣads* is purely a matter of interpretation, and if people differ in their capacities to understand subtle things the meaning of truth will be unstable (*avyavasthā*), or it will have no definable meaning or essence. If the truth of the *Upaniṣads* or the meaning of the Upaniṣadic language is purely a matter of individual's interpretation then any enquiry into the nature of the truth of the *Upaniṣads* will be futile. And at the same time what is not really intelligible and valid to one's own understanding is not really significant and helpful to him. In that case truth is either subjective and relativistic or there is no objectively valid truth at all. If the truth is subjective, or is a matter of one's understanding no one can help the other, and the *Śruti* will have no authority in revealing the truth.

If the *Upaniṣads* are a source of knowledge of what is objectively existing that knowledge should be the same to all, or its validity should be universal. The language of the *Upaniṣads* cannot have more than one meaning, but how to arrive at that meaning? In knowing the meaning of the *Upaniṣads*, besides direct realisation or *anubhava*, reasoning is also important. Though reasoning on its own cannot give us definite knowledge of *Brahman* as people who base their understanding of the nature of *Brahman* on reason alone differ significantly among themselves, for there are different and mutually opposed rational systems of metaphysics, like *Sāṁkhya* and *Vaiśeṣika*. Nevertheless, it can help or guide us in discriminating the right meaning of the *Śruti* texts and sentences. Though reason on its own cannot help us in attaining definite knowledge of *Brahman*, being guided by or based on experience or *Śruti*, as ultimately *Śruti* stands for experience in transcendental matters, reason can help us in knowing the right meaning of *Śruti*. Thus we find in all the writings of Śaṅkara the use of reason in discerning the right meaning of the *Upaniṣads*, and in harmoniously reconciling the apparently conflicting and even contradictory statements of the *Upaniṣads*. This is what we tried to do in the previous chapters. Thus the principle of context, direct realisation of *Brahman* or tradition, as tradition stands for the wisdom of those who had directly realised *Brahman*, and reason are of great help, or are the guiding principles in understanding and determining the meaning of the *Upaniṣads*. Tradition is often used to refer to those who had realised *Brahman* directly (*brahmavidāh*). All the three are resorted to by Śaṅkara in interpreting the *Śruti* texts. While the principle of context helps us in determining the relative significance and authority of the various statements, and in comprehending the unity of meaning of the *Upaniṣads*, reason helps us in knowing what the *Śruti* statements cannot mean, and also in reconciling the apparent conflict among the various *Śruti* statements. For instance, different sentences may mean different things in isolation but their true import is discerned in the light of the context of the total Upaniṣadic meaning or vision. Basing on this principle we can know whether a sentence is to be understood literally or metaphorically. And reason, for instance, can tell us what a statement like 'I am *Brahman*' cannot mean though apparently it may mean something. The statement 'I am *Brahman*' cannot be true literally or in its direct sense as what is connoted by the term 'I' is completely different from and is even opposed to the connotation of the word *Brahman*. If there is to be identity between the two it cannot be at the surface or direct level.

Ultimately it is direct realisation of *Brahman* or *anubhava*, which is not only the culmination of our understanding of the *Upaniṣads* but also the chief object of the *Upaniṣads*, that reveals the true meaning of the *Upaniṣads*. The enquiry into the nature of *Brahman* comes to a fruitful end or is fulfilled supremely in realising *Brahman* directly, and that is the real or intended purpose and meaning of the *Upaniṣads*.

The main concern of Śaṅkara in interpreting the *Vedānta* texts is to show that *Advaita* is the true meaning of the texts. And our attempt in the previous chapters was to show the meaningfulness and intelligibility of the concept of *advaita* though it is not completely comprehensible to man's rational or empirical understanding. Now we face certain problems in accepting *advaita* as the true meaning of the *Upaniṣads*. If *advaita* is free from all distinctions and differences or duality how in the first place it could be expressed in language, or how could it be the object or import of language? Several mystics have felt the difficulty of expressing their experiences in language as the nature of experience, or its object is so profound and dissimilar to the empirical experience the ordinary language fails to express the mystic experience adequately and meaningfully. It is mainly due to the very structure of language and its limitations a mystic finds it difficult to express his experience in language, but the basic requirement of expressing anything in language, that is, the distinction between the experiencer and the experienced or the speaker and the spoken is present in all the mystical experiences. But the object of mystic experience is so profound and majestic that the language in its ordinary form is not adequate to express it. Therefore the mystics often resort to analogical or symbolic mode of expression. But *advaita* as an experience or realisation, though we name it as experience or realisation, transcends the duality of subject and object, or the speaker and the spoken. It is therefore logically not possible to describe *advaita* or to express it in language. *Advaita* is not basically an object of experience or realisation, and it is only that which is an object of knowledge or experience that can be expressed in language or communicated through some other means. In knowing or experiencing something we know it or experience it as having certain qualities or functions or as belonging to a class of objects, and on that basis we not only distinguish it from other objects of knowledge and experience but we can also say something about it significantly. To be meaningful we have to say something about the object of knowledge or experience.

I am Brahman

The basic reason why there can be no description of *advaita* in language is that it is not an object of knowledge or experience as it is to realise the true or objective nature of *ātman* which is one's own inner reality; and one's own nature cannot be an object of knowledge or experience. Since one cannot be without one's nature there is no meaning in saying that one experience it or knows it. It is known but in a way different from the way the objects are known. Though in language we say that a boy has attained his adulthood the attainment is not something new. Or when we say that fire burns we are not saying anything significant about fire as fire is burning. Similarly in realising as it were one's own true nature, which is not something to be attained or shunned, one is not attaining anything that is not already attained, or one is not realising or experiencing anything that is not already realised or experienced. The parable of the prince brought up by a hunter is significant in this context.[4] A prince was brought up by a hunter, and therefore he identified himself as a hunter. But when he was told that he was not a hunter but a prince, and realised his true identity there is no positive gain as in reality he was never a hunter. The realisation that he is a prince but not a hunter is however meaningful negatively in that he gives up his wrong identity. In realising that he is a prince he has not gained or attained anything positively as he is in reality a prince.

Similarly in realising *advaita* or *Brahman* which is objectively or ontologically real, and is the same as the true nature of oneself nothing that is not already known or attained is known or attained. *Advaita* is not something that is to be known or realised as if it is something other than oneself. As it means the realisation of one's own true nature it does not involve knowing or realising something other than oneself. And if *advaita* is the realisation of one's own true nature, which is never unattained or unrealised, and if it is to be attained it cannot be one's own true nature, there is no meaning in saying that it is realised or experienced. To say therefore that the realisation of one's own true nature means to be oneself in its true nature is superfluous. It does not say anything as one is never without one's true nature. Thus knowing *Brahman* by being *Brahman* does not mean that *Brahman* is something other than one's own true nature, and one has to be that. It is to realise that *Brahman* is no other than the true nature of oneself. Such realisation does not involve subject-object duality. It is not an object of realisation on the part of someone, and what is not an object of realisation or experience cannot also be the object of description. But we may say that one can describe one's true nature after its realisation. This would be possible and meaningful only if one's true nature is the object of one's knowledge or experience. If one knows oneself as *Brahman* as one can know oneself as this or that in which case one knows something about oneself it can be described and communicated. But the statement expressing the realisation of *Brahman* as 'I am *Brahman*' does not mean one knowing oneself as *Brahman* which is impossible as 'I' cannot be identified with *Brahman*. Can we say then that one knows oneself to be *Brahman* means what one knows or thinks of oneself to be, as one can say that one is such and such. But the 'I' in the statement 'I am *Brahman*' does not mean the individual or subject who realises himself to be *Brahman* but the state of undifferentiated consciousness which we may name *Brahman*. The state of realisation in which the consciousness of oneself as distinct from the consciousness of *Brahman* is absent does not or cannot mean the consciousness of someone as being *Brahman*. But when such realisation is to be expressed in language one has to say following the convention of using language that one is *Brahman* as if they are two things, as otherwise it cannot be expressed in language. This cannot be avoided as otherwise language cannot express it. In the realisation of *advaita* there is no consciousness of either I or of *Brahman*, but the statement 'I am *Brahman*' is meaningful not as directly referring to the state of realisation but from the point of view of non-realisation or ignorance. It conveys its meaning by negating the duality of I and *Brahman*, or by denying the idea that *Brahman* is something other than one's own true nature, or is an object of one's search and realisation. It also negates the idea that the reality commonly expressed by the word I is the true nature of oneself. Thus if the true or intended meaning of the statement 'I am *Brahman*' is to deny the reality of both I and *Brahman* it cannot mean what it apparently means, that is, the relation of identity between I and *Brahman*. The idea of *Brahman* with all that it means, and which is an object of enquiry and knowledge on the part of someone is transcended in realising *advaita*. Similarly the idea of I in the sense of a subject or knower is also transcended in realising *advaita*. And what transcends the notions of I and *Brahman* cannot be expressed in terms of I and *Brahman*, and their relation. But if such realisation is to be presented in language one has to use the terms of I and *Brahman* as the context of making the statement 'I am *Brahman*' is empirical knowledge or ignorance in which one thinks one is different from *Brahman*, and *Brahman* is something other than oneself. And independently of the context of ignorance the statement has no meaning as its meaning consists in denying the reality of both I and *Brahman*. Let us consider the parable of hunter-prince. Before his realisation that he is a prince he knows himself as a hunter, and after realisation he knows himself as a prince. Thus at no time he is conscious of himself as both hunter and prince. If a hunter being a hunter knows himself as a prince he can say 'I am a prince' in which 'I' stands for his hunter identity and prince for his assumed identity. But when the prince after realisation of his true identity asserts that he is a prince its meaning lies in what it implicitly denies or negates, namely, that he is not a hunter which he thought himself to be. On the other hand, a prince who has never lost his identity as prince will have no context to assert that he is prince, and even if he asserts it says nothing. It will be superfluous.

Similarly if one asserts that one is *Brahman* by retaining his individual identity, which is conveyed by the term 'I', the statement cannot be true and meaningful as one having the qualities and characteristics of 'I' cannot be *Brahman*. And when the I consciousness is transcended in realising *advaita* there is no question of 'I' being identified with *Brahman*. Then there would be neither the consciousness of 'I' nor of '*Brahman*', and that is *advaita*. And if such state of realisation is to be expressed in language as 'I am *Brahman*' the meaning of the statement does not consist in asserting any kind of relation between 'I' and '*Brahman*' but to show that both 'I' and '*Brahman*', which we ordinarily accept as real, are not there in reality. However, as the realisation is significant in the context of one's previous state of non-realisation or ignorance the statement 'I am *Brahman*' gains its meaning by denying the duality of I and *Brahman* which amounts to saying that both are unreal in relation to *Advaita*. Thus as *advaita* is taught in the context of duality or ignorance, as otherwise there is no need to teach it, the meaning of the statements expressing *advaita* consists in what they deny or negate. Any positive assertion cannot be true of *advaita* as it involves the duality of one who asserts and the reality asserted, and without this distinction language cannot function. But then the denial is as meaningful as assertion as both are context bound. *Advaita* cannot be expressed in language without observing the rules of language in which nothing can be said in a sentence form without a subject and an object. For instance, when we want to express in language the fact that Rāhu (planet) is head only, or a stone statue is body only we say following the conventions of using language 'Rāhu's head' or 'the body of a statue'.

All is Brahman

Similarly the meaning of the other statement expressing *advaita* 'all is *Brahman*' is to be understood. There is no 'all' different from *Brahman* so that both can be identified. If we admit the reality of all as something different from *Brahman*, and try to relate them we will be landing ourselves in contradictions. This was discussed fully in the previous chapter. In fact or ontologically there is no 'all' which is other than or different from *Brahman*, and *Brahman* is not a reality which is other than and different from the world or 'all'. *Brahman* is all that is, and the differences which we empirically experience and believe to be real are not ontologically real as everything is *Brahman* and its self-expression. How to express this in language? If *Brahman* is all that is nothing can be attributed to *Brahman*, and *Brahman* cannot be distinguished from anything else. Since the statement 'all is *Brahman*' is not a statement of identity no relation of any kind is asserted in the statement. There are no two realities of 'all' and '*Brahman*' which are identified or otherwise related in the statement 'all is *Brahman*'. At the same time we cannot say that the terms 'all' and '*Brahman*' refer to the same reality though it cannot be termed either as 'all' or as '*Brahman*'. In a similar statement, like 'this is that Devadatta', though there are no two persons referred to by 'this' and 'that' yet the same person 'Devadatta' is qualified by two different contexts. The Devadatta who was seen long ago is the same person who is seen now. Can we say likewise that what was seen as world during empirical experience is seen as *Brahman* in the state of *advaita* or *Brahman* realisation? Here we admit that in both the contexts only one reality, either the world or *Brahman*, is experienced. Or if we consider the familiar example of rope-snake we say that what was seen as snake is objectively rope. Can we say that the illusory snake is identical with the real rope? We cannot do this as at the time of asserting their identity only one reality, that is, rope is objectively there, and the snake exists only in one's memory. Both are not perceived together or both do not exist at the same time. They are not real in the same sense. Even otherwise there can be no identity between a snake and a rope. However, the statement is significant psychologically as one sees the illusory nature of snake, and there can be no identity between what is illusory and what is objectively real.

In both the analogies of Devadatta and rope-snake both are experiences of someone or both are objects of knowledge of someone, whereas *advaita* is not the object of realisation of someone as in realising *advaita* the notion or sense of 'I' is also transcended. On the other hand, if the knower or experiencer persists in both the experiences he can think of and assert any kind of relation between them. We cannot therefore say that the one who had seen world sees it later as *Brahman*. Furthermore, one who sees the world sees the world only, and never thinks that he is seeing *Brahman* as world, and when *Brahman* realisation takes place there is no world consciousness. On the other hand, if the 'I' to which the world is given as an object of experience persists in *Brahman* realisation he can assert any kind of relation between the world and *Brahman*. But in realising *advaita* the notion of I is transcended, and therefore we cannot say that the statement 'all is *Brahman*' expresses the wisdom of someone. *Advaita* which transcends all the terms and concepts like 'I', *Brahman*' and 'all' cannot be expressed in terms of any terms and concepts, and their relation. But that is how we can talk of it as otherwise no expression of it is possible in language. All the analogies and examples are meaningful and relevant in the context of empirical experience of duality, and when *advaita* is presented in language, which cannot function without the distinction of knower and knower or the speaker and spoken to be communicative and meaningful, it ends up in distorting the meaning of *advaita.*

The statements 'I am *Brahman*' and 'all is *Brahman*' refer to the same state of realisation. But the language which expresses it gives rise to the idea that it is the realisation of someone and is about something. To prevent such misunderstanding the nature of realisation is expressed in two different ways. For instance, when it is said in the *Upaniṣads*, 'where one sees nothing' the use of the words 'where' and 'sees' may make one think of *Brahman* in spatial terms, and also that one has to see it.[5] To prevent such wrong understanding that *Brahman* is something out there it is said 'I am *Brahman*' or 'you are That'. But the statement 'I am *Brahman*' may equally give rise to the wrong understanding that *Brahman* is one's own self only, and to obviate the possibility of such wrong understanding it is said that *Brahman* is all. Therefore the true import of all the statements is to show that what is there is one only without a second, and such knowledge or realisation cannot be the object of someone's knowledge as it is the true nature of one who wants to know it.

Can such knowledge or realisation be expressed positively in language? Language in its ordinary sense or use is suited to express a thing which is having certain qualities or functions, and which can be distinguished in terms of those qualities and functions from other things. In other words, whatever that can be known or thought of in terms of the categories of class, quality and function can also be expressed in language. And more basically something can be said in language when the distinction between the speaker and spoken is available. Just as seeing or the capacity to see cannot be an object of sight, thinking an object of thought and knowing an object of knowledge the very capacity to express in language cannot be expressed in language. Secondly if all that is is one only without a second the language based on distinctions and differences cannot express it. For instance, the assertion that something is real is possible and meaningful only if we can distinguish it from what is unreal, and if there is nothing that is unreal there is no point in saying that something is real. This is the case with the meaning of the word truth also. Likewise all the words which are meant to describe a thing either independently or as distinguished from other things in terms of a quality or function can convey a thing which is differentiated by other things. But this is not the case with *advaita*. For example, it is meaningful to say that one goes from one place to another as there are different places on earth. But if there is nothing but earth without different places it would not be meaningful to say that one goes from place to place.

Now we cannot say that the all is in any way related to *Brahman* as we have shown in the previous chapter that all is the nature of *Brahman*, and *Brahman* cannot be differentiated from its own nature and then related. And the nature of a thing is not something that can qualify a thing or be its attribute so that both can be related in any way. Therefore to say that all is *Brahman* is to say that *Brahman* is the only reality. And about such reality, which is devoid of all differences, either internal or external, any characterisation is meaningless.

We now try to discuss the relation of language to *advaita* in a different way. Supposing that the world or all is the self-expression or nature of *Brahman*, and is therefore not something different from *Brahman* cannot we express it in language and say that 'all is *Brahman*'. 'All' is a term with no determinable meaning as the meaning of all cannot be determined in terms of enumerating all that was and all that is. For instance, when one says to his wife to cook all the rice it means all the rice available in the house but not all the rice available in the world. Even then 'all' cannot include all the rice that is going to be. Thus the meaning of all is in relation to the context of its use though it appears to include all. If we consider in this context the self and its varied expressions the problem is easy to comprehend. We may say that the self is all its expressions expressed so far as well as those that are yet to be expressed as the possibility of its future expressions is always there. Can we then identify the self with any of its expressions? As the self means all the expressions that are already expressed, and the possibility of future expressions it is more than or transcends all its expressions at any time. It cannot therefore be identified with any of its expressions as if the self is the sum total of its expressions, for the possibility of expressing itself in newer and newer forms, which cannot be anticipated, is always there. That means, the self is all its expressions and yet is something more than them. How to express this in language? All the expressions expressed at any given time is self, and yet the self is more than or transcends all its expressions, and at the same time the expressions are not different from the self as they express its nature. They are self, and yet self is more than all its expressions. Therefore we cannot say that the expressions describe the self. However, they point to self instead of describing it. Similarly all the names and forms which constitute the world or all point to *Brahman* as the source of their expression but do not describe *Brahman*. Only *Brahman* can know all the forms of its possible expression as they constitute its nature which is infinite. Similarly all the conceptions of *Brahman* point to it without making it their object. In this sense even the concepts like *ātman*, *Brahman*, truth, oneness, infinite, etc., can only point to reality without making it an object of their meaning.

Language as Revelation of Brahman

We now discuss the nature of language as revelation of *Brahman*, or language in its revelatory function. As *prajñā* or knowledge, which is the nature of *ātman*, is also the revelation of *ātman* (*prajñapti prakāśa svarūpa*), language (*vāk*) which is co-extensive with knowledge or *prajñā* is the very expression of *Brahman* or *ātman*. The Upaniṣadic language is not about

Brahman or does not represent *Brahman* as its object but is the very expression or revelation of *Brahman*.

Vāk, which is wider in its meaning than language, can ordinarily mean either the organ of speech or the letters arranged in an order to form a word which is intended to mean or designate a thing, or a quality, or a function, or a class.[6] However, in relation to *advaita* the language of *Śruti* is revelatory in its function. The language of *Śruti* is not meant to designate or represent *Brahman*, but is the revelation of *Brahman*. *Vāk* is identified with the *rasa* or essence of reality (*vāgvai puruṣo rasaḥ*) in the *Veda*.[7] As the abode of speech (*āyatanam*) the *Vedas* are the essence of reality because they have issued forth out of the worlds, or they are the truth of the world.[8] Ordinarily language refers to something other than itself, or it represents reality. But in the case of Vedic speech it is an expression of the state of realisation or *Brahman*. Does it not then represent the state of realisation? Though in a sense it does represent the state of realisation in a deeper sense it is the self-expression of truth in the sense that it is a spontaneous outflow or revelation of the state of realisation. Raising a problem whether the realised person is bound by the *Veda*, Śaṅkara says that he is not bound by the *Veda* as it emanates from him, and no one is bound by his own wisdom which is his nature.[9] Since the state of realisation or being *Brahman* does not have an object the language that expresses it is not the expression of something by someone. Since in the case of *advaita* language does not serve the function of representing something by someone, as it is a spontaneous outflow or expression of the non-dualistic state of realisation, the object of Vedic speech is not to reveal something other than itself. Speech reveals itself through itself. In this sense the Vedic statement that *Brahman* is speech itself (*vāgvai brahman*) is significant.[10] Here speech means what is expressed as well as the expression. And since *Brahman* is not different from its self-expression speech is not different from *Brahman*. Just as knowing is not an object of knowledge, but because of which all knowledge is possible, and at the same time it is revealed in and through all knowledge or as consciousness is not an object of knowledge but is revealed by all knowledge, *Brahman*, the source of all speech, is not the object of speech but is nevertheless revealed by all speech. *Brahman* is not that which is expressed by speech but because of which speech is expressed or uttered (*yat vācānabhyuditam yena vāk abhyuditam*).[11] Therefore the function of Vedic knowledge and language is not to reveal *Brahman* as their object but as that which is being revealed and expressed in and through all knowledge and language. Unlike the function or use of language in the empirical context to represent something, the Vedic language serves its purpose by directing the hearer's attention to *Brahman* or *ātman* which is the true nature of one's own reality without referring to it as an object of itself. It is the nature of light of consciousness (*vāk caitanya jyoti mātra svarūpa*).[12] It has consciousness as its existence or essence (*caitanya mātra sattākam*) and is able to reveal by the light of consciousness (*caitanya jyotiṣā prakāśate*).[13] Consciousness illumines language, and language helps in revealing consciousness. Thus the extension of *Brahman* is the extension of language, or one is co-extensive with the other.

Brahman and Speech

The primary form of manifestation of *Brahman* is speech, or the world consisting of name and form which as the nature of *Brahman* is not ultimately different from *Brahman*. The Vedic classification of language into *parā*, *paśyanti*, *madhyamā* and *vaikhari* in which the *parā* state is identified with reality is highly significant in this context. If *Brahman* is pure spirit or consciousness it does not require or depend on another reality for its revelation as it is eternally self-revealing by its very nature, and that self-revelatory nature of *Brahman* or the revelation of *Brahman*, which is its nature, is language or *vāk*. It is not therefore different from the reality which it reveals as it is the self-revelation of reality. However, when the revelation of reality which is spontaneous and natural is sought to be expressed in terms of ordinary use of language the *Veda* is born. Thus the primary function of language in relation to *advaita* is to reveal the nature of reality which it does by revealing itself. It reveals the reality which is embodied or embedded in itself while revealing itself. It is therefore said that in the case of Vedic speech the meaning follows language instead of language following the meaning as in the case of ordinary use of language.[14] In other words, the meaning of the Vedic speech is intrinsic to Vedic speech. And the *Veda* as the self-revelation of reality, clothed in a form of language, is as eternal as reality, and impersonal. *Veda* is not the knowledge or wisdom of someone but the revealation of reality which is its nature. This type of understanding of language gave rise to *śabda-advaita* school of philosophy in which the word or speech is identified with *Brahman*. In its capacity to express or reveal reality language is free from the distinction between name and named. Language itself is the revelation of *Brahman*, and therefore it is by understanding the meaning of language (*śabdārtha vicāra*) one knows *Brahman*, the source of its expression.

But when we try to understand the meaning of *Śruti* language in the way we understand the meaning of ordinary language, which is mostly representative, we fail to understand the meaning of Vedic language. The ordinary language is based on differences and distinctions, and can operate only when they are admitted. At times it itself is the source of creating the illusion of difference as in the examples cited already, like the sun and light and gem and its lusture. While the differences are accepted as ultimately or ontologically real by others, *advaita* admits their reality only for the practical purpose of teaching non-duality. There is no non-*ātman* or anything other than *ātman* or *Brahman* in reality, as all that is is *Brahman*, but to teach it some differences are to be superimposed on it so that instruction about it is possible. But what was superimposed initially for the purpose of instruction or as a means to teach *advaita* is ultimately negated to make one realise the non-dual nature of *Brahman*, or when *Brahman* is realised directly what was negated as other than *Brahman* is seen as not-different from *Brahman*. *Śruti* itself superimposes certain qualities on *Brahman*, and thus distinguishes *Brahman* from what is not-*Brahman* for the purpose of imparting knowledge about *Brahman*, as otherwise no instruction is possible. It teaches people according to the levels of their understanding and maturity; it does not teach *advaita* as soon as one is born. Thus the context of teaching *advaita* is duality, and therefore *Śruti* has to teach *advaita* by taking into consideration the dualistic ways of thinking and understanding of people. While *advaita* admits duality only as a means to teach *advaita* ordinary peoples' belief in it is due to ignorance, and *advaita* is required to be taught for them only. Therefore the object of *advaita* as a philosophy, or *Śruti* as an assemblage of words is not to describe *Brahman* or *advaita* but with the help of the ordinary or dualistic mode of thinking and language to help one to see the unreality of duality, and realise *advaita*. It is to direct one's attention to the fact of *advaita* but not to represent it either in knowledge or in language.[15] On the other hand, if we understand the meaning of the Upaniṣadic language as describing reality we miss its real intention. What is asserted and what is denied in the *Upaniṣads* are meaningful only as a methodological device or means to teach *advaita*. But if they are taken to be real, as that is the apparent meaning of *Śruti*, not only one fails to understand the true meaning of *Śruti* but also distorts its meaning. When the realisation dawns, which is the real object of *Śruti*, one sees the unreality of all the distinctions like *Śruti*, *Brahman* and oneself, and then *Śruti* dissolves itself along with ignorance which it removes.

References

1. *MuUpBh*, 1.1.5.
2. *MāKāBh*, 3.14.
3. *ChāUpBh*, 8.9.2.

4. *BṛUpBh*,2.1.20.
5. *ChāUpBh*, 7.24.1.
6. *KenaUpBh*, 1.5.
7. *ChāUpBh*, 1.1.2.
8. *Ibid.*, 3.5.4.
9. *AitUpBh*, chapter I introduction; **see also** *TaitUpBh*, 2.3.1.
10. *BṛUpBh*, 1.3.21.
11. *KenaUp*, 1.5.
12. *Ibid.*, 1.5.
13. *Ibid.*, 1.5.
14. *laukikānām hi sādhunām vāg artham anudhāvati*
    ṛṣinām punar ādyānām vācam artho anudhāvati.

    — *Bhavabhuti in Uttararāmacaritram.*
15. *SūBh*, 3.2.21. "What then, it may be asked, is the meaning of those Vedic passages which speak of the highest *Brahman* as something to be seen, to he heard, and so on? They aim, we reply, not at enjoying the knowledge of truth, but merely at directing our attention to it. Similarly in ordinary life imperative phrases such as 'listen to this!' 'look at this!' are frequently meant to express not that we are immediately to cognise this or that, but only that we are to direct our attention to it. Even when a person is face to face with some object of knowledge, knowledge may either arise or not; all that another person wishing to inform him about the object can do is to point it out to him."

Bibliography

Primary Sources (Sanskrit)

Śaṅkara, *Brahmasūtra Bhāṣya*, V. Ramaswamy Sastrulu & Sons, Madras, 1937.

——, *Upaniṣad Bhāṣya; Ten Principal Upaniṣads with Śaṅkara Bhāṣya*, Motilal Banarsidass, Delhi, 1964.

——, *Bhagavadgītā Bhāṣya*, V. Ramaswamy Sastrulu & Sons, Madras, 1953.

Ṛg-veda Saṁhitā with the commentary of Sāyaṇācārya, five volumes, Vaidika Samsodhana Mandala, Poona, 1946.

Translations

Śaṅkara, *Bhagavadgītā Bhāṣya*, Tr. by A. Mahadevasastry, V. Ramaswamy Sastrulu & Sons, Madras, 1961.

——, *Bṛhadāraṇyaka Upaniṣad Bhāṣya*, Tr. by Swāmī Mādhavānanda, Advaita Ashrama, Mayavati, Almora, Himalayas, 1950.

——. *Eight Upaniṣads with* commentary of Śaṅkara, Tr. by Swāmī Gambhīrānanda, Vol.I (1957) & Vol.II (1958) Advaita Ashrama, Calcutta, 1957-58.

——, *Chāndogya Upaniṣad* with Śaṅkara's commentary, Tr. by Swāmī Gambhīrānanda, Advaita Ashrama. 5 Delhi Entally Road, Calcutta.

———, *Sūtra Bhāṣya*, Tr. by George Thibaut, Motilal Banarsidass, Delhi, in two Vols. 1962.

Glossary

advaita — Non-dualistic interpretation of *Vedānta.*

antarātmā — Inward reality or self of a person.

antaryāmī — Internal ruler. *Ātman* which rules or regulates all by being within all.

ātman — Self, essence and inner reality and unity of all that is.

ādhyātmika — Relating to man's inward life.

adhyātma yoga — Method of knowing *ātman* or *Brahman* through an analysis and understanding of man's inner reality.

ādhibhautika — Relating to the realm of physical nature or phenomenal world.

ādhidaivika — Relating to the realm of deities.

aparokṣa — That which is known or experienced directly or immediately which is meaningful in relation to *ātman* or *Brahman* only.

avidyā or *ajñāna* — Absence of perfect or objective knowledge.

Aśvins — Divine physicians.

Brahmā — In the *Veda* it means devotion or its expression in the form of a hymn, and is

	due to divine inspiration.
Brahman	Literally means that which is great or that which grows. Upaniṣadic term for ultimate reality.
brahmānubhava	Direct and immediate experience or realisation of *Brahman*, the culmination of *Vedānta* philosophy. It is synonymous with *turīya* and *moksa*.
citta	Psyche of which mind and intellect are functionnal names.
devaḥ	Deity.
dvaita	Dualistic interpretation of *Vedānta* in which the reality of differences is accepted.
hṛdaya	Heart, the seat of human emotions and feelings, and also the seat of faith and devotion.
Indra	A principal Vedic deity primarily representing divine power.
Īśvara	Qualified form of *Brahman* or *Brahman* conceived as the creator and Lord of the universe.
kalpanā	Mental construction and hence lacking objective reality.
kavi	A poet; in the *Veda* it means the one who sees the richness and creativity involved in the process of world creation; and when applied to a deity it means the creative wisdom of the deity.
kāvya	The creation of a poet. The whole creation

	is a *kāvya* of God or an expression of His creativity.
laukika	Mundane. Pertaining to the empirical world.
māyā	Mystery, a kind of knowledge or wisdom, that which is both real and unreal.
Prajāpati	Lord of creation but not the ultimate reality.
pralaya	Final dissolution of the world.
prajñā	Wisdom, consciousness, intelligence.
prajñapti	Consciousness.
pāramārthika	What is completely objective and universal.
puruṣa	Person; ultimate reality conceived as personal.
rasa	*Brahman*'s creativity and its expression.
ṛṣi	Seer or one who sees the divine unity amidst phenomenal multiplicity.
Rāhu	A planet.
Sāyaṇa	A Vedic commentator of high repute.
sākṣātkāra	Direct knowledge or realisation of *Brahman.*
Soma	A Vedic deity connected with divine inspiration; a plant and its juice.
Śruti	The entire Vedic literature including the *Upaniṣads*; that which is orally transmitted or communicated.

skamba	A post, support or pillar and is used in the *Veda* to mean the ultimate ground and support of the universe.
turīya	Fourth or final state of experience or realisation, the other three being waking, dream and deep sleep. It is the same as *mokṣa* and *brahmānubhava*.
Upaniṣad	The basic texts of *Vedānta* philosophy, and part of *Śruti* literature.
vastu	Objective reality.
vāk	Speech or language, and in its transcendental or *parā* aspect it is the self-revelation of *Brahman*. In its conception it is similar to the Greek word Logos.
Veda	The entire Vedic literature including *Saṁhitās*, *Brāhmaṇas* and *Āraṇyakas*.
Vedānta	The *Upaniṣads* or the philosophy of the *Upaniṣads*.
vyavahāra	Pertaining to conduct and having only pragmatic validity.
vikalpa	Same as *kalpanā*.
vāsanā	Mental impressions of things experienced.
vijñānavāda	A school of Buddhism which upholds the reality of *vijñāna* or consciousness only and denies reality to the external world.
vyakti	Individualised manifestation.

yajña	Worship, Vedic sacrifice which is the Vedic mode of worship.
Yāska	Interpreter of the *Veda* belonging to the school of etymologists.

Index